How to Form a Corporation in Minnesota

How to Form a Corporation in Minnesota

D-M Boulay
Mark Warda
Attorneys at Law

SPHINX® PUBLISHING
AN IMPRINT OF SOURCEBOOKS, INC.®
NAPERVILLE, ILLINOIS

Copyright © 2002 by D-M Boulay and Mark Warda

All rights reserved. No part of this book may be reproduced in any form or by any electronic or mechanical means including information storage and retrieval systems—except in the case of brief quotations embodied in critical articles or reviews, or in the case of the exercises in this book solely for the personal use of the purchaser—without permission in writing from its publisher, Sourcebooks, Inc.® Purchasers of the book are granted a license to use the forms contained herein for their own personal use. No claim of copyright is made in any official government forms reproduced herein. Portions of the text were previously published in the book *How to Form a Corporation in Florida*, by Mark Warda.

First Edition, 2002

Published by: **Sphinx® Publishing, An Imprint of Sourcebooks, Inc.®**

Naperville Office
P.O. Box 4410
Naperville, Illinois 60567-4410
630-961-3900
Fax: 630-961-2168
http://www.sphinxlegal.com
http://www.sourcebooks.com

This publication is designed to provide accurate and authoritative information in regard to the subject matter covered. It is sold with the understanding that the publisher is not engaged in rendering legal, accounting, or other professional service. If legal advice or other expert assistance is required, the services of a competent professional person should be sought.
*From a Declaration of Principles Jointly Adopted by a Committee of the
American Bar Association and a Committee of Publishers and Associations*

This product is not a substitute for legal advice.
Disclaimer required by Texas statutes.

Library of Congress Cataloging-in-Publication Data

Boulay, D.-M. (Donna-Marie), 1942-
   How to form a corporation in Minnesota / D.-M. Boulay, Mark Warda.-- 1st ed.
      p. cm. -- (Legal survival guides)
   Includes index.
   ISBN 1-57248-179-X (pbk. : alk. paper)
    1. Incorporation--Minnesota--Popular works. I. Warda, Mark. II. Title. III. Series.

KFM5613.5.Z9 B678 2002
346.776'06622--dc21

2001049902

Printed and bound in the United States of America.

VHG Paperback — 10 9 8 7 6 5 4 3 2 1

Contents

Using Self-Help Law Books vii
Introduction xi

Chapter 1: Corporations in General 1
    Shareholders
    Officers
    Board of Directors
    Registered Agent
    Articles of Incorporation
    Bylaws

Chapter 2: Advantages and Disadvantages of Incorporating 5
    Advantages
    Disadvantages

Chapter 3: Types of Corporations 11
    Minnesota Corporation versus Foreign Corporation
    S Corporation versus C Corporation
    Closely Held Corporation Election
    Corporation versus Professional Firm
    Nonprofit Corporations

Chapter 4: Start-Up Procedures 19
    Name Check
    Articles of Incorporation
    Shareholder Agreement
    Organizational Paperwork
    Tax Forms

Corporate Supplies
Organizational Meeting
Minute Book
Bank Accounts
Licenses

CHAPTER 5: SELLING CORPORATE STOCK 45
Securities Laws
Federal Exemptions from Securities Laws
Minnesota Securities Laws
Internet Stock Sales
Payment for Shares

CHAPTER 6: RUNNING A CORPORATION 53
Day-to-Day Activities
Corporate Records
Shareholder Meetings
Board of Directors Meetings
Annual Registration

CHAPTER 7: AMENDING A CORPORATION 59
Articles of Incorporation
Bylaws
Registered Agent or Registered Office

CHAPTER 8: DISSOLVING A CORPORATION 61
Automatic Dissolution
Formal Dissolution
Bankruptcy

GLOSSARY 63

APPENDIX A: SELECTED MINNESOTA CORPORATION STATUTES 69

APPENDIX B: CHECKLISTS 91

APPENDIX C: CORPORATE NAME AVAILABILITY 95

APPENDIX D: FEE SCHEDULE 101

APPENDIX E: BLANK FORMS 105

INDEX 195

Using Self-Help Law Books

Before using a self-help law book, you should realize the advantages and disadvantages of doing your own legal work and understand the challenges and diligence that this requires.

The Growing Trend

Rest assured that you won't be the first or only person handling your own legal matter. For example, in some states, more than seventy-five percent of divorces and other cases have at least one party representing him or herself. Because of the high cost of legal services, this is a major trend and many courts are struggling to make it easier for people to represent themselves. However, some courts are not happy with people who do not use attorneys and refuse to help them in any way. For some, the attitude is, "Go to the law library and figure it out for yourself."

We at Sphinx write and publish self-help law books to give people an alternative to the often complicated and confusing legal books found in most law libraries. We have made the explanations of the law as simple and easy to understand as possible. Of course, unlike an attorney advising an individual client, we cannot cover every conceivable possibility.

Cost/Value Analysis

Whenever you shop for a product or service, you are faced with various levels of quality and price. In deciding what product or service to buy, you make a cost/value analysis on the basis of your willingness to pay and the quality you desire.

When buying a car, you decide whether you want transportation, comfort, status, or sex appeal. Accordingly, you decide among such choices as a Neon, a Lincoln, a Rolls Royce, or a Porsche. Before making a decision, you usually weigh the merits of each option against the cost.

When you get a headache, you can take a pain reliever (such as aspirin) or visit a medical specialist for a neurological examination. Given this choice, most people, of course, take a pain reliever, since it costs only pennies; whereas a medical examination costs hundreds of dollars and takes a lot of time. This is usually a logical choice because it is rare to need anything more than a pain reliever for a headache. But in some cases, a headache may indicate a brain tumor and failing to see a specialist right away can result in complications. Should everyone with a headache go to a specialist? Of course not, but people treating their own illnesses must realize that they are betting on the basis of their cost/value analysis of the situation. They are taking the most logical option.

The same cost/value analysis must be made when deciding to do one's own legal work. Many legal situations are very straight forward, requiring a simple form and no complicated analysis. Anyone with a little intelligence and a book of instructions can handle the matter without outside help.

But there is always the chance that complications are involved that only an attorney would notice. To simplify the law into a book like this, several legal cases often must be condensed into a single sentence or paragraph. Otherwise, the book would be several hundred pages long and too complicated for most people. However, this simplification necessarily leaves out many details and nuances that would apply to special or unusual situations. Also, there are many ways to interpret most legal questions. Your case may come before a judge who disagrees with the analysis of our authors.

Therefore, in deciding to use a self-help law book and to do your own legal work, you must realize that you are making a cost/value analysis. You have decided that the money you will save in doing it yourself outweighs the chance that your case will not turn out to your satisfaction. Most people handling their own simple legal matters never have a problem, but occasionally people find that it ended up costing them more to have an attorney straighten out the situation than it would have if they had hired an attorney in the beginning. Keep this in mind if you decide to handle your own case, and be sure to consult an attorney if you feel you might need further guidance.

LOCAL RULES

The next thing to remember is that a book which covers the law for the entire nation, or even for an entire state, cannot possibly include every procedural difference of every county court. Whenever possible, we provide the exact form needed; however, in some areas, each county, or even each judge, may require unique forms and procedures. In our *state* books, our forms usually cover the majority of counties in the state, or provide examples of the type of form that will be required. In our *national* books, our forms are sometimes even more general in nature but are designed to give a good idea of the type of form that will be needed in most locations. Nonetheless, keep in mind that your *state*, county, or judge may have a requirement, or use a form, that is not included in this book.

You should not necessarily expect to be able to get all of the information and resources you need solely from within the pages of this book. This book will serve as your guide, giving you specific information whenever possible and helping you to find out what else you will need to know. This is just like if you decided to build your own backyard deck. You might purchase a book on how to build decks. However, such a book would not include the building codes and permit requirements of every city, town, county, and township in the nation; nor would it include the lumber, nails, saws, hammers, and other materials and tools you would need to actually build the deck. You would use the book as your guide, and then do some work and research involving such matters as whether you need a permit of some kind, what type and grade of wood are available in your area, whether to use hand tools or power tools, and how to use those tools.

Before using the forms in a book like this, you should check with your court clerk to see if there are any local rules of which you should be aware, or local forms you will need to use. Often, such forms will require the same information as the forms in the book but are merely laid out differently, use slightly different language, or use different color paper so the clerks can easily find them. They will sometimes require additional information.

Changes in the Law

Besides being subject to state and local rules and practices, the law is subject to change at any time. The courts and the legislatures of all fifty states are constantly revising the laws. It is possible that while you are reading this book, some aspect of the law is being changed or that a court is interpreting a law in a different way. You should always check the most recent statutes, rules and regulations to see what, if any changes have been made.

In most cases, the change will be of minimal significance. A form will be redesigned, additional information will be required, or a waiting period will be extended. As a result, you might need to revise a form, file an extra form, or wait out a longer time period; these types of changes will not usually affect the outcome of your case. On the other hand, sometimes a major part of the law is changed, the entire law in a particular area is rewritten, or a case that was the basis of a central legal point is overruled. In such instances, your entire ability to pursue your case may be impaired.

Again, you should weigh the value of your case against the cost of an attorney and make a decision as to what you believe is in your best interest.

Introduction

After you experience the first flush of excitement when you realize you want to start a business, all sorts of concerns come to mind. These days, one of the first is often "How do I do what I want but not put my personal finances at risk?" In other words, how can you protect yourself from liability? The first answer lies in the existence of a corporation. A corporation is the legal entity that can act as a shield to prevent its owners from jeopardizing their personal assets.

The purpose of this book is to explain in as plain language as possible how you can create a simple corporation. By a *simple corporation*, we mean one in which there are five or fewer shareholders and all of them are active in the business.

In Chapter 1 you will find a brief explanation of some of the most significant legal terms used by corporations. These are terms that we use throughout the book.

Chapter 2 gives you a concise description of the pluses and minuses of having a corporation, from personal liability prevention to the tax issues.

One of the decisions you need to make is where you want to incorporate. You can choose to start a Minnesota type of corporation or you can choose another state or territory. It all depends on your goals, your need for convenience, and the image you want to build. Chapter 3 covers the advantages and disadvantages of where you locate the corporation's existence no matter where you operate the actual business. This chapter also gives you information on corporate forms, such as professional firms, nonprofits and others. Your choice depends on your situation and your objectives.

You will find a road map in Chapter 4. It marks your beginning (how to get a safe name choice) and plots your route through the rest of the trip, one landmark at a time. You will explore the procedures to go through to get your corporation into shape as a legal entity.

An essential part of a corporation's existence is money. When you first start out, you need to raise the amount that you have calculated will meet your needs for the time period you decide upon. This often means selling stock in the corporation. For the simple types of corporations that are covered in this book, you may never want to sell to persons other than the 1-5 persons who are active in the business. But if you do decide to sell stock to an outsider or if you have 6 or more shareholders, you should seek advice of an attorney who specializes in securities law.

Selling a few thousand shares of stock to friends and neighbors may sound like an easy way to raise capital for your business, but it is not. Since the stock market crash of the 1930's there have been federal laws that regulate the sale of *securities*. There are harsh criminal and financial penalties for violators. And these complicated laws don't have many loopholes. The basic rules are explained in Chapter 5.

Once you commit to creating a corporation, there are things you will need to take care of to keep its legal existence healthy. Chapter 6 contains the information you will need for these tasks.

Change happens. Even to corporations. For example, if you incorporate your business under one name you may later decide it makes good business sense to change it. Chapter 7 tells you about the process and the costs to amend your corporate documents and covers other processes necessary to go through to make changes to the corporate existence.

Sometime change in the operations of a corporation is so vast that the corporation must come to an end. Chapter 8 outlines the choices you have if you choose to dissolve your corporation.

In the glossary is a list of terms to which you can refer at anytime to refresh your memory or clear up the meaning on any of the specialized words we use in the text. In the appendices you will find such practical items as check lists, name-choice issues, federal and state tear out forms, costs for filing forms and some of the Minnesota laws that control corporations.

If your situation is in any way complicated or involves factors not mentioned in this book, you should seek the advice of an attorney who practices corporate law. Remember that this book has limitations because it is general in scope. Consultation with a lawyer who knows about corporate law can help you put together a business entity that reflects your specific needs and desires. This type of lawyer can help you with the details to build a safe legal structure that tailored to your business and particular situation. The cost of a consultation can be a lot cheaper that the financial and emotional consequences of violating the law.

No basic book is complete without an explanation of taxes. And although we do have tax information in here, you should discuss your own particular situation with your financial advisor and accountant before you decide what is best for you. Your accountant can also set you up with an efficient system of bookkeeping and tax payments that can save time, money and minimize stress.

Good luck with your new business!

Corporations in General 1

A *corporation* is a legal "person" that is created under state law. As a person, a corporation has certain rights and obligations such as the right to do business and the obligation to pay taxes. Sometimes one hears of a law referring to *natural persons*. That is to differentiate them from corporations, which are only legal persons, and not natural persons.

Business corporations were invented hundreds of years ago to promote risky ventures. Prior to the use of corporations, persons engaged in business faced the possibility of unlimited liability. By using a corporation, many people could put up a fixed sum of money for a new venture such as a voyage to explore the new world. If the venture made money, they shared the profits. If the venture went into debt, the most they could lose was the initial investment they put up.

The reasons for having a corporation are the same today. They allow investors to put up money for new ventures without risk of further liability. While our legal system is making more and more people liable for more and more things, the corporation remains one of the few innovations that has not yet been abandoned.

Before forming a corporation, you should be familiar with common corporate terms that will be used in the text.

Shareholders

A *shareholder* is a person who owns stock in a corporation. In most small corporations the shareholders are the same as the officers and directors, but in large corporations most shareholders are not officers or directors. Sometimes small corporations have shareholders who are not officers, such as when the stock is in one spouse's name and the other spouse runs the business. Specific laws regarding issuance of shares and shareholders' rights are in the Minnesota Statutes Annotated (Minn. Stat. Ann.), Chapter (Ch.) 302A in Appendix A of this book.

Officers

Officers are usually the president, secretary, treasurer, and vice president. These persons run the day-to-day affairs of the business. They are elected each year by a vote of the board of directors. In Minnesota, one person can hold all of the offices of a corporation.

Board of Directors

The *board of directors* is the controlling body of a corporation that makes major corporate decisions and elects the officers. It usually meets just once a year. A corporation can have one director (who can also hold all offices and own all the stock). In a small corporation the board members are usually also officers.

Registered Agent

The *registered agent* is the person designated by the corporation to receive legal papers that must be served on the corporation. The registered agent should be regularly available at the registered office of the corporation. The registered office can be the corporate office or the office of the corporation's attorney or other person or company who is the registered agent. Registered agents are optional in Minnesota.

The address for the registered office must be maintained somewhere in Minnesota. It cannot be a post office box. But, it can be:

- a street address;
- a rural route and rural box or fire number; or
- directions from a landmark.

All addresses must have a zip code.

Articles of Incorporation

Articles of Incorporation is the name of the document that is filed with the Secretary of State to start the corporation. In most cases it legally needs to contain only five basic statements. Some corporations have lengthy articles of incorporation, but this just makes it harder to make changes in the corporate structure. It is usually better to keep the articles short and put the details in the bylaws.

Bylaws

Bylaws are the rules governing the structure and operation of the corporation. Typically the bylaws will set out rules for the board of directors, officers, shareholders, and corporate formalities.

Minnesota Statutes Annotated, Chapter 302A contains most of Minnesota's laws regarding general corporate activities. For example, it lists all of the powers of corporations so they do not have to be recited again in the articles or bylaws. Sections of Chapter 302A will be referred to throughout the text like this: (Minn. Stat. Ann., Sec. 302A.001.)

Legal definitions of other corporate terms are included in Minnesota Statutes Annotated, Section 302A.011 contained in Appendix A.

Advantages and Disadvantages of Incorporating

Before forming a corporation, the business owner or prospective business owner should become familiar with the advantages and disadvantages of incorporating.

Advantages

The following are some of the advantages that a corporation has over other forms of businesses such as sole proprietorships and partnerships.

Limited Liability

The main reason for forming a corporation is to limit the liability of the owners. In a sole proprietorship or partnership the owners are personally liable for the debts and liabilities of the business, and creditors can go after all of their assets to collect. If a corporation is formed and operated properly, the owners can be protected from all such liability.

Example 1: If several people are in partnership and one of them makes many large extravagant purchases in the name of the partnership, the other partners can be held liable for the full amount of all such purchases. The creditors can take the bank accounts, cars, real estate, and other property of any partner to pay the debts of the partnership. If only one partner has money, he or she may have to pay all of the debts accumulated by all the other partners. When doing business in the corporate form, the corporation may go bankrupt and the shareholders may lose their initial investment, but the creditors cannot touch the assets of the owners.

Example 2: If a person runs a taxi business and one of the drivers causes a terrible accident, the owner can be held liable for the full amount of the damages. If the taxi driver was on drugs and killed several people and the damages amount to millions of dollars more than the insurance coverage, the owner may lose everything he owns. With a corporation, only the corporation would be liable and if there was not enough money the owner still could not be touched.

One true example is a business owner who owned hundreds of taxis. He put one or two in each of hundreds of different corporations which he owned. Each corporation only had minimum insurance and when one taxi was involved in an accident the owner only lost the assets of that corporation.

> *Warning:* If a corporate officer or shareholder does something negligent himself, or signs a debt personally, or guarantees a corporate debt, the corporation will not protect him from the consequences of his own act or from the debt. Also, if a corporation does not follow the proper corporate formalities, it may be ignored by a court and the owners or officers may be held personally liable. The formalities include having separate bank accounts, holding meetings, and keeping minutes. When a court ignores a corporate structure and holds the owners or officers liable it is called *piercing the corporate veil*. A good explanation of Minnesota law on piercing the corporate veil is contained in the Minnesota Supreme Court Case, *West Concord Conservation Club, Inc. v. Chilson*, 306, N.W. 2d 893 (Minn. 1981).

CONTINUOUS EXISTENCE

A corporation may have a perpetual existence. When a sole proprietor or partner dies, the assets of their business may go to their heirs but the business does not exist any longer. If the surviving spouse or other heirs of a business owner want to continue the business in their own names, they will be considered a new business even if they are using the assets of the old business. With a partnership, the death of one partner may cause a dissolution of the business.

Example 1: If a person dies owning a sole proprietorship, his or her spouse may want to continue the business. That person may inherit all of the assets but will have to start a new business. This means getting new licenses and tax numbers, registering the name and establishing credit from scratch. With a corporation, the business continues with all of the same licenses, bank accounts, etc.

Example 2: If one partner dies, the partnership may be forced out of business. The heirs of the deceased partner can force the sale of their share of the assets of the partnership even if the surviving partner needs them to continue the business. If he does not have the money to buy the heirs out, the business may have to be dissolved. With a corporation, the heirs would only inherit stock. With properly drawn documents the business could continue.

EASE OF TRANSFERABILITY

A corporation and all of its assets and accounts may be transferred by the simple assignment of a stock certificate. With a sole proprietorship or partnership, each of the individual assets must be transferred and the accounts, licenses, and permits must be individually transferred.

Example: If a sole proprietorship is sold, the new owner will have to get a new occupational license, set up his own bank account and apply for a new taxpayer identification number. The title to any vehicles and real estate will have to be put in his name and all open accounts will have to be changed to his name. He will probably have to submit new credit applications. With a corporation, all of these items remain in the same corporate name. As the new shareholder he would elect himself director and as director he would elect himself president, treasurer, and any other offices he wanted to hold.

NOTE: *In some cases, the new owners will have to submit personal applications for such things as credit lines or liquor licenses.*

TRANSFER OF OWNERSHIP

By distributing stock, the owner of a business can share the profits of a business without giving up control. This is done by keeping a majority of stock or by issuing different classes of stock some with voting rights and others without.

Example: If a person wants to give his children some of the profits of his business, he can give them stock and pay dividends to them without giving them any control over the management. This would not be practical with a partnership or sole proprietorship.

EASE OF RAISING CAPITAL

A corporation may raise capital by selling stock or borrowing money. A corporation does not pay taxes on money it raises by the sale of stock.

Example: If a corporation wants to expand, the owners can sell off 10%, 50%, or 90% of the stock and still remain in control of the business. The people putting up the money may be more willing to invest if they know they will have a piece of the action than if they were making a loan with a limited return. They may not want to become partners in a partnership.

NOTE: *There are strict rules about the sale of stock with criminal penalties and triple damages for violators. See Chapter 5, page 45.*

SEPARATE RECORD KEEPING

A corporation has all its own bank accounts and records. A partner or sole proprietor may have trouble differentiating which of his expenses were for business and which were for personal items.

TAX ADVANTAGES

There are some tax advantages that are available only to corporations, including the following:

- Medical insurance for your family may be fully deductible.

- A tax deferred trust can be set up for a retirement plan.

- Losses are fully deductible for a corporation whereas an individual must prove there was a profit motive before deducting losses.

EASE OF ESTATE PLANNING

With a corporation, shares of a company can be distributed more easily than with a partnership. Different heirs can be given different percentages and control can be limited to those who are most capable.

PRESTIGE

The name of a corporation sounds more prestigious than the name of a sole proprietor to some people. John Smith d/b/a Acme Builders sounds like one lone guy. Acme Builders, Incorporated, sounds like it might be a large operation.

SEPARATE
CREDIT RATING

A corporation has its own credit rating, which can be better or worse than the owner's credit rating. A corporate business can go bankrupt while the owner's credit remains unaffected, or an owner's credit may be bad but the corporation may maintain a good rating.

DISADVANTAGES

EXTRA
TAX RETURN

A corporation is required to file its own tax return. This is a bit longer and more complicated than the form required by a sole proprietorship and may entail additional expenses if the services of an accountant are required. (A partnership must also file its own tax return so there is no advantage or disadvantage over a partnership as far as tax returns are concerned.)

ANNUAL
REGISTRATION

A corporation must file a one-page annual registration with the state. There is no fee, unless the filing is late. Then it is $25.00. Preprinted forms are sent out in March and you are expected to use these.

SEPARATE
CREDIT RATING

The owners of a corporation must be careful to keep their personal business separate from the business of the corporation. The corporation must have its own records and have minutes of meetings. Money must be kept separate. But in every business, records should be separate, so the corporate structure might make it easier to do so.

EXTRA
EXPENSES

There are, of course, expenses in operating a corporation compared to not operating one. People who employ an attorney to form their corporation pay a lot more than people who use this book. A corporation owner will have to pay unemployment compensation for himself which he wouldn't have to pay as a sole proprietor.

Most new employers must register with the State within 30 days after wages are paid for the first time and must pay a quarterly state unemployment tax into the Minnesota Unemployment Insurance Trust Fund. Each year, the State of Minnesota sets the amount an employer must pay.

To help you to learn about current Minnesota rates, requirements and your obligations, the State publishes a handbook every two or three years with updated information. This handbook is available in regular size print, large print, Braille, audiotape, or on computer disk. To obtain copies of the handbook, entitled "Minnesota Employer's Unemployment Handbook" contact:

> The Minnesota Department of Economic Security
> Tax Office
> 390 North Robert Street
> St. Paul, MN 55101
> 651-296-6141, Voice
> 651-297-3944, TTY
> Email: mdes.tax@state.mn.us

Also, they can send you the forms they describe in the handbook or you can download them from:

> http://www.mnworkforcecenter.org/tax

Most employers who pay Minnesota unemployment tax must also pay federal unemployment tax. The good news is that employers who have paid the state tax receive a credit that lowers the amount of federal tax due.

To get the federal unemployment tax information and forms, call 800-829-1040 (to get your Employer Identification Number (EIN)).

Download forms from:

> http://www.irs.ustreas.gov

FTP (*file transfer protocol*, which is a method some computers use to download material) at:

> http://ftp.irs.ustreas.gov

You can also call IRS at FedWorld: 703-321-8020 or fax them at 703-487-4160

CHECKING ACCOUNTS

Checks made out to a corporation cannot be cashed; they must be deposited into a corporate account. Some banks have higher fees just for businesses that are incorporated. See Chapter 4, page 19 for tips on avoiding high bank fees.

Types of Corporations 3

You have several options for the type of legal entity you want to have for your business. Which one you choose will depend upon your situation, the type of products or services you have, the people who are in it with you and your goals. You also have a choice for where you want to locate the legal presence of your office. This chapter outlines those choices.

Minnesota Corporation versus Foreign Corporation

A person wishing to form a corporation must decide whether the corporation will be a Minnesota corporation or a *foreign* corporation. A foreign corporation is one incorporated in another state that does business in Minnesota.

DELAWARE CORPORATIONS
In the past there was some advantage to incorporating in Delaware, since that state had very liberal laws regarding corporations, and many national corporations are incorporated there. However, in recent years most states have liberalized their corporation laws—so today there is no advantage to incorporating in Delaware for most people.

NEVADA CORPORATIONS
Nevada has liberalized its corporation laws recently to attract businesses. It allows bearer stock and other rules that allow more

privacy to corporate participants. It also does not share information with the Internal Revenue Service and does not have a state income tax.

MINNESOTA CORPORATIONS

Today Minnesota has very favorable corporate laws. If you form a corporation in a state other than Minnesota, you will probably have to have an agent or an office in that state and will have to register as a foreign corporation doing business in Minnesota. This is more expensive and more complicated than just registering as a Minnesota corporation to begin with. Also, if you are sued by someone who is not in your state, they can sue you in the state in which you are incorporated which would probably be more expensive for you than a suit filed in your local court. In some states your corporation may be required to pay state income tax.

S CORPORATION VERSUS C CORPORATION

A corporation has a choice of how it wants to be taxed. It can make the election at the beginning of its existence or at the beginning of a new tax year. The choices follow.

S CORPORATION

Formerly called a *"Subchapter S corporation,"* an *S corporation* pays no income tax and may only be used for small businesses. All of the income or losses of the corporation for the year are passed through to the shareholders who report them on their individual returns. At the end of each year the corporation files an *information return* listing all of its income, expenses, depreciation, etc., and sends to each shareholder a notice of his or her share as determined by percentage of stock ownership.

Advantages. Using this method avoids double taxation and allows pass-through of losses and depreciation. The business is treated like a partnership. Since many businesses have tax losses during the first years due to start-up costs, many businesses elect S status and switch over to C corporation status in later years. Once a corporation terminates its S status, there is a five year waiting period before it can switch back. S corporations do not have to pay Minnesota corporate income tax. They may have to pay a minimum fee to the state, based on property, payroll and sales attributed to Minnesota.

Disadvantages. If stockholders are in high income brackets, their share of the profits will be taxed at those rates. Shareholders who do not "materially participate" in the business cannot deduct losses. Some fringe benefits such as health and life insurance may not be tax deductible in an S corporation.

Requirements. To qualify for S corporation status the corporation must:

- have no more than seventy-five shareholders, none of whom are non-resident aliens or corporations, all of whom consent to the election (shares owned by a husband and wife jointly are considered owned by one shareholder);

- have only one class of stock;

- not be a member of an "affiliated group;"

- generate at least 20% of its income in this country and have no more than 20% of its income from "passive" sources (interest, rents, dividends, royalties, securities transactions); and

- file ELECTION BY A SMALL BUSINESS CORPORATION (IRS FORM 2553) before the end of the 15th day of the third month of the tax year for which it is to be effective and have it approved by the IRS. (see form 20, p.153.)

Multiple Corporations. The IRS has approved the use of two or more S corporations in partnership to increase the number of allowable investors in a venture. It may also be possible for an S corporation to form a partnership with a C corporation.

C CORPORATION

A C *corporation* has to pay taxes on its net earnings at corporate tax rates. It may also have to pay taxes based on its property, payroll and sales. The minimum fee schedule is:

Minnesota Payroll, Property and Sales	Fee
Less than $500,000	$0
$500,000 to $900,000	$100
$1,000,000 to $4,999,999	$300
$5,000,000 to $9,999,999	$1,000
$10,000,000 to $19,999,999	$2,000
$20,000,000 or more	$5,000

Call the Corporations Unit at the Minnesota Department of Revenue at 651-297-7000 for information about how to determine what taxes you will owe and when they must be paid. You can also write to:

Department of Revenue
600 North Robert Street
St Paul, MN 55416

You may find it necessary to get detailed tax advice on your specific business and situation from a competent tax advisor.

Salaries of officers, directors, and employees are deducted from income so are not taxed to the corporation, but money paid out in dividends is taxed twice. It is taxed at the corporation's rate as part of its profit, and then the stockholders must include the amounts they receive as dividends in their income.

Advantages. If taxpayers are in a higher tax bracket than the corporation and the money will be left in the company for expansion, taxes are saved. Fringe benefits such as health, accident, and life insurance are deductible expenses.

Disadvantages. Double taxation of dividends by the federal government is the biggest problem with a C corporation. Also, Minnesota has an income tax of 9.8% which only applies to C corporations.

NOTE: *Neither of these taxes applies to money taken out as salaries, and many small business owners take all profits out as salaries to avoid double taxation and the Minnesota income tax. But there are rules requiring that salaries be reasonable and if a stockholder's salary is deemed to be too high, relative to his or her job, the salary may be considered dividends and subject to the double taxation.*

Depending on your business activities, your business may have sales and use taxes to pay.

Requirements. None. All corporations are C corporations unless they specifically elect to become S corporations.

Closely Held Corporation Election

A closely held corporation election is beneficial for many small businesses. It's purpose is to place restrictions on the transferability of stock. Often it obligates a shareholder to offer to the corporation or the shareholders the opportunity to purchase the stock before offering it to any outside purchaser. If the corporation and shareholders reject the offer, they typically must still consent to who the transferee (buyer) of the shares will be.

To elect to have these restrictions, they will need to be imposed in the articles, in the BYLAWS, by a resolution adopted by the shareholders, by an agreement among or other written action by a number of shareholders or holders of other securities, or among them and the corporation. A restriction should be noted conspicuously on the certificate or transaction statement.

Corporation versus Professional Firm

Certain types of services can only be rendered by a corporation if it is a *Professional Firm*. These are such businesses as attorneys, nurses, physicians, certified public accountants, veterinarians, architects, life insurance agents, chiropractors, and similarly licensed, registered, or certified professionals.

A professional firm comes under nearly all of the rules of Minnesota Statutes Annotated, Chapter 302A or 317A regarding profit and non-profit corporations in general, unless they conflict with Chapter 319B, which specifically governs professional firms. The differences between the two include their purpose, name, merger, and type of legal entity.

PURPOSE A professional firm must provide one or more categories of professional services that are spelled out in the organizing document. Which organizing document you use will depend upon the choice of legal entity you choose. The most frequently used legal entities in Minnesota for professional firms are corporations, limited liability companies and partnerships. See Appendix E at the back of this book for these blank forms:

- ARTICLES OF INCORPORATION (form 5)
- ARTICLES OF ORGANIZATION FOR A LIMITED LIABILITY COMPANY (form 7)
- LIMITED LIABILITY PARTNERSHIP STATEMENT OF QUALIFICATION (form 8)

Those services must be the practice of one or more authorized professions in Minnesota. It may not engage in any other business, but it may invest its funds in real estate, stocks, bonds, mortgages or other type of investment. A professional firm may change its purpose to another legal, non-professional purpose, but it will then no longer be a professional firm and may be dissolved by the Minnesota Attorney General.

NAME The name of a professional firm, if it is a corporation, must end with any one of the following phrases, words, or abbreviations:

Professional Corporation	Professional Service Corporation
Service Corporation	Professional Association
Chartered	Limited
P.C.	P.S.C
S.C.P.A.	Ltd.

It may contain the name of some or all of the shareholders and the names of deceased or retired shareholders, or it may be an assumed name that has none of its shareholders in the title.

MERGER	A professional firm may merge with any other corporation. If it merges with a nonprofessional firm, the new entity cannot then become a professional firm and must be considered a corporation under the relevant general corporation or nonprofit corporation laws.
TYPE OF LEGAL ENTITY	Professional firms may choose the type of legal form that they want to operate as. They can choose to be either a C or S corporation, a limited liability company, or a limited liability partnership.

NONPROFIT CORPORATIONS

Nonprofit corporations are intended to be used to return something to the community, such as social clubs, churches, and charities, and are beyond the scope of this book. While they are similar to for-profit corporations in many aspects, such as limited liability and the required formalities, there are additional state and federal requirements which must be met.

In some cases, a business with a public service mission can be formed as a nonprofit corporation. However, it would not be allowed to have shareholders or distribute profits to its founders or anyone else. But, it could pay market rate salaries for services rendered to the corporation and enjoy numerous tax advantages. Nonprofits have their own Minnesota incorporation and Federal Tax-exempt application forms and a special unemployment tax payment option.

START-UP PROCEDURES 4

In this chapter you find the very specific tasks you must do to get your type of business form put into the legal system. There are phone numbers, addresses and websites listed for you to contact at each step of the way. Although this phase of your business is mostly paperwork, it's critical. To help you off to an easy start we begin with some fun: the name you want to use.

NAME CHECK

The very first thing to do before starting a corporation is to thoroughly check out the name you wish to use to be sure it is available. Many business have been forced to stop using their name after spending thousands of dollars promoting it.

ASSUMED NAMES

Any person or business organization that conducts a commercial business in Minnesota under a name other than his or her full name must file a CERTIFICATE OF ASSUMED NAME with the Secretary of State. (see form 3, p.111.) Forms for this certificate are available by calling 651-296-2803, pressing 1, then 1 again, and entering 444-2406, then entering your fax number, or by going to the Secretary's website at:

http://www.sos.state.mn.us/business/forms.html

To check for other corporations using the name you want, you should call the corporate records office of the Secretary of State's office at 651-296-2803, or tollfree 877-551-6767. If your name is too similar to another corporate name then you will not be allowed to register it.

The filing fee for original and assumed names is $25.00. The filing must be published in a legal newspaper qualified for the county of the business's location for two successive issues after the filing is made with the Secretary of State. (See page 19 for more information).

It is also advisable to check local phone books.

BUSINESS LISTINGS
Because some businesses neglect to properly register their name (yet still may have superior rights to the name) you should also check phone books and business directories. Many libraries have phone books from around the country as well as directories of trade names.

YELLOW PAGE LISTINGS
If you have a computer with Internet access you can search every yellow pages listing for free. Just search for "yellow pages" with any web search engine (i.e., Yahoo, WebCrawler, Lycos, etc.). You can select a state, enter your business name and it will tell you if any other companies are listed with that name. One site that allows you to search all states at once is:

http://www.infoseek.com

If you do not have access to a computer you may be able to use one at your public library or have the search done at your library for a small fee.

TRADEMARK SEARCH
To be sure that you are not violating a registered trademark you should have a search done of the records of the United States Patent and Trademark Office. This can be done at their offices in Arlington, Virginia, or at one of the Patent and Trademark Depository Libraries listed at the end of this chapter. You can also have a search done for a small fee at some libraries if they subscribe to Dialog Information Services or a similar service.

Another alternative is to order a search from a trademark search firm. This is usually the most thorough but the cost can range from $100 to $500 or more. Some firms that do searches are:

Government Liaison Services, Inc.
200 North Glebe Road, Suite 321
P.O. BOX 3292, Arlington, VA 22203
800-642-6564, 703-524-8200
Fax: 703-525-8451
http://www.trademarkinfo.com

start-up procedures

Thomson & Thomson
500 Victory Road
North Quincy, MA 02171-3145
fax 617-479-5398
http://www.thomson_thomson.com/

Blomberg Excelsior
62 White Street
New York, NY 10013
800-221-2972, ext. 570

Name Reservation
It is possible to reserve a name for a corporation for a period of twelve months for a fee of $35. However, this is usually unnecessary because it is just as easy to file the ARTICLES OF INCORPORATION as it is to reserve the name. (see form 5, p.115.) One possible reason for reserving a name would be to hold it while waiting for a trademark name search to arrive.

Similar Names
Sometimes it seems like every good name is taken. But a name can often be modified slightly or used on a different type of goods. If there is a "TriCounty Painting, Inc." in Minneapolis, it may be possible to use something like "TriCounty Painting of Tonka Bay, Inc." if you are in a different part of the state. Try different variations if your favorite is taken. Another possibility is to give the corporation one name and then do business under an assumed name. (See "Assumed Names" on page 19.)

Example: If you want to use the name "Flowers by Freida" in Minneapolis and there is already a "Flowers by Freida, Inc." in St. Paul, you might incorporate under the name "Freida Jones, Inc." and then register the corporation as doing business under the fictitious name "Flowers by Freida." Unless "Flowers by Freida, Inc." has registered a trademark for the name either in Minnesota or nationally, you will probably be able to use the name.

NOTE: *You should realize that you might run into complications later, especially if you decide to expand into other areas of the state. One protection available would be to register the name as a trademark. This would give you exclusive use of the name anywhere that someone else was not already using it. (See "Trademarks", page 22.)*

21

FORBIDDEN
NAMES

A corporation may not use certain words in its name if there would be a likelihood of confusion. There are state and federal laws which control the use of these words. In most cases, your application will be rejected if you use a forbidden word. Some of the words that may not be used without special licenses or registration are:

Assurance	Target Center
Bank	Insurance
Banker	Olympic
Banking	St. Paul Port Authority
Credit Union	Trust Company
3M	

SECRETARY OF
STATE

If you perform a name check with the Secretary of State and discover that because of the similarity with a name on file prevents that Office from allowing you to use your choice, you still may have a course of action you can take to secure that name. You may be able to get permission to use it from the business or make an effort to find the people who could give permission and then register the name. The forms and information can be obtained from:

Secretary of State
180 State Office Building
100 Constitution Ave.
St. Paul, MN 55155-1299
http://www.sos.state.mn/business/forms.html
Or from the Fax Forms Library at 651-296-2803

TRADEMARKS

The name of a business can not be registered as a trademark, but if the name is used in connection with goods or services it may be registered and such registration will grant the holder exclusive rights to use that name except in areas where someone else has already used the name. A trademark may be registered either in Minnesota or in the entire country.

Each trademark is registered for a certain "class" of goods. If you want to sell "Zapata" chewing gum, it doesn't matter that someone has registered the name "Zapata" for use on shoes. If you want to register the mark for several types of goods or services, you must register it for each different class into which the goods or services fall, and pay a separate fee for each category.

For protection within the state of Minnesota the mark may be registered with the Minnesota Secretary of State. The cost is $50.00. Application forms and instructions can be obtained from:

>Secretary of State
>100 Constitution Ave.
>180 State Office Building
>St. Paul, MN 55155-1299
>651-296-2803

For protection across the entire United States the mark can be registered with the United States Patent and Trademark Office and the cost is about $245.

ARTICLES OF INCORPORATION

The act which creates the corporation is the filing of ARTICLES OF INCORPORATION with the Secretary of State in St. Paul. (see form 5, p.115.) Some corporations have long, elaborate articles that spell out numerous powers and functions, but most of this is unnecessary. The powers of corporations are spelled out in Minnesota law (See Minn. Stat., Ch. 302A in Appendix A) and do not have to be repeated. (In fact the statute says that the powers do not have to be repeated in the articles, but they often are.)

The main reason to keep the ARTICLES OF INCORPORATION short is to avoid having to amend them later. By putting all but the operational basics in the BYLAWS of the corporation, you can make changes in the corporate structure much more easily. The ARTICLES OF INCORPORATION included in this book are as simple as possible for this purpose. (see form 5, p.115.)

REQUIREMENTS   Minnesota law requires that only five things be included in the ARTICLES OF INCORPORATION. Some things, such as the purpose of the corporation, regulations for the operation of the corporation, and a par value of the stock may be spelled out in the ARTICLES OF INCORPORATION, but this is not advisable since any changes would then require the complicated process of amending the articles. It is better to spell these things out in the BYLAWS. The articles must contain the following five provisions. These provisions are included in form 5 of this book.

Name of the corporation. The corporation name must include one of the following six words:

Incorporated	Corp.
Inc.	Company
Corporation	Co.

You cannot use "and" or "&" immediately before the word "company." The reason is that persons dealing with the business will be on notice that it is a corporation. This is important in protecting the shareholders from liability. "Company" is not as good as the others because it is not clear notice to the public that the business is incorporated.

Address of the corporation. The address of the principal office and the mailing address of the corporation must be provided. If there is a registered agent, the agent's name and address must be listed and make changes at bottom of page as marked.

The number of shares of stock the corporation is authorized to issue. This is usually an even number such as 100, 1000 or 1,000,000. A lot of people authorize 1,000,000 shares (with a par value of $0.01 or 0.001) because it sounds impressive.

In some cases, it may be advantageous to issue different classes of stock such as *common* and *preferred*, or *voting* and *non-voting*, but such matters should be discussed with an attorney or accountant.

If there are different classes of stock, the ARTICLES OF INCORPORATION must contain a designation of the classes and a statement of the preferences, limitations, and relative rights of each class. In addition, if there are to be any preferred or special shares issued in series, the articles must explain the relative rights and preferences and/or any authority of the board of directors to establish preferences. Any preemptive rights must also be spelled out.

This book will explain how to form a corporation with one class of stock. It is usually advisable to authorize double or quadruple the amount of stock that will be initially issued. The unissued stock can be issued later if more capital is contributed by a shareholder or by a new member of the business.

One important point to keep in mind when issuing stock is that the full par value must be paid for the shares. If this is not done then the shareholder can later be held liable for the full par value. For more important information about issuing stock see Chapter 5.

The name of the registered agent and the address of the registered agent. Each corporation may have a registered agent and a registered office. The registered agent can be any individual or a corporation. The registered office can be the business office of the corporation or it can be the office of another individual who is the registered agent (such as an attorney) or it may be a corporate registered agent's office. The business address of the registered agent is considered the registered office of the corporation.

The name and address of the incorporator of the corporation. This may be any person who is at least 18 years old, even if that person has no future interest in the corporation. For people who need to be incorporated quickly, there are companies in the Twin Cities that can, on a moment's notice, have someone sign and run over to the Secretary of State to file corporate articles which are later assigned to the real parties in interest.

Duration. The duration of the corporation need not be mentioned if it is to be perpetual. If not, the duration must be in the articles.

OPTIONAL

Effective date. A specific effective date may be in the articles but is not required. They are effective upon filing. If an effective date is specified it may not be more than five days prior to filing or more than ninety days after.

PROFESSIONAL
FIRMS

There are two additional requirements for corporations which will be professional firms (see pages 15-17). These are:

Purpose. The purpose of the corporation must be stated and must be limited to the practice of one profession.

Designation. The name must contain the designation:

Professional Corporation	Professional Service Corporation
Service Corporation	Professional Association
Chartered	Limited
P.C.	P.S.C.
S.C.	P.A.
Ltd.	

EXECUTION

The ARTICLES OF INCORPORATION must be signed by the incorporator and dated. There is no longer a need to have them notarized. Anyone can be the incorporator, and there is no need to have more than one person sign. Rights of other parties can be spelled out at the incorporation meeting.

FORMS

ARTICLES OF INCORPORATION need not be on any certain form. They can be typed on blank paper or can be on a fill-in-the-blank form. In the back of this book is a form for ARTICLES OF INCORPORATION. It can be used for both a regular corporation and a Professional Firm. (see form 5, p.115.)

FILING

The ARTICLES OF INCORPORATION must be filed with the Secretary of State of Minnesota. Send the originals to:

Secretary of State
100 Constitution Ave.
180 State Office Building
St. Paul, MN 55155-1299

You should mail them along with a TRANSMITTAL LETTER and the filing fees (see form 4, p.113.) The fee (as of 2001) is $135.00.

The return time for the articles is usually a week or two. If there is a need to have them back quickly, you may have them expedited for a

$20.00 fee if you have them filed at the Secretary of State's Office counter. Then, they will be processed immediately.

You may also fax them to 651-297-5844 if payment is made by automated clearinghouse (ACH). Certificates are $5.00 each. Certified copies are $5.00 each plus the Secretary's photocopying fee. Certified copies are rarely needed and you may want to wait to order one until you need it.

Minnesota's Secretary of State files and records original and amendment documents for all businesses: corporations, partnership, limited liability companies, including professional firms, that are formed in Minnesota. It also records trademark and assumed names. The Secretary of State's forms that you will need are at the back of the book in Appendix E. Appendix D contains the various fees for the filing and recording of documents with that office.

LEGAL NEWSPAPER STATUS

Each year, including the first, you must make an application to have the name of the corporation published in a Legal Newspaper between September 1st and December 31st. New corporations usually submit this when they file the incorporation papers. An application for legal newspaper status may be obtained from:

> Secretary of State
> Records Processing Section
> 180 State Office Building
> 100 Constitution Avenue
> St. Paul, MN 55155-1299
> 651-296-927

There is a $25.00 filing fee for the application.

SHAREHOLDER AGREEMENT

Whenever there are two or more shareholders in a corporation, they should consider drawing up a SHAREHOLDER AGREEMENT. (see form 37, p.191.) This is a document that spells out the rights and obligations of the parties in the event disagreements come up. Even family corporations should consider a SHAREHOLDER AGREEMENT since it could make, say, a future divorce much less costly by settling some issues without the expense of litigation.

Because a SHAREHOLDER AGREEMENT is a fairly complicated document you should consider having one drafted by an attorney. (Be sure the attorney drafts it to fit your needs and does not just have an assistant print out a standard form.)

Some of the issues that are usually included in a SHAREHOLDER AGREEMENT are discussed below and a simple SHAREHOLDER AGREEMENT form is included in Appendix E. (see form 37, p.191.) This might suit your needs while your corporation is small. Be sure to review it as your company grows to be sure it still fits your needs.

When deciding on a SHAREHOLDER AGREEMENT you will consider your options during the expansion of your company, but also be sure to consider the possibility of negative events, such as bankruptcy or death of a participant. These are the times when a SHAREHOLDER AGREEMENT is most needed.

RIGHTS OF MINORITY

The biggest risk in a small corporation with unequal ownership is that an owner of a minority interest will be shut out of decision-making. Unless some rights are spelled out in a SHAREHOLDER AGREEMENT, any shareholder with less than 50% interest risks having that investment tied up indefinitely. Many of the clauses in a SHAREHOLDER AGREEMENT address various rights (salary, withdrawal) of shareholders with a minority interest.

SUPERMAJORITY VOTE OR UNANIMOUS CONSENT

In order to allow shareholders with minority interests to have a say in major changes in the corporation, you can require unanimous consent or a larger than simple majority vote (*supermajority*) on such issues. One danger to keep in mind is that requiring unanimous consent can allow one disgruntled shareholder to sabotage the efforts of the majority.

Example: If the majority wants to sell the company you would not want one shareholder with 10% interest to kill the deal. You should seek an agreement that can balance the rights of the majority and the minority. If a 10% owner is the only one who does not want to sell, then he or she can be given the right to buy out the other 90%.

DEVOTING BEST EFFORTS

One problem that sometimes comes up in the life of a corporation is that one shareholder loses interest and no longer contributes the time that was originally expected. Or, a shareholder might become a part of a competing enterprise. To avoid disagreements you should spell out what is expected of each shareholder. You could spell out how many hours a week each person is expected to work, or you could just have a general agreement that each shareholder will devote his best efforts to the company.

RIGHT TO SERVE AS DIRECTOR

An effective protection for minority shareholders is the right of each to serve as a director. This enables them to take part in directors' meetings without being elected and to stay informed of activities of the corporation. However being a director alone does not guarantee a right to control decisions. That is covered by the following clause.

SALARY

If there is a chance that some of the shareholders will later vote themselves higher salaries than others you can include an agreement as to what the salaries will be and include a requirement that any change must be agreed to by everyone or by more than a simple majority.

NOMINATING OFFICERS AND EMPLOYEES

One common provision in a SHAREHOLDER AGREEMENT is to agree as to which office will be held by each shareholder. Any change could require unanimous consent or a supermajority vote. However, be sure to provide for the possibility that someone may become unable or unwilling to do the job.

COMPULSORY BUY-OUT

A way to end a dispute between shareholders is to provide for a compulsory buyout. This can be open-ended in which either party can buy out the other, or it can be specific in which one persons shares are subject to a buyout. A formula for determining the buyout price should be in the agreement to avoid disagreements later.

Most small corporations limit the ability of shareholders to sell their shares. This protects the corporation from violations of securities laws and from persons whom they might not want as shareholders. A limitation on the ability to sell shares is usually combined with a buyout plan.

ADDITIONAL SHARES   To maintain a balance of power among the shareholders it is important to have provisions covering the issuance of new shares or a merger with another corporation. Besides a clause that provides a majority or unanimous consent (see above) for decisions concerning these events, a provision to issue new shares on a pro-rata basis can solve some situations.

TRANSFER OF SUBSTANTIAL ASSETS   To protect the shareholder's value—a clause should be added that any transfer of substantial assets for any consideration other than cash is not allowed.

ENDORSEMENT   An endorsement on the shares that informs a potential transferee about the circumstance that the shares are subject to certain restrictions concerning their transfer. It warns the transferee and improves the chances of the corporation in case of a lawsuit on account of a transfer not being in accordance with the provisions of the SHAREHOLDER AGREEMENT.

FORMALITIES   To avoid any misunderstanding, the formalities as to how the SHAREHOLDER AGREEMENT should be complied with can be included. This also avoids problems such as a shareholder who is obliged to inform the others about his intention to sell his shares sending letters to the other shareholder's summer house in Canada while they are here.

MEDIATION   If shareholders cannot negotiate their way through a misunderstanding, then they need to go into *mediation*. Mediation is the process that allows the corporation and its shareholders to have a professional facilitate their negotiations. Mediation is unlike arbitration or litigation because it allows the parties to keep control of the outcome. It also gives the parties their best opportunity to resolve matters without creating ill will. You will find it helpful to make the mediation requirement the first paragraph in the dispute resolution section of the shareholder agreement.

A *mediator* can help you find a creative, quick and inexpensive solution. The big advantage to mediation is that you can craft solutions that cannot be obtained in arbitration or court. Another benefit of mediation is the opportunity to resolve disputes in a way that relationships can be preserved. But if mediation fails then it's on to the next step, arbitration.

ARBITRATION   Because going to court is so expensive and can take years, it is a good idea to put an arbitration clause in your agreement. Arbitrators are often lawyers or former judges so you get a decision similar to what you would have gotten court without the expense or delay.

BOILERPLATE   Most SHAREHOLDER AGREEMENTS contain standard legal boilerplate language, such as Entire Agreement (there are no verbal additions to this agreement), Severability (if one clause is invalid that would not be reason to throw out the entire agreement), and Choice of Law (which state's laws will be used to interpret the agreement).

Minnesota has specific rules on shareholder agreements. (Minn. Stat. Ann., Secs. 302A.455 and 302A.457.) The most important of these is that the existence of a SHAREHOLDER AGREEMENT should be noted:

- on the face or back of each stock certificate;
- on each transaction statement; and
- filed with the corporation.

These steps must be taken to make the SHAREHOLDER AGREEMENT binding.

ORGANIZATIONAL PAPERWORK

Every corporation must have bylaws and must maintain a set of minutes of its meetings. The bylaws must be adopted at the first meeting and the first minutes of the corporation will be of the organizational meeting.

BYLAWS   The BYLAWS are the rules for organization and operation of the corporation. They are required by Minnesota law. (Minn. Stat., Sec. 302A.461.) Two sets of BYLAWS are included with this book. Form 14 is for simple corporations and form 15 is for professional firms. To complete form 14:

- Fill in the name of the corporation at the top blank.
- Write the city of the main office of the corporation, and the state in the Article I blanks.

☛ Write the proposed date and time of the annual meeting (this can be varied each year as needed) in Article II, Section 1.

☛ Fill in the number of directors to be on the board in Article III, Section 1.

☛ In Article VI, Section 1, fill in the blank for how many months the board has to issue a report

☛ Articles XI and XII both require a state in the blanks. Most likely you will fill in Minnesota because you incorporated in Minnesota.

☛ The secretary will date and sign the form.

To complete form 15:

☛ Fill in the name of the corporation in the top blank.

☛ Write in the city of the corporation's main office in Article I.

☛ Write in the profession in Article II.

☛ Fill in the proposed date and time of the annual meeting in Article III, Section 2.

☛ Write the number of directors in Article IV, Section 2.

☛ Fill in the number of shares and the par value at Article VIII, Section 1.

☛ The secretary will sign and date the form.

WAIVER OF NOTICE

Before a meeting of the incorporators, the board of directors or the shareholders can be held to transact lawful business, formal notice must be given to the parties ahead of time. Since small corporations often need to have meetings on short notice and do not want to be bothered with formal notices, it is customary to have all parties sign written WAIVERS OF NOTICE. Minnesota law allows the waiver to be signed at any time, even after the meeting has taken place, for both shareholders and for directors. (Minn. Stat., Secs. 302A.435 and 302A.182.) WAIVERS OF NOTICE are included in this book for the organizational meeting (form 12 for shareholders) and for the annual meetings (form 22 for directors and form 24 for shareholders) and special meetings. (form 26 for the directors and form 28 for shareholders.)

MINUTES   As part of the formal requirements of operating a corporation, MINUTES must be kept of the meetings of shareholders and the board of directors. Usually only one meeting of each is required per year (the annual meeting) unless there is some special need for a meeting in the interim (such as the resignation of an officer). The first MINUTES that will be needed are the MINUTES OF THE ORGANIZATIONAL MEETING OF INCORPORATORS AND DIRECTORS. (see form 13, p.130.) At this meeting the officers and directors are elected; the BYLAWS, corporate seal and STOCK CERTIFICATES are adopted; and other organizational decisions made.

To complete form 13:

- Fill in the name of the corporation at the top blank.

- Write the date, address, and time of the meeting in the first blank.

- Write the names of all attendees in the second paragraph.

- In the fourth paragraph, write the name of the Incorporator that called the meeting, and the names of the elected chairperson and temporary secretary.

- In the fifth paragraph, write what state (most likely Florida) in which the articles were filed and the date they were filed.

- Next, write the names of the Board of Directors next to their respective titles of President, Vice President, Secretary and Treasurer.

- On page two, affix the corporate seal at the top right side.

- In the paragraph beginning with RESOLVED, write in the blanks the bank that will hold the corporate accounts. In the last blank of that paragraph write in how many signatures of authority are required to make transactions with the bank account. Then list in the blanks below that all those that potentially has the authority to make transactions.

- In the second to the last paragraph on that page, check one of the boxes at item 2. Indicating C or S status of the corporation.

- On page 3, list the names of the board of directors.

- Next, list in the three columns who wants to buy shares, how many shares, and the total of what they will owe. (Example: John Smith, 100 shares, $100 (if the shares were $1.00 each.))

- The President and Secretary (not the chairperson and temporary secretary) should sign and date the form.

RESOLUTIONS

When the board of directors or shareholders make major decisions it is usually done in the form of a resolution. At the organizational meeting the important resolutions are those choosing a bank with a BANKING RESOLUTION. (see form 16, p.145.) Another is a RESOLUTION (Adopting S Corporation Status). (see form 21, p.159.)

WAIVER OF MEETING

Minnesota law allows corporate officers to execute incorporation papers without a meeting, but it is better to have a formal meeting to prove to possible future creditors that you conducted the corporation in a formal manner. (Minn. Stat. Ann., Sec. 308A.181.)

TAX FORMS

If the idea of taxes has you trembling, this section will help you calm down. If you follow these steps and use the resources listed in this section, you still might not like paying your taxes, but the process will be tolerable.

IRS FORM SS-4 (EMPLOYER IDENTIFICATION NUMBER)

Prior to opening a bank account the corporation must obtain a "taxpayer identification number," which is the corporate equivalent of a social security number. This is done by filing APPLICATION FOR EMPLOYER IDENTIFICATION NUMBER (IRS FORM SS-4), included in this book. (see form 11, p.125.) Processing usually takes four or five weeks, so it should be filed early. Send the form to:

Internal Revenue Service Center
Attn: Entity Control
Stop 6800
2306 E. Bannister Rd.
Kansas City, MO 64999

If you need the number quickly you may be able to obtain the number by phone by calling the IRS at 816-926-5999. Be sure to have your **IRS Form SS-4** complete and in front of you before calling. To use the fax to obtain your number, call 816-926-5999 to ask for it.

When you apply for this number you will probably be put on the mailing list for other corporate tax forms. If you do not receive these, you should call your local IRS forms number and request the forms for new businesses. These include Circular E explaining the taxes due, the W-4 forms for each employee, the tax deposit coupons and the Form 941 quarterly return for withholding.

IRS Form 2553 (S Corporation)

If your corporation is to be taxed as an S corporation, you must file **Election by a Small Business Corporation (IRS Form 2553)** with the IRS within seventy-five days of incorporation. (see form 20, p.153.) As a practical matter you should sign and file this at your incorporation meeting; otherwise, you may forget. To make the S corporation status "official" you should also adopt a corporate **Resolution** (Adopting S Corporation Status) and keep it in your minute book. (see form 21, p.159.)

State Sales Tax Registration

You must collect the appropriate Minnesota Sales and Use Tax if your corporation will be selling goods at retail or providing taxable services. Some services. For information on what services are taxable or to request the special fact sheets written for corporations that provide taxable services, contact the Department of Revenue at 651-296-6181 or 800-657-3777.

Before any taxes are collected, you must register your corporation with the Department of Revenue to obtain a tax number. When you contact them, you will be asked for information for the ABR form (Application for Business Registration), which they will also send to you. At the time you enter the information for the form, you will need to have your taxpayer identification number or EIN number (Federal Employment Identification Number).

To register with Minnesota and get your State tax number, call the Minnesota Department of Revenue at 651-282-5225 or 800-657-3605 or go to their website at:

http://www.taxes.state.mn.us

CORPORATE SUPPLIES

In addition to the paper work that others must have, the corporation must have certain things for its own use. For example there is the charter, minutes of meetings and stock certificates, to mention a few.

A corporation needs to keep a permanent record of its legal affairs. This includes:

- the original charter;
- minutes of all meetings;
- records of the stock issued, transferred and cancelled;
- fictitious names registered; and any other legal matters.

CORPORATE KITS
The records are usually kept in a ring binder. Any ring binder will do, but it is possible to purchase a specially prepared *corporate kit* that has the name of the corporation printed on it and usually contains forms such as minutes, stock certificates, etc. Most of these items are included with this book so purchasing such a kit is unnecessary unless you want to have a fancy leather binder or specially printed stock certificates.

Some sources for corporate kits are:

Blumberg Excelsior
62 White Street
New York, NY 10013
800 529-6278
http://www.blumberg.com

Corpex
1440 Fifth Avenue
Bay Shore, NY 11706
800-221-8181
email: Corpex@CorpexNet.com

CorpKit Legal Supplies
888-888-9120
email: info@corpkit.com
http://www.corpkit.com/

Miller Davis Company
2515 West University Avenue
St. Paul, MN 55114
651-642-1988

CORPORATE SEAL
One thing that is not included with this book is a *corporate seal*. Minnesota does not require them. It must be specially made for each corporation. Often corporations use a metal seal like a notary's seal to

emboss the paper. These can be ordered from many office supply companies. In recent years, many have been using rubber stamps for corporate seals. These are cheaper, lighter, and easier to read. Rubber stamp seals can also be ordered from office supply stores, printers, and specialized rubber stamp companies. The corporate seal should contain the full, exact name of the corporation, the word "SEAL" and the year of incorporation. It may be round or rectangular.

Stock Certificates and Offers to Purchase Stock

Minnesota corporations are no longer required to issue STOCK CERTIFICATES to represent shares of ownership. (Minn. Stat. Ann., Sec. 302A.417.) However, as a practical matter it is a good idea to do so. This shows some formality and gives each person tangible evidence of ownership.

If you do issue shares, the face of each certificate must show:

- the corporate name;
- that the corporation was organized under Minnesota law;
- the name of the shareholder(s); and
- the number, class, and series of the stock.

The certificate must be signed by one or more officers designated by the bylaws or the board of directors.

If there are two or more classes or series of stock, the front or back of the certificate must disclose that upon request and without charge the corporation will provide to the shareholder the preferences, limitations, and relative rights of each class or series; the preferences of any preferred stock; and the board of directors' authority to determine rights for any subsequent classes or series. If there are any restrictions they must be stated on the certificate, or a statement must be included that they are available without charge.

The STOCK CERTIFICATES can be fancy, with engraved eagles, or they can be typed or even handwritten. STOCK CERTIFICATE forms are included at the end of this book. (see form 34, p.177.) They should be completed like the sample on the next page. For professional firms the following statement should be typed on the certificate: "The transfer of the shares represented by this certificate is restricted by the bylaws of the corporation."

Before any stock is issued, the purchaser should submit an **OFFER TO PURCHASE STOCK**. (see form 17, p.147.) The offer states that it is made pursuant to IRS Code, Section 1244. The advantage of this section is that in the event the business fails or the value of the stock drops, the shareholder can write off up to $50,000 ($100,000 for married couples) as ordinary income, rather than as a long term capital lose which would be limited to $3,000 a year.

Some thought should be given to the way in which the ownership of the stock will be held. Stock owned in one person's name alone is subject to probate upon death. Making two persons joint owners of the stock (joint tenants with full rights of survivorship) would avoid probate upon the death of one of them. However, taking a joint owner's name off in the event of a disagreement (such as divorce) could be troublesome. Where a couple jointly operates a business, joint ownership would be best. But where one person is the sole party involved in the business the desire to avoid probate should be weighed against the risk of losing half the business in a divorce. Another way to avoid probate is to put ownership of the stock in a living trust.

LIMITED OFFERINGS
Minnesota levies a tax on the issue or transfer of stock. (Minnesota Statutes Chapter 80A). The issuance of stock is governed by Federal and State laws that are complex. The advice of professionals knowledgeable in this area should be sought before you make an attempt to issue corporate securities.

ORGANIZATIONAL MEETING

The real birth of the corporation takes place at the initial meeting of the incorporators and the initial board of directors. At this meeting the stock is issued and the officers and board of directors are elected. Other business may also take place, such as opting for S corporation status or adopting employee benefit plans.

Usually MINUTES, STOCK CERTIFICATES and tax and other forms are prepared before the organizational meeting and used as a script for the meeting. They are then signed at the end of the meeting. Otherwise, they may be forgotten until it is too late.

The agenda for the initial meeting is usually as follows:

1. Signing the WAIVER OF NOTICE OF ORGANIZATIONAL MEETING (form 12);

2. Noting persons present;

3. Presentation and acceptance of articles of incorporation (the copy returned by the Secretary of State);

4. Election of Directors;

5. Adoption of BYLAWS (form 14 or form 15);

6. Election of officers;

7. Presentation and acceptance of corporate seal;

8. Presentation and acceptance of STOCK CERTIFICATE (form 34);

9. Designation of bank with BANKING RESOLUTION (form 16);

10. Acceptance of OFFERS TO PURCHASE STOCK (form 17); (Use form 19, BILL OF SALE, if property is traded for stock.)

11. Resolution to pay expenses;

12. Adoption of special resolutions such as S corporation status (form 21);

13. Adjournment.

At the end of the meeting the stock certificates are usually issued, but in some cases, such as when a prospective shareholder does not yet have money to pay for them, they are issued when paid for.

To issue the stock, the certificates at the end of this book should be completed by adding the name of the corporation, a statement that the corporation is organized under the laws of Minnesota, the number of shares the certificate represents and the person to whom the certificate is issued. Each certificate should be numbered in order to keep track of them. A record of the stock issuance should be made on the STOCK TRANSFER LEDGER. (see form 32, p.173.) It should also be made on the STOCK CERTIFICATE STUBS. (see form 33, p.175.) The STOCK CERTIFICATE STUBS should be cut apart on the dotted lines, punched and inserted in the ring binder.

MINUTE BOOK

After the organizational meeting you should set up your minute book. This can be a fancy leather book or a simple ring binder. The minute book usually contains the following:

1. A title page ("Corporate Records of _____")
2. A table of contents
3. The letter from the Secretary of State acknowledging receipt and filing of the articles of incorporation
4. Copy of the ARTICLES OF INCORPORATION
5. Copy of any fictitious name registration
6. Copy of any trademark registration
7. WAIVER OF NOTICE OF ORGANIZATIONAL MEETING
8. MINUTES OF ORGANIZATIONAL MEETING OF INCORPORATORS AND DIRECTORS
9. BYLAWS
10. Sample STOCK CERTIFICATE
11. OFFER TO PURCHASE STOCK
12. Tax forms:

    IRS FORM SS-4 and Employer Identification Number certificate

IRS Form 2553 and acceptance

State tax number certificate

13. STOCK TRANSFER LEDGER

14. STOCK CERTIFICATE STUBS

BANK ACCOUNTS

A corporation must have a bank account. Checks payable to a corporation cannot be cashed; they must be deposited into an account.

FEES Unfortunately, many banks charge ridiculous rates to corporations for the right to put their money in the bank. You can tell how much extra a corporation is being charged when you compare a corporate account to a personal account with similar activity.

> **Example**: For similar balance and activity, an individual might earn $6.00 interest for the month while a corporation pays $40.00 in bank fees. Surely the bank is not losing money on every personal account. Therefore, the corporate account is simply generating $46.00 more in profit for the bank.

Usually, there is a detailed system of fees with charges for each transaction. Many banks today even charge companies for the right to make a deposit. (Twenty-five cents for the deposit plus 10¢ for each check that is deposited. Deposit thirty checks and this will cost you $3.25.) Often the customer is granted an interest credit on the balance in the account, but it is usually small and if the credit is larger than the charges, you lose the excess. In some banks the officers cannot even tell you how the fees are figured because the system is so complicated.

Fortunately, some banks have set up reasonable fees for small corporations such as charging no fees if a balance of $1000 or $2500 is maintained. Because the fees can easily amount to hundreds of dollars a year, it pays to shop around. Even if the bank is relatively far from the business, using bank-by-mail can make the distance meaningless. But do not be surprised if a bank with low fees raises them. (One company changed banks four times in one year as each one raised its fees or was bought out by a bank with higher fees.)

As the banking industry got deeper into trouble, fewer and fewer banks were offering reasonable fees for corporate checking accounts. Even with their balance sheets improving, they are not eager to give up this new source of wealth. But you can usually find loopholes if you use your imagination. One trick is to open a checking account and a money market account. (Money market accounts pay higher interest and do not charge for making deposits. You can only write three checks a month but you can usually make unlimited withdrawals.) Then make all of your deposits into the money market account and just pay bills out of the regular checking account, transferring funds as needed. However, because banks are catching on to this and starting to charge for deposits into money market accounts, you may choose to start one at a brokerage firm.

Another way to save money in bank charges is to order checks from a private source rather than through the bank. These are usually much cheaper than those the bank offers because the bank makes a profit on the check printing. If the bank officer does not like the idea when you are opening the account, just wait until your first batch runs out and switch over without telling the bank. They probably will not even notice, as long as you get the checks printed correctly. While most "business checks" are large (and expensive), there is no reason you cannot use small "personal size" checks for your business.

PAPERWORK

All you should need to open a corporate bank account is a copy of your **ARTICLES OF INCORPORATION** and your federal tax identification number. Some banks, however, want more.

Example: After opening numerous corporate accounts with only the two items listed above, Larry once encountered a bank employee who wanted "something certified so we know who your officers are. Your attorney will know what to draw up." Larry explained that he was his own attorney and was the president, secretary, and treasurer of the corporation. He offered to write out and sign and seal whatever they wanted. When the bank insisted that it had to be a nice certificate signed by the secretary of the corporation and sealed, Larry typed out a statement in legalese, put a gold foil seal on it, and the bank opened the account.

If you have trouble opening the account, you can use the **Banking Resolution** included with this book, or you can make up a similar form. (see form 16, p.145.)

Licenses

Counties and municipalities are authorized to levy a license tax on the "privilege" of doing business. Before opening your business, check with the city and county to see if you should obtain a county occupational license. Businesses that perform work in several cities, such as builders, must obtain a license from each city they work in. This does not have to be done until you actually begin a job in a particular city.

County occupational licenses can be obtained from the tax collector in the county courthouse. City licenses are usually available at city hall. Be sure to find out if zoning allows your type of business before buying or leasing property because the licensing departments will check the zoning before issuing your license.

Home Businesses

Problems occasionally arise when persons attempt to start a business in their home. Small new businesses cannot afford to pay rent for commercial space and cities often try to forbid business in residential areas. Getting a county occupational license often gives notice to the city that a business is being conducted in a residential area.

Some people avoid the problem by starting their businesses without occupational licenses, figuring that the penalties are nowhere near the cost of office space. Others get the county license and ignore the city rules. If a person has commercial trucks and equipment parked on his property, there will probably be complaints by neighbors and the city will most likely take legal action. But if a person's business consists merely of making phone calls out of the home and keeping supplies inside the house, the problem may never come up.

If the problem does come up regarding a home business that does not disturb the neighbors, a good argument can be made that the zoning law that prohibits the business is unconstitutional. When zoning laws were first instituted they were not meant to stop people from doing things in a residence that had historically been part of the life in a residence. Consider a painter. Should a zoning law prohibit a person from sitting in his home and painting pictures? If he sells them for a living is there a difference? Can the government force him to rent commercial space?

Similar arguments can be made for many home businesses. But court battles with a city are expensive and probably not worth the effort for a small business. It is prudent to check with your local government about their requirements.

Selling Corporate Stock 5

When you want to sell stock in your corporation, you need to be aware that there are many rules that control your transactions. It is just not the same as selling a service or a product. Special laws govern the sale of stock. You need to follow them or you could wind up with big financial penalties or even jail time. With that in mind, the following gives you a good idea of what those laws are all about.

Securities Laws

The issuance of securities is subject to both federal and state securities laws. A *security* is stock in the company (common and preferred) and debt (notes, bonds, etc.). The laws covering securities are so broad that any instrument that represents an investment in an enterprise, where the investor is relying on the efforts of others for profit, is considered a security. Even a promissory note has been held to be a security. Once an investment is determined to involve a security, strict rules apply. There can be criminal penalties, and civil damages can also be awarded to purchasers, if the rules are not followed.

The rules are designed to protect people who put up money as an investment in a business. In the stock market crash in the 1930s many people lost their life savings in swindles, and the government wants to be sure that it will not happen again. Unfortunately, the laws can also make it difficult to raise capital for many honest businesses.

The goal of the laws covering sales of securities is that investors be given full disclosure of the risks involved in an investment. To accomplish this, the law usually requires that the securities must either be registered with the federal Securities and Exchange Commission and/or a similar state regulatory body, and that lengthy disclosure statements be compiled and distributed.

The law is complicated and strict compliance is required. The penalties are so harsh that most lawyers will not handle securities matters. You most likely would not be able to get through the registration process on your own. But, like your decision to incorporate without a lawyer, you may wish to consider some alternatives when attempting to raise capital without a lawyer:

One option is to borrow the money as a personal loan from friends or relatives. The disadvantage is that you will have to pay them back personally if the business fails. However, you may have to do that anyway if they are close relatives or if you don't follow the securities laws.

Another option is to tailor your stock issuance to fall within the exemptions in the securities laws. There are some exemptions in the securities laws for small businesses that may apply to your transaction. (The anti-fraud provisions always apply, even if the transaction is exempt from registration.) Some exemptions are explained below, but you should make at least one appointment with a securities lawyer to be sure you have covered everything and that there have not been any changes in the law. Often you can pay for an hour or so of a securities lawyer's time for $100 or $200 and just ask questions about your plans. He or she can tell you what not to do and what your options are. Then you can make an informed decision.

You can get information on federal securities registration requirements and a pamphlet from:

Publications Office of the United States Securities
and Exchange Commission,
450 5th Street NW Mail Stop 3-4,
Washington, D.C. 20549.
800-SEC-0330 or
202-942-2950.

To get information about state securities regulations, contact:

Minnesota Department of Commerce Registration
and Analysis Division
133 7th Street East
St. Paul, MN 55101
651-296-4026

FEDERAL EXEMPTIONS FROM SECURITIES LAWS

In most situations where one person, a husband and wife or a few partners run a business, and all parties are active in the enterprise, securities laws do not apply to their issuance of stock to themselves. These are the simple corporations that are the subject of this book. As a practical matter, if your father or aunt wants to put up some money for some stock in your business you probably will not get in trouble. They probably will not seek triple damages and criminal penalties if your business fails.

However, you may wish to obtain money from additional investors to enable your business to grow. This can be done in many circumstances as long as you follow the rules carefully. In some cases you do not have to file anything with the SEC but in others you must file some sort of notice.

PRIVATE PLACEMENT

If you sell your stock to a small group of people without any advertising you can fall into the private offering exemption.

- All persons to whom offers are made are financially astute, are participants in the business or have a substantial net worth.

- No advertising or general solicitation is used to promote the stock.

- The number of persons to whom the offers are made is limited.

- The shares are purchased for investment and not for immediate resale.

- The persons to whom the stock is offered are given all relevant information (including financial information) regarding the corporation and the issuance of stock.

- A filing claiming the exemption is made upon the United States Securities and Exchange Commission.

There are numerous court cases explaining each aspect of these rules, including such questions as what is a "financially astute" person.

INTRASTATE OFFERING

If you only offer your securities to residents of one state you may be exempt from federal securities laws. This is because federal laws usually only apply to interstate commerce. Intrastate offerings are covered by SEC Rule 147 and if it is followed carefully, your sale will be exempt from federal registration.

SMALL OFFERINGS

In recent years the SEC has liberalized the rules in order to make it easier for businesses to grow. Under *Regulation D*, adopted by the Securities and Exchange Commission, there are three types of exemptions under Rules 504, 505, and 506.

The offering of securities of up to $1,000,000 in a twelve-month period can be exempt under SEC Rule 504. Offers can be made to any number of persons, no specific information must be provided, and investors do not have to be sophisticated.

Under Rule 505, the offering of up to $5,000,000 can be made in a twelve-month period, but no public advertising may be used and only thirty-five non-accredited investors may purchase stock. Any number of accredited investors may purchase stock. *Accredited investors* are sophisticated individuals with high net worth or high income, large trusts or investment companies, or persons involved in the business.

Rule 506 has no limit on the amount of money that may be raised. Like Rule 505, it does not allow advertising and limits non-accredited investors to thirty-five.

MINNESOTA SECURITIES LAWS

The simplification of federal requirements has been accompanied by similar changes at the state level.

MINNESOTA LIMITED OFFERINGS OF ISOLATED SALES

No person may make more than ten sales of securities of the same corporation during any consecutive 12-month period. In the case of sales by a corporation, unless the securities are registered under the Federal Securities laws, the seller must reasonably believe that all buyers are purchasing for investment and the securities must not be advertised for sale to the general public.

A sale will be excluded from the total if made within 48 hours of a previous sale to another purchaser, if the first sale is included in the computation and the second sale is to:

1. any relative or spouse sharing the home of the other purchaser; or

2. any estate or trust in which the first purchaser and a relative sharing the home of the other purchaser or a related entity (described in 3.) collectively have more than 50 percent of the "beneficial interest in the corporation; or

3. any corporation or other organization of which the other purchase and related persons are beneficial owners of more than 50 percent of the securities or equity interests.

Sales to any *accredited investor* are also excluded in the total.

These rules may sound fairly straightforward on the surface, but there are many more rules, regulations and court cases explaining each one in great detail. For example, a sale to any corporation will be counted as one sale unless the corporation was organized for the specific purpose of acquiring the securities offered.

Internet Stock Sales

With the advent of the Internet, promoters of stock have a new way of reaching large numbers of people, most of whom are financially able to afford investments in securities. However, all securities laws apply to the Internet and they are being enforced. Recently state attorneys general have issued cease and desist orders to promoters not registered in their states.

Under current law you must be registered in a state in order to sell stock to its residents. If you are not registered in a state you must turn down any residents from that state that want to buy your stock.

You may wonder how the famous Spring Street Brewing raised $1.6 million for its Wit Beer on the internet. The main reason they were successful was perhaps because their president is a lawyer and could prepare his own prospectus to file with the SEC and the states.

Payment for Shares

When issuing stock, it is important that full payment be made by the purchasers. If the shares have a par value and the payment is in cash, then the cash must not be less than the par value. In most states promissory notes cannot be used in payment for shares. The shares must not be issued until the payment has been received by the corporation.

Trading Property for Shares
In many cases organizers of a corporation have property they want to contribute for use in starting up the business. This is often the case where an on-going business is incorporated. To avoid future problems, the property should be traded at a fair value for the shares. The directors should pass a resolution stating that they agree with the value of the property. When the stock certificate is issued in exchange for the property, a bill of sale should be executed by the owner of the property detailing everything that is being exchanged for the stock.

TAXABLE TRANSACTIONS

In cases where property is exchanged for something of value, such as stock, there is often income tax due as if there had been a sale of the property. Fortunately, Section 351 of the IRS Code allows tax-free exchange of property for stock if the persons receiving the stock for the property or for cash *end up owning* at least 80% of the voting and other stock in the corporation. If more than 20% of the stock is issued in exchange for services instead of property and cash, then the transfers of property will be taxable and treated as a sale for cash.

TRADING SERVICES FOR SHARES

The founders of a corporation may issue stock to one or more persons in exchange for services rendered to the corporation in the past or in the future. This practice is allowed by Minnesota Statutes Annotated, Section 302A.405.

Running a Corporation

6

In this chapter, you will see that running a corporation means something different than running the operations of a business. It refers to the duties that must be performed to keep the existence of a corporation legal.

Day-to-Day Activities

There are not many differences between running a corporation and any other type of business. The most important point to remember is to keep the corporation separate from your personal affairs. Do not be continuously making loans to yourself from corporate funds and don't commingle funds.

Another important point to remember is to always refer to the corporation as a corporation. Always use the suffix designation that you have chosen, such as "Inc." or "Corp." on everything. Always sign corporate documents with your corporate title. If you do not, you may lose your protection from liability. There have been many cases where a person forgot to put the word "pres." after his or her name and was held personally liable for a corporate debt.

Corporate Records

MINUTES Minnesota Statutes require that a corporation keep the following records for three years: proceedings of the Board of Directors and reports made to any government agency as a matter of public record. (Minn. Stat. Ann., Sec. 302A.461.)

ACCOUNTING RECORDS Accurate accounting records must be kept by the corporation. (Minn. Stat. Ann., Sec. 302A.46.)

RECORD OF SHAREHOLDERS The corporation must keep a record of its shareholders including the names and addresses and the number, class, and series of shares owned. (Minn. Stat. Ann., Sec. 302A.457.) This can be kept at the registered office or principal place of business.

CORPORATE DOCUMENTS The corporation must maintain copies of its ARTICLES OF INCORPORATION and all amendments, BYLAWS and all amendments, resolutions regarding stockrights, minutes of shareholders' meetings and records of actions taken without a meeting for the last three years, written communications to all shareholders for the last three years, financial statements furnished to shareholders for the last three years, names and usual business addresses of all current directors and officers, and the most recent annual report.

FORM OF RECORDS The records may be in writing or computerized. The key is that they must be able to be reproduced, so safety and secure storage is essential.

EXAMINATION OF RECORDS Any shareholder of a corporation has the right to examine and copy the corporation's books and records after giving written notice at least 10 days before the date on which he wishes to inspect and copy them, if he has a good faith reason for a proper purpose and he describes his purpose and the records (if the purpose is related to the records). (Minn. Stat. Ann., Sec. 302A.461.)

The shareholder may have his attorney or agent examine the records and may receive photocopies of the records. (Minn. Stat. Ann., Sec. 302A.461.) The corporation may charge a reasonable fee for making photocopies. If the records are not in written form, the corporation must convert them to written form. The corporation must bear the cost of:

- converting the ARTICLES OF INCORPORATION and any amendments, BYLAWS and any amendments;

- resolutions by the board of directors creating different rights in the stock;

- minutes of all shareholders' meetings and records of any action taken by the shareholders without a meeting for the past three years;

- written communications to all shareholders generally or of any class, names and addresses of all officers and directors; and

- the most recent annual registration filed with the Secretary of State.

The shareholder must pay for converting any other records.

If the corporation refuses to allow a shareholder to examine the records then the shareholder may get an order from the District Court and in such case the corporation may have to pay the shareholder' costs and attorney fees.

BALANCE SHEETS Within 180 days of the close of each fiscal year, the corporation must, upon request, furnish its shareholders with financial statements including an end of the year balance sheet and yearly income and cash flow statements. (Minn. Stat. Ann., Sec. 302A.463.) The corporation must furnish the statements no later than 10 business days after receipt of a shareholder's written request.

SHAREHOLDER MEETINGS

Each year the corporation must hold an annual meeting of the shareholders. These meetings may be formal and held in a restaurant or they may be informal and held in the swimming pool. A sole officer and director can hold them in his mind without reciting all the verbiage or taking a formal vote. But the important thing is that the meetings are held and that minutes are kept. Regular minutes and meetings are evidence that the corporation is legitimate if the issue ever comes up in court. Minute forms for the annual meetings are included with this book. (form 25.) You can use them as master copies to photocopy each year, changing the date and other old information.

SPECIAL MEETINGS When important decisions must be made by the board of shareholders between the annual meetings, the corporation can hold special meetings.

ACTION WITHOUT A MEETING
Under the procedures of Minnesota Statutes Annotated, Section 302A.441, action may be taken by the shareholders without a formal meeting. However, for a small corporation it is best to use formal meetings in case someone later tries to pierce the corporate veil.

NOTICE OF MEETINGS
Under Minnesota law, shareholders with voting rights must be notified of the date, time, and place of annual and special meetings at least ten but not more than sixty days prior. (Minn. Stat. Ann., Sec. 302A.435.) No description of the purpose of an annual meeting need be given, but the purpose for a special meeting must be stated in the notice.

A shareholder may waive notice either before or after the meeting if done in writing and included in the minutes. Unless a shareholder objects, attendance at a meeting waives objection to the notice or lack thereof.

VOTING
The following rules apply to voting at the shareholders' meeting:

- Unless otherwise provided in the articles of incorporation or bylaws, a quorum consists of a majority of the shares entitled to vote (Minn Stat. Ann., Sec. 302A.443);

- Once a share is represented at a meeting for any purpose it is deemed present for quorum purposes for the rest of the meeting (Minn. Stat. Ann., Sec. 302A.443);

- Holders of a majority of the shares represented may adjourn the meeting (Minn. Stat. Ann., Sec. 302A.443);

- The ARTICLES OF INCORPORATION or BYLAWS must authorize a quorum (Minn. Stat. Ann., Sec. 302A.443).

VOTING FOR DIRECTORS
Unless otherwise provided in the ARTICLES OF INCORPORATION, directors are elected by a plurality of votes. Shareholders do not have a right to cumulative voting unless provided in the articles.

BOARD OF DIRECTORS MEETINGS

Each year the corporation must hold an annual meeting of the directors. These meetings also may be formal and held in a restaurant or they may be informal and held in the swimming pool. A sole officer and director can hold them in his mind without reciting all the verbiage or taking a formal vote. But the important thing is that the meetings are held and that minutes are kept. Regular minutes and meetings are evidence that the corporation is legitimate if the issue ever comes up in court.

A MINUTES OF THE ANNUAL MEETINGS OF THE BOARD OF DIRECTORS form is included with this book. (see form 23, p.161.) You can use it as master copies to photocopy each year. All that needs to be changed is the date, unless you change officers or directors or need to take some other corporate action.

SPECIAL MEETINGS
When important decisions must be made by the board of shareholders between the annual meetings, the corporation can hold special meetings. MINUTES OF SPECIAL MEETING OF THE BOARD OF DIRECTORS is in this book. (see form 27, p.165.)

ACTION WITHOUT A MEETING
Under the procedures of Minnesota Statutes Annotated, Section 302A.435, action may be taken by the directors without a formal meeting. However, for a small corporation it is best to use formal meetings in case someone later tries to *pierce the corporate veil*. (see page 6.)

NOTICE OF MEETINGS
Under Minnesota law regular meetings of the board of directors may be held without notice unless the articles of incorporation or bylaws provide otherwise. (Minn. Stat. Ann., Sec. 302A.435.) Special meetings must be preceded by at least 10 days notice of the time, date, and place unless the articles or bylaws provide for a longer or shorter period.

VOTING
The following rules apply to voting at the directors' meeting:

- Unless otherwise provided in the ARTICLES OF INCORPORATION or BYLAWS, a quorum consists of a majority of the number of directors prescribed in the articles or bylaws.

- The ARTICLES OF INCORPORATION may authorize a quorum of less than a majority.

- If a quorum is present for a vote, a vote by a majority of those present constitutes an act of the board of directors unless otherwise provided in the ARTICLES OF INCORPORATION or BYLAWS.

- A director present at a meeting of the board or a committee is deemed to have assented to an action taken unless he or she objects at the beginning of the meeting or the vote to the meeting or the business, or votes against it.

COMMITTEES Unless prohibited by the bylaws, the board of directors may designate a committee of its members that can exercise all authority of the board except that it may not:

- approve or recommend actions which by law must be approved by the shareholders;

- fill vacancies on the board or committees thereof;

- adopt, repeal, or amend the BYLAWS;

- authorize reacquisition of shares except under a formula approved by the board;

- authorize sale of shares or shareholder rights except within limits set by the board.

Also, meeting rules of committees must comply with the rules for the board itself. Setting up a committee does not relieve a member of his duty to act in good faith in the best interests of the corporation.

ANNUAL REGISTRATION

A corporation must file an annual registration form with the Secretary of State. There is no fee unless you do not file, then your corporation loses its good standing. You can resume good standing by completing a current registration and paying a $25.00 Fee. But not registering for three consecutive years results in automatic dissolution of your corporation, unless you a registration is submitted with the $25.00 fee. If your corporation is dissolved this way, you must reincorporate.

Amending a Corporation 7

With any luck at all, you will not have to use this chapter. If you work hard to create a realistic framework at the outset, you will minimize your need to make any changes in the articles, bylaws and registered agent. But, in new businesses, things do not always go as planned. That is why this chapter is here for your use if and when you need it.

Articles of Incorporation

Because the ARTICLES OF INCORPORATION included in this book are so basic, they will rarely have to be amended. The only reasons for amending them would be to change the name or the number of shares of stock, or to add some special clause such as a higher than majority voting requirement for directors as provided in Minnesota Statutes Annotated, Section 302A.115.

If the amendment is made before any shares are issued, it may be done by the incorporator or directors by filing articles of amendment signed by the incorporators or director stating the name of the corporation, the amendment and date adopted. The AMENDMENT OF ARTICLES OF INCORPORATION form at the back of the book in Appendix E can be used. (see form 6, p.117.)

If the amendment is made after shares have been issued, the articles of amendment must be signed by the president or vice president, and the secretary or assistant secretary. The articles of amendment must contain the name of the corporation, the amendments, the date of adoption by the shareholders (pursuant to a meeting subject to all notice and quorum requirements under Minnesota law), and, if the change affects the outstanding shares, a statement of how the change will be affected.

The articles of amendment must be filed with the Secretary of State along with the filing fee of $35. For a copy of this form, see form 6 in Appendix E. The procedure for amending corporate articles depends upon who is doing the amending and at what point in time the amendment is adopted. For more information you should refer to Minnesota Statutes Annotated, Sections 302A.131 through 302A.139 which are included in Appendix A of this book.

Bylaws

The board of directors may adopt, amend, or repeal the BYLAWS unless the articles provide that the BYLAWS may be amended by the shareholders. (Minn. Stat. Ann., Sec. 302A.181.)

The ARTICLES OF INCORPORATION may allow a bylaw that requires a greater quorum or voting requirement for shareholders. (Minn. Stat. Ann., Sec. 302A.001.)

A bylaw that fixes a greater quorum or voting requirement for the board of directors that was adopted by the shareholders may be amended or repealed only by the shareholders, but if it was adopted by the board, it may be amended or repealed by the board. (Minn. Stat. Ann., Sec. 302A.001.)

Registered Agent or Registered Office

To change the registered agent or registered office, a form must be sent to the Secretary of State with the fee of $50. This form called CHANGE OF REGISTERED OFFICE/REGISTERED AGENT is included in this book (see form 31, p.171.) This form can be used to change both the registered agent and the registered office, or to just change one of them. If you are changing just one, such as the agent, then list the registered office's new address only.

Dissolving a Corporation 8

Even when you start a business it is prudent to think about the end. You may find it comforting to know that you are not hooked forever to the corporation. You can get out of it if you find that things go wrong or if you just do not want to have the corporation continue to exist. Even if you put perpetual duration in the articles you can still end it. Many people discover that the businesses they set up just do not work out.

The end of your corporation will be through what the State of Minnesota calls *dissolution*. And, you may decide that *bankruptcy* (this process is governed by federal laws) is a sensible course.

Automatic Dissolution

If your corporation has ceased to do business and you no longer need to keep it active there is no reason to take any special action to dissolve it because it will be automatically dissolved if you fail to file your annual report for three years in a row. Be sure that you will not need the corporation again because you must reincorporate and incur all those expenses again.

If your corporation has some debts that it is unable to pay at the time of dissolution, then you would be better off formally dissolving the corporation or having it file bankruptcy.

Formal Dissolution

An advantage of formal dissolution is that if you give proper notice to creditors, after a period of time there is no risk that they can come back against the directors.

To formally dissolve a corporation, ARTICLES OF DISSOLUTION must be filed with the Secretary of State. (see form 30, p.169.) If the corporation has not issued shares or commenced business the ARTICLES OF DISSOLUTION must be authorized by a majority of the incorporators or directors and signed by the chairman or vice chairman of the board of directors, or by an officer, or if there are no officers or directors, then by an incorporator. (see form 30, p.169.) If shares have been issued then the ARTICLES OF DISSOLUTION must be authorized by the shareholders at a duly noticed meeting and signed by the chairman or vice chairman of the board of directors or by an officer. (see form 30, p.169.)

Bankruptcy

If your corporation is in debt beyond its means it can file for bankruptcy. Chapter 7 bankruptcy is for liquidation and Chapter 11 for reorganization of debts.

If the debts are small and there is little chance the creditors will pursue collection, then bankruptcy is unnecessary. You can allow the state to dissolve the corporation for failure to file the annual report. However, if the debts are large and you fear the creditors will attempt to collect the debt from the officers or directors you should go through formal bankruptcy and/or dissolution. Such a scenario is beyond the scope of this book and you should consult an attorney or bankruptcy text for further guidance.

Glossary

A

articles of incorporation. The document that enables the corporation to do business legally. It usually contains only basic information, such as a name and address of the corporation.

assumed name. A corporation that does business under a name that is different from the full, true name of each business owner.

B

banking resolution. This is the written proof of the corporation's decision to keep its bank accounts at a specified financial institution. Many banks provide free copies of resolutions that they prefer you to use.

bylaws. Rules and regulations that a corporation uses to govern itself.

C

C corporation. Pays corporate state and federal taxes. Any compensation paid to owners is taxed via personal income tax.

common stock. The basic ownership shares of a corporation.

consideration. Compensation that must paid by purchasers of stock.

contract. An agreement between two or more parties.

corporation. An organization that the law recognizes as a person. It is set up to conduct a business owned by shareholders and run by officers and directors.

D

dissolution. Even in corporations whose Articles provide that they are perpetual, the owners or the State can terminate them.

E

employee. Person who works for another under that person's control and direction.

employer identification number (EIN). The federal taxpayer identification number.

estate planning. Preparing such documents as a will, trust and other arrangements to control the passing of one's property at death.

exemption. The ability to sell certain limited types of securities without full compliance with securities registration laws.

F

fictitious name. A name used by a business that is not its personal or legal name.

foreign corporation. One that is not incorporated in Minnesota but is incorporated in another U.S. State, territory or Possession (Guam or the Virgin Islands) or the District of Columbia.

G

general partnership. A business that is owned by two or more persons.

I

incorporator. Any person 18 years of older may sign the Articles of Incorporation and file the paper work with the Secretary of State.

L

liable. To be financially responsible for the legal wrongs of the corporation. The corporation usually acts as a liability shield for its owners, unlike a "sole proprietorship".

limited liability company. An entity recognized as a legal "person" that is set up to conduct a business owned and run by members.

limited liability partnership. An entity recognized as a legal "person" that is set up to conduct a business owned and run by professionals, such as attorneys or doctors.

M

minutes. The formal record of the corporation's decisions. It includes the name of each Board member who attended, who did not, the date of the meeting, the time it started and adjourned, each action taken and the reason for it.

N

nonprofit corporation. An entity recognized as a legal "person" that is set up to run an operation in which none of the profits are distributed to controlling members.

O

occupational license. A government-issued permit to transact business.

organizational meeting. The meeting of the founders of a corporation or limited liability company in which the company is structured and ready to begin business.

organizing document. This term refers to the Articles of Incorporation or other legal entity and is filed with the Secretary of State to launch the legal life of the business.

P

par value. A value given to newly-issued stock, which used to have legal significance, but now usually does not relate to anything except, in some states, taxation.

partnership. A business formed by two or more persons.

perpetual. Corporations are presumed to have an eternal existence. But, the owners may bring them to an end. And, under certain circumstances, so can the State.

piercing the corporate veil. When a court is allowed to ignore the liability shield for a corporate director and hold that person responsible for the legal wrongs of the corporation. One of the ways that enable a court to ignore the shield is if personal funds are mingled with corporate funds.

professional firm. A corporation, limited liability company or partnership composed of licensed professionals who provide the professional services listed in the charter.

promoters. Persons who start a business venture and usually offer interests for sale to investors.

proprietorship. A business that is owned by one person.

R

registered. Corporations need to record their existence and names with the Secretary of State at the beginning and each year thereafter. The Department of Revenue has several registration requirements. Protection for service and trademarks is enhanced by registration with the State of Minnesota and the U.S. Patent and Trademark Office.

registered office. The legal address of a corporation. The corporation must always maintain a legal address in Minnesota. It is the address where someone who files a lawsuit against the corporation must send the legal papers. For many businesses it is the only address where official notices from the state can be received.

resolution. The record kept of each major decision at Board and shareholders meetings.

S

S corporation. Pays no income tax and owner pays the corporate income via personal tax forms and gets the losses.

securities. These are documents that represent stock ownership in a corporation. Every aspect of them are tightly regulated by the State and the Federal Governments according to complex laws, rules and regulations.

service mark. Any mark used to designate the origin of a service, such as D-M BOULAY WIDGETS.

shareholder agreement. A contract among the owners of a corporation that spells out their rights.

shareholders. Those who own the corporation.

shares. Another word for Securities.

stock. Another word for Securities and for Shares.

T

trademark. Used to protect the brand name of the items you sell and can be registered with the State and Federal governments. Examples of former trademarks are aspirin and escalator. They are former trademarks that lost their proprietary significance because their owners allowed them to be used by the public as common names for certain lines of goods.

W

waiver. To give up or forgo a legal right, such as one to have the meeting of the Board to form the corporation.

withholding. Money taken out of an employee's salary and remitted to the government.

Z

zoning. Local governmental control of the use of land and buildings through a system of rules and permits. In most locales, business activities must conform to zoning laws.

Appendix A
Selected Minnesota Corporation Statutes

Included in this appendix are the Minnesota corporation statutes that will be most useful in organizing your corporation. The italicized ones in the beginning list means they are included in this appendix. The non-italicized ones are other statutes that cover such things as mergers, buyback of shares, share dividends, proxies, voting trusts and other matters which might come up at a future time. You can download all of Minnesota's Corporate Statutes from:

http://www.revisor.leg.state.mn.us/stats

This appendix includes the following:

Selections from Minnesota Statutes Chapter 302A, 319B, and 333.

CHAPTER 302A
BUSINESS CORPORATIONS

302A.001	Citation.
302A.011	*Definitions.*
302A.021	Application and election.
302A.031	Transition.
302A.041	*Reservation of right.*
302A.101	*Purposes.*
302A.105	*Incorporators.*
302A.111	*Articles.*
302A.115	Corporate name.
302A.117	Reserved name.
302A.121	Registered office; registered agent.
302A.123	Change of registered office or registered agent; change of name of registered agent.
302A.131	Amendment of articles.
302A.133	Procedure for amendment when no shares are outstanding.
302A.135	Procedure for amendment after issuance of shares.
302A.137	Class or series voting on amendments.
302A.139	Articles of amendment.
302A.141	Effect of amendment.
302A.151	Filing articles.
302A.153	Effective date of articles.
302A.155	Presumption; certificate of incorporation.
302A.161	Powers.
302A.163	Corporate seal.
302A.165	Effect of lack of power; ultra vires.
302A.171	Organization.
302A.181	Bylaws.
302A.201	Board.
302A.203	Number.
302A.205	Qualifications; election.
302A.207	Terms.
302A.209	Acts not void or voidable.
302A.211	Compensation.
302A.213	Classification of directors.
302A.215	Cumulative voting for directors.
302A.221	Resignation.
302A.223	Removal of directors.
302A.225	Vacancies.
302A.231	Board meetings.
302A.233	Absent directors.
302A.235	*Quorum.*
302A.237	*Act of the board.*
302A.239	*Action without meeting.*
302A.241	Committees.
302A.243	Repealed, 1989 c 172 s 11
302A.251	Standard of conduct.
302A.255	Director conflicts of interest.
302A.301	*Officers required.*
302A.305	Duties of required officers.
302A.311	Other officers.
302A.315	Multiple offices.
302A.321	Officers deemed elected.
302A.331	Contract rights.
302A.341	Resignation; removal; vacancies.
302A.351	Delegation.
302A.361	Standard of conduct.
302A.401	*Authorized shares.*
302A.402	Share dividends, divisions, and combinations.
302A.403	*Subscriptions for shares.*
302A.405	*Consideration for shares; value and payment; liability.*
302A.409	*Rights to purchase.*
302A.413	Preemptive rights.
302A.417	*Share certificates; issuance and contents; uncertificated shares.*
302A.419	Lost share certificates; replacement.
302A.423	Fractional shares.
302A.425	*Liability of subscribers and shareholders with respect to shares.*
302A.429	*Restriction on transfer or registration of securities.*
302A.431	Regular meetings of shareholders.
302A.433	Special meetings of shareholders.
302A.435	Notice.
302A.436	Electronic communications.
302A.437	Act of the shareholders.
302A.441	Action without a meeting.
302A.443	Quorum.
302A.445	Voting rights.
302A.447	Voting of shares by organizations and legal representatives.
302A.449	Proxies.
302A.453	Voting trusts.
302A.455	Shareholder voting agreements.
302A.457	Shareholder control agreements.
302A.461	Books and records; inspection.
302A.463	Financial statements.
302A.467	Equitable remedies.
302A.471	Rights of dissenting shareholders.
302A.473	Procedures for asserting dissenters' rights.
302A.501	Loans; guaranties; suretyship.
302A.505	Advances.
302A.521	Indemnification.
302A.551	Distributions.
302A.553	Power to acquire shares.
302A.557	Liability of shareholders for illegal distributions.
302A.559	Liability of directors for illegal distributions.
302A.601	Merger, exchange, transfer.
302A.611	Plan of merger or exchange.
302A.613	Plan approval.
302A.615	Articles of merger or exchange; certificate.
302A.621	Merger of subsidiary.
302A.631	Abandonment.
302A.641	Effective date or time of merger or exchange; effect.
302A.651	Merger or exchange with foreign corporation or limited liability company.
302A.661	Transfer of assets; when permitted.
302A.671	Control share acquisitions.
302A.673	Business combinations.
302A.675	Takeover offer; fair price.
302A.701	*Methods of dissolution.*
302A.711	*Voluntary dissolution by incorporators or directors.*
302A.721	*Voluntary dissolution by shareholders.*
302A.723	*Filing notice of intent to dissolve; effect.*
302A.725	*Procedure in dissolution.*
302A.727	*Dissolution procedure for corporations that give notice to creditors and claimants.*
302A.729	Repealed, 1991 c 49 s 28
302A.7291	*Dissolution procedure for corporations that do not give notice.*

302A.730	Repealed, 1991 c 49 s 28		333.13	Violations; penalties.
302A.731	Revocation of dissolution proceedings.		333.135	Improper use of insignia.
302A.733	Repealed, 1991 c 49 s 28		333.14	Unauthorized use is a crime.
302A.734	Effective date of dissolution; certificate.		333.15	Threatened use may be restrained.
302A.741	Supervised voluntary dissolution.		333.16	Vested rights not affected.
302A.751	Judicial intervention; equitable remedies or dissolution.		333.17	Forbidden in business; "marine" exception.
			333.18	Definitions.
302A.753	Procedure in involuntary or supervised voluntary dissolution.		333.19	Unregistrable matter; collective and certification marks.
302A.755	Qualifications of receivers; powers.		333.20	Application; form, signature, specimen of mark, fee.
302A.757	Action by attorney general.			
302A.759	Filing claims in proceedings to dissolve.		333.21	Certificate of registration, issuance, evidentiary effect.
302A.761	Discontinuance of dissolution proceedings.			
302A.763	Decree of dissolution.		333.22	Term of registration; renewal, notice, fee.
302A.765	Filing decree.		333.23	Conveyances of marks; recordation, fee, necessity.
302A.771	Deposit with state treasurer of amount due certain shareholders.			
			333.24	Secretary of state's record of marks.
302A.781	Claims barred; exceptions.		333.25	Cancellation of marks.
302A.783	Right to sue or defend after dissolution.		333.26	Must use U.S. patent and trademark office system.
302A.791	Omitted assets.			
302A.801	Extension after duration expired.		333.27	Improper registration; liability.
302A.805	Effect of extension.		*333.28*	*Identical or similar marks; liability for misuse.*
302A.821	*Minnesota corporate registration.*		333.285	Dilution of distinctive famous mark may be enjoined.
302A.901	Service of process on corporation.			
302A.917	State interested; proceedings.		333.29	Remedies.
			333.30	Marks acquired at common law.
	CHAPTER 319B		333.305	Forum is district court; service on nonresident registrant.
	PROFESSIONAL FIRMS			
319B.01	Professional Firms Act; citation.		333.31	Service of process upon nonresident registrants.
319B.02	*Definitions.*		333.40	Trademark; when deemed affixed.
319B.03	Authority of Minnesota firms to furnish professional services; election by Minnesota firms to invoke the act.		333.41	Trademarks of workers' unions.
			333.42	Counterfeiting or dealing in counterfeits; how punished.
319B.04	Authority of foreign firms to furnish professional services; election by foreign firms to invoke the act.			
			333.43	Registration.
319B.05	*Firm name.*		333.44	Fraudulent registration or use; penalty.
319B.06	*Furnishing services.*		333.45	Illegal use of certificate of registration.
319B.07	Ownership interests.		333.50	Unauthorized use is a crime.
319B.08	Effect of death or disqualification of owner.		333.51	Threatened use may be restrained.
319B.09	Governance.		333.52	Vested rights not affected.
319B.10	Mergers and other reorganizations.		333.53	Unauthorized use is a crime.
319B.11	Professional regulation.		333.54 Threatened use may be restrained.	
319B.12	Transition provisions.			
319B.40	Professional health services.			

CHAPTER 333
ASSUMED NAMES, INSIGNIA, AND MARKS

333.001	*Definitions.*
333.01	*Commercial assumed names.*
333.02	*Filing of certificate.*
333.03	Repealed, 1978 c 698 s 9
333.035	Amendment of certificate.
333.04	Secretary of state; duties, fees.
333.05	Repealed, 1978 c 698 s 9
333.055	Term of certificate; renewal, notices, fees.
333.06	Pleading failure to file certificate; costs.
333.065	*Penalty for violation.*
333.07	Lodges, societies and the like may register.
333.08	Application.
333.09	Secretary of state to keep record and index.
333.10	Duplicates not registered.
333.11	Issuance of certificates.
333.12	Fees.

302A.011 Definitions

Subdivision 1. Scope. For the purposes of this chapter, unless the language or context clearly indicates that a different meaning is intended, the words, terms, and phrases defined in this section have the meanings given them.

Subd. 2. Acquiring corporation. "Acquiring corporation" means the domestic or foreign corporation that acquires the shares of a corporation in an exchange.

Subd. 3. Address. "Address" means mailing address, including a zip code. In the case of a registered office or principal executive office, the term means the mailing address and the actual office location which shall not be a post office box.

Subd. 4. Articles. "Articles" means, in the case of a corporation incorporated under or governed by this chapter, articles of incorporation, articles of amendment, a resolution of election to become governed by this chapter, a demand retaining the two-thirds majority for shareholder approval of certain transactions, a statement of change of registered office, registered agent, or name of registered agent, a statement establishing or fixing the rights and preferences of a class or series of shares, a statement of cancellation of authorized shares, articles of merger, articles of abandonment, and articles of dissolution. In the case of a foreign corporation, the term includes all documents serving a similar function required to be filed with the secretary of state or other officer of the corporation's state of incorporation.

Subd. 5. Board. "Board" means the board of directors of a corporation.

Subd. 6. Class. "Class", when used with reference to shares, means a category of shares that differs in designation or one or more rights or preferences from another category of shares of the corporation.

Subd. 6a. Closely held corporation. "Closely held corporation" means a corporation which does not have more than 35 shareholders.

Subd. 7. Constituent corporation. "Constituent corporation" means a corporation or a foreign corporation that:

(1) in a merger is either the surviving corporation or a corporation that is merged into the surviving organization; or

(2) in an exchange is either the acquiring corporation or a corporation whose shares are acquired by the acquiring organization.

Subd. 8. Corporation. "Corporation" means a corporation, other than a foreign corporation, organized for profit and incorporated under or governed by this chapter.

Subd. 9. Director. "Director" means a member of the board.

Subd. 10. Distribution. "Distribution" means a direct or indirect transfer of money or other property, other than its own shares, with or without consideration, or an incurrence or issuance of indebtedness, by a corporation to any of its shareholders in respect of its shares. A distribution may be in the form of a dividend or a distribution in liquidation, or as consideration for the purchase, redemption, or other acquisition of its shares, or otherwise.

Subd. 11. Filed with the secretary of state. "Filed with the secretary of state" means that a document meeting the applicable requirements of this chapter, signed and accompanied by a filing fee of $ 35, has been delivered to the secretary of state of this state. The secretary of state shall endorse on the document the word "Filed" and the month, day, and year of filing, record the document in the office of the secretary of state, and return a document to the person who delivered it for filing.

Subd. 12. Foreign corporation. "Foreign corporation" means a corporation organized for profit that is incorporated under laws other than the laws of this state for a purpose or purposes for which a corporation may be incorporated under this chapter.

Subd. 13. Good faith. "Good faith" means honesty in fact in the conduct of the act or transaction concerned.

Subd. 14. Intentionally. "Intentionally" means that the person referred to either has a purpose to do or fail to do the act or cause the result specified or believes that the act or failure to act, if successful, will cause that result. A person "intentionally" violates a statute if the person intentionally does the act or causes the result prohibited by the statute, or if the person intentionally fails to do the act or cause the result required by the statute, even though the person may not know of the existence or constitutionality of the statute or the scope or meaning of the terms used in the statute.

Subd. 15. Know; knowledge. A person "knows" or has "knowledge" of a fact when the person has actual knowledge of it. A person does not "know" or have "knowledge" of a fact merely because the person has reason to know of the fact.

Subd. 16. Legal representative. "Legal representative" means a person empowered to act for another person, including, but not limited to, an agent, officer, partner, or associate of, an organization; a trustee of a trust; a personal representative; an executor of a will; an administrator of an estate; a trustee in bankruptcy; and a receiver, guardian, custodian, or conservator of the person or estate of a person.

Subd. 17. Notice. "Notice" is given by a shareholder of a corporation to the corporation or an officer of the corporation when in writing and mailed or delivered to the corporation or the officer at the registered office or principal executive office of the corporation. In all other cases, "notice" is given to a person when mailed to the person at an address designated by the person or at the last known address of the person, or when communicated to the person orally, or when handed to the person, or when left at the office of the person with a clerk or other person in charge of the office, or if there is no one in charge, when left in a conspicuous place in the office, or if the office is closed or the person to be notified has no office, when left at the dwelling house or usual place of abode of the person with some person of suitable age and discretion then residing therein. Notice by mail is given when deposited in the United States mail with sufficient postage affixed. Notice is deemed received when it is given.

Subd. 18. Officer. "Officer" means a person elected, appointed, or otherwise designated as an officer by the board, and any other person deemed elected as an officer pursuant to section 302A.321.

Subd. 19. Organization. "Organization" means a domestic or foreign corporation, limited liability company, whether domestic or foreign, partnership, limited partnership, joint venture, association, business trust, estate, trust, enterprise, and any other legal or commercial entity.

Subd. 20. Outstanding shares. "Outstanding shares" means all shares duly issued and not reacquired by a corporation.

Subd. 21. Parent. "Parent" of a specified corporation means a corporation that directly, or indirectly through related corporations, owns more than 50 percent of the voting power of the shares entitled to vote for directors of the specified corporation.

Subd. 22. Person. "Person" includes a natural person and an organization.

Subd. 23. Principal executive office. "Principal executive office" means an office where the elected or appointed chief executive officer of a corporation has an office. If the corporation has no elected or appointed chief executive officer, "principal executive office" means the registered office of the corporation.

Subd. 24. Registered office. "Registered office" means the place in this state designated in the articles of a corporation as the registered office of the corporation.

Subd. 25. Related organization. "Related organization" of a specified corporation means:

(1) a parent or subsidiary of the specified corporation;

(2) another subsidiary of a parent of the specified corporation;

(3) a limited liability company owning, directly or indirectly, more than 50 percent of the voting power of the shares entitled to vote for directors of the specified corporation;

(4) a limited liability company having more than 50 per-

cent of the voting power of its membership interests entitled to vote for governors owned directly or indirectly by the specified corporation;

(5) a limited liability company having more than 50 percent of the voting power of its membership interests entitled to vote for governors owned directly or indirectly either (i) by a parent of the specified corporation or (ii) a limited liability company owning, directly or indirectly, more than 50 percent of the voting power of the shares entitled to vote for directors of the specified corporation; or

(6) a corporation having more than 50 percent of the voting power of its shares entitled to vote for director owned directly or indirectly by a limited liability company owning, directly or indirectly, more than 50 percent of the voting power of the shares entitled to vote for directors of the specified corporation.

Subd. 26. Security. "Security" has the meaning given it in section 80A.14, subdivision 18.

Subd. 27. Series. "Series" means a category of shares, within a class of shares authorized or issued by a corporation by or pursuant to its articles, that have some of the same rights and preferences as other shares within the same class, but that differ in designation or one or more rights and preferences from another category of shares within that class.

Subd. 28. Share. "Share" means one of the units, however designated, into which the shareholders' proprietary interests in a corporation are divided.

Subd. 29. Shareholder. "Shareholder" means a person registered on the books or records of a corporation or its transfer agent or registrar as the owner of whole or fractional shares of the corporation.

Subd. 30. Signed. (a) "Signed" means that the signature of a person has been written on a document, as provided in section 645.44, subdivision 14, and, with respect to a document required by this chapter to be filed with the secretary of state, means that the document has been signed by a person authorized to do so by this chapter, the articles or bylaws, or a resolution approved by the directors as required by section 302A.237 or the shareholders as required by section 302A.437.

(b) A signature on a document may be a facsimile affixed, engraved, printed, placed, stamped with indelible ink, transmitted by facsimile or electronically, or in any other manner reproduced on the document.

Subd. 31. Subsidiary. "Subsidiary" of a specified corporation means a corporation having more than 50 percent of the voting power of its shares entitled to vote for directors owned directly, or indirectly through related corporations, by the specified corporation.

Subd. 32. Surviving corporation. "Surviving corporation" means the domestic or foreign corporation resulting from a merger.

Subd. 33. Repealed, 1997 c 10 art 1 s 33

Subd. 34. Vote. "Vote" includes authorization by written action.

Subd. 35. Repealed, 1982 c 497 s 73

Subd. 36. Written action. "Written action" means a written document signed by all of the persons required to take the action described. The term also means the counterparts of a written document signed by any of the persons taking the action described. Each counterpart constitutes the action of the persons signing it, and all the counterparts, taken together, constitute one written action by all of the persons signing them.

Subd. 37. Acquiring person. "Acquiring person" means a person that makes or proposes to make a control share acquisition.

When two or more persons act as a partnership, limited partnership, syndicate, or other group pursuant to any written or oral agreement, arrangement, relationship, understanding, or otherwise for the purposes of acquiring, owning, or voting shares of an issuing public corporation, all members of the partnership, syndicate, or other group constitute a "person." "Acquiring person" does not include (a) a licensed broker/dealer or licensed underwriter who (1) purchases shares of an issuing public corporation solely for purposes of resale to the public and (2) is not acting in concert with an acquiring person, or (b) a person who becomes entitled to exercise or direct the exercise of a new range of voting power within any of the ranges specified in section 302A.671, subdivision 2, paragraph (d), solely as a result of a repurchase of shares by, or recapitalization of, the issuing public corporation or similar action unless (1) the repurchase, recapitalization, or similar action was proposed by or on behalf of, or pursuant to any written or oral agreement, arrangement, relationship, understanding, or otherwise with, the person or any affiliate or associate of the person or (2) the person thereafter acquires beneficial ownership, directly or indirectly, of outstanding shares entitled to vote of the issuing public corporation and, immediately after the acquisition, is entitled to exercise or direct the exercise of the same or a higher range of voting power under section 302A.671, subdivision 2, paragraph (d), as the person became entitled to exercise as a result of the repurchase, recapitalization, or similar action.

Subd. 38. Control share acquisition. "Control share acquisition" means an acquisition, directly or indirectly, by an acquiring person of beneficial ownership of shares of an issuing public corporation that, except for section 302A.671, would, when added to all other shares of the issuing public corporation beneficially owned by the acquiring person, entitle the acquiring person, immediately after the acquisition, to exercise or direct the exercise of a new range of voting power within any of the ranges specified in section 302A.671, subdivision 2, paragraph (d), but does not include any of the following:

(a) an acquisition before, or pursuant to an agreement entered into before, August 1, 1984;

(b) an acquisition by a donee pursuant to an inter vivos gift not made to avoid section 302A.671 or by a distributee as defined in section 524.1-201, clause (10);

(c) an acquisition pursuant to a security agreement not created to avoid section 302A.671;

(d) an acquisition under sections 302A.601 to 302A.661, if the issuing public corporation is a party to the transaction;

(e) an acquisition from the issuing public corporation;

(f) an acquisition for the benefit of others by a person acting in good faith and not made to avoid section 302A.671, to the extent that the person may not exercise or direct the exercise of the voting power or disposition of the shares except upon the instruction of others;

(g) an acquisition pursuant to a savings, employee stock ownership, or other employee benefit plan of the issuing public corporation or any of its subsidiaries, or by a fiduciary of the plan acting in a fiduciary capacity pursuant to the plan; or

(h) an acquisition subsequent to January 1, 1991, pursuant to an offer to purchase for cash pursuant to a tender offer all shares of the voting stock of the issuing public corporation:

(i) which has been approved by a majority vote of the members of a committee comprised of the disinterested members of the board of the issuing public corporation formed pursuant to section 302A.673, subdivision 1, paragraph (d), before the commencement of, or the public announcement of the intent to commence, the tender offer; and

(ii) pursuant to which the acquiring person will become the owner of over 50 percent of the voting stock of the issuing public corporation outstanding at the time of the transaction.

For purposes of this subdivision, shares beneficially owned by a plan described in clause (g), or by a fiduciary of a plan described in clause (g) pursuant to the plan, are not deemed to be beneficially owned by a person who is a fiduciary of the plan.

Subd. 39. Issuing public corporation. "Issuing public corporation" means either: (1) a publicly held corporation that has at least 50 shareholders; or (2) any other corporation that has at least 100 shareholders, provided that if, before January 1, 1998, a corporation that has at least 50 shareholders elects to be an issuing public corporation by express amendment contained in the articles or bylaws, including bylaws approved by the board, that corporation is an issuing public corporation if it has at least 50 shareholders.

Subd. 40. Publicly held corporation. "Publicly held corporation" means a corporation that has a class of equity securities registered pursuant to section 12, or is subject to section 15(d), of the Securities Exchange Act of 1934.

Subd. 41. Beneficial owner; beneficial ownership.

(a) "Beneficial owner," when used with respect to shares or other securities, includes, but is not limited to, any person who, directly or indirectly through any written or oral agreement, arrangement, relationship, understanding, or otherwise, has or shares the power to vote, or direct the voting of, the shares or securities or has or shares the power to dispose of, or direct the disposition of, the shares or securities, except that:

(1) a person shall not be deemed the beneficial owner of shares or securities tendered pursuant to a tender or exchange offer made by the person or any of the person's affiliates or associates until the tendered shares or securities are accepted for purchase or exchange; and

(2) a person shall not be deemed the beneficial owner of shares or securities with respect to which the person has the power to vote or direct the voting arising solely from a revocable proxy given in response to a proxy solicitation required to be made and made in accordance with the applicable rules and regulations under the Securities Exchange Act of 1934 and is not then reportable under that act on a Schedule 13D or comparable report, or, if the corporation is not subject to the rules and regulations under the Securities Exchange Act of 1934, would have been required to be made and would not have been reportable if the corporation had been subject to the rules and regulations.

(b) "Beneficial ownership" includes, but is not limited to, the right to acquire shares or securities through the exercise of options, warrants, or rights, or the conversion of convertible securities, or otherwise. The shares or securities subject to the options, warrants, rights, or conversion privileges held by a person shall be deemed to be outstanding for the purpose of computing the percentage of outstanding shares or securities of the class or series owned by the person, but shall not be deemed to be outstanding for the purpose of computing the percentage of the class or series owned by any other person. A person shall be deemed the beneficial owner of shares and securities beneficially owned by any relative or spouse of the person or any relative of the spouse, residing in the home of the person, any trust or estate in which the person owns ten percent or more of the total beneficial interest or serves as trustee or executor or in a similar fiduciary capacity, any corporation or entity in which the person owns ten percent or more of the equity, and any affiliate of the person.

(c) When two or more persons act or agree to act as a partnership, limited partnership, syndicate, or other group for the purposes of acquiring, owning, or voting shares or other securities of a corporation, all members of the partnership, syndicate, or other group are deemed to constitute a "person" and to have acquired beneficial ownership, as of the date they first so act or agree to act together, of all shares or securities of the corporation beneficially owned by the person.

Subd. 42. Interested shares. "Interested shares" means the shares of an issuing public corporation beneficially owned by any of the following persons: (1) the acquiring person, (2) any officer of the issuing public corporation, or (3) any employee of the issuing public corporation who is also a director of the issuing public corporation.

Subd. 43. Affiliate. "Affiliate" means a person that directly or indirectly controls, is controlled by, or is under common control with, a specified person.

Subd. 44. Announcement date. "Announcement date," when used in reference to any business combination, means the date of the first public announcement of the final, definitive proposal for the business combination.

Subd. 45. Associate. "Associate," when used to indicate a relationship with any person, means any of the following:

(1) any corporation or organization of which the person is an officer or partner or is, directly or indirectly, the beneficial owner of ten percent or more of any class or series of shares entitled to vote or other equity interest;

(2) any trust or estate in which the person has a substantial beneficial interest or as to which the person serves as trustee or executor or in a similar fiduciary capacity;

(3) any relative or spouse of the person, or any relative of the spouse, residing in the home of the person.

Subd. 46. Business combination. "Business combination," when used in reference to any issuing public corporation and any interested shareholder of the issuing public corporation, means any of the following:

(a) any merger of the issuing public corporation or any subsidiary of the issuing public corporation with (1) the interested shareholder or (2) any other domestic or foreign corporation (whether or not itself an interested shareholder of the issuing public corporation) that is, or after the merger would be, an affiliate or associate of the interested shareholder, but excluding (1) the merger of a wholly-owned subsidiary of the issuing public corporation into the issuing public corporation, (2) the merger of two or more wholly-owned subsidiaries of the issuing public corporation, or (3) the merger of a corporation, other than an interested shareholder or an affiliate or associate of an interested shareholder, with a wholly-owned subsidiary of the issuing public corporation pursuant to which the surviving corporation, immediately after the merger, becomes a wholly-owned subsidiary of the issuing public corporation;

(b) any exchange, pursuant to a plan of exchange under section 302A.601, subdivision 2, or a comparable statute of any other state or jurisdiction, of shares or other securities of the issuing public corporation or any subsidiary of the issuing corporation or money, or other property for shares, other securities, money, or property of (1) the interested shareholder or (2) any other domestic or foreign corporation (whether or not itself an interested shareholder of the issuing public corporation) that is, or after the exchange would be, an affiliate or associate of the interested shareholder, but excluding the exchange of shares of a corporation, other than an interested shareholder or an affiliate or associate of an interested shareholder, pursuant to which the corporation, immediately after the exchange, becomes a wholly-owned subsidiary of the issuing public corporation;

(c) any sale, lease, exchange, mortgage, pledge, transfer, or other disposition (in a single transaction or a series of transactions), other than sales of goods or services in the ordinary course of business or redemptions pursuant to section 302A.671, subdivision 6, to or with the interested shareholder or any affiliate or associate of the interested shareholder, other than to or with the issuing public corporation or a wholly-owned subsidiary of the issuing public corporation, of assets of the issuing public corporation or any subsidiary of the issuing public corporation (1) having an aggregate market value equal to ten percent or more of the aggregate market value of all the assets, determined on a consolidated basis, of the issuing public corporation, (2) having an aggregate market value equal to ten percent or more of the aggregate market value of all the outstanding shares of the issuing public corporation, or (3) representing ten percent or more of the earning power or net income, determined on a consolidated basis, of the issuing public corporation except a cash dividend or distribution paid or made pro rata to all shareholders of the issuing public corporation;

(d) the issuance or transfer by the issuing public corporation or any subsidiary of the issuing public corporation (in a single transaction or a series of transactions) of any shares of the issuing public corporation or any subsidiary of the issuing public corporation that have an aggregate market value equal to five percent or more of the aggregate market value of all the outstanding shares of the issuing public corporation to the interested shareholder or any affiliate or associate of the interested shareholder, except pursuant to the exercise of warrants or rights to purchase shares offered, or a dividend or distribution paid or made, pro rata to all shareholders of the issuing public corporation other than for the purpose, directly or indirectly, of facilitating or effecting a subsequent transaction that would have been a business combination if the dividend or distribution had not been made;

(e) the adoption of any plan or proposal for the liquidation or dissolution of the issuing public corporation, or any reincorporation of the issuing public corporation in another state or jurisdiction, proposed by or on behalf of, or pursuant to any written or oral agreement, arrangement, relationship, understanding, or otherwise with, the interested shareholder or any affiliate or associate of the interested shareholder;

(f) any reclassification of securities (including without limitation any share dividend or split, reverse share split, or other distribution of shares in respect of shares), recapitalization of the issuing public corporation, merger of the issuing public corporation with any subsidiary of the issuing public corporation, exchange of shares of the issuing public corporation with any subsidiary of the issuing public corporation, or other transaction (whether or not with or into or otherwise involving the interested shareholder), proposed by or on behalf of, or pursuant to any written or oral agreement, arrangement, relationship, understanding, or otherwise with, the interested shareholder or any affiliate or associate of the interested shareholder, that has the effect, directly or indirectly, of increasing the proportionate share of the outstanding shares of any class or series of shares entitled to vote, or securities that are exchangeable for, convertible into, or carry a right to acquire shares entitled to vote, of the issuing public corporation or any subsidiary of the issuing public corporation that is, directly or indirectly, owned by the interested shareholder or any affiliate or associate of the interested shareholder, except as a result of immaterial changes due to fractional share adjustments;

(g) any receipt by the interested shareholder or any affiliate or associate of the interested shareholder of the benefit, directly or indirectly (except proportionately as a shareholder of the issuing public corporation), of any loans, advances, guarantees, pledges, or other financial assistance, or any tax credits or other tax advantages provided by or through the issuing public corporation or any subsidiary of the issuing public corporation.

Subd. 47. Consummation date. "Consummation date," with respect to any business combination, means the date of consummation of the business combination or, in the case of a business combination as to which a shareholder vote is taken, the later of (1) the business day before the vote or (2) 20 days before the date of consummation of the business combination.

Subd. 48. Control. "Control," including the terms "controlling," "controlled by," and "under common control with," means the possession, directly or indirectly, of the power to direct or cause the direction of the management and policies of a person, whether through the ownership of voting securities, by contract, or otherwise. A person's beneficial ownership of ten percent or more of the voting power of a corporation's outstanding shares entitled to vote in the election of directors creates a presumption that the person has control of the corporation. Notwithstanding the foregoing, a person is not considered to have control of a corporation if the person holds voting power, in good faith and not for the purpose of avoiding section 302A.673, as an agent, bank, broker, nominee, custodian, or trustee for one or more beneficial owners who do not individually or as a group have control of the corporation.

Subd. 49. Interested shareholder. (a) "Interested shareholder," when used in reference to any issuing public corporation, means any person that is (1) the beneficial owner, directly or indirectly, of ten percent or more of the voting power of the outstanding shares entitled to vote of the issuing public corporation or (2) an affiliate or associate of the issuing public corporation and at any time within the four-year period immediately before the date in question was the beneficial owner, directly or indirectly, of ten percent or more of the voting power of the then outstanding shares entitled to vote of the issuing public corporation. Notwithstanding anything stated in this subdivision, if a person who has not been a beneficial owner of ten percent or more of the voting power of the outstanding shares entitled to vote of the issuing public corporation immediately prior to a repurchase of shares by, or recapitalization of, the issuing public corporation or similar action shall become a beneficial owner of ten percent or more of the voting power solely as a result of the share repurchase, recapitalization, or similar action, the person shall not be deemed to be the beneficial owner of ten percent or more of the voting power for purposes of clause (1) or (2) unless:

(i) the repurchase, recapitalization, conversion, or similar action was proposed by or on behalf of, or pursuant to any agreement, arrangement, relationship, understanding, or otherwise (whether or not in writing) with, the person or any affiliate or associate of the person; or

(ii) the person thereafter acquires beneficial ownership, directly or indirectly, of outstanding shares entitled to vote of the issuing public corporation and, immediately after the acquisition, is the beneficial owner, directly or indirectly, of ten percent or more of the voting power of the outstanding shares entitled to vote of the issuing public corporation.

(b) Interested shareholder does not include:

(1) the issuing public corporation or any of its subsidiaries; or

(2) a savings, employee stock ownership, or other employee benefit plan of the issuing public corporation or its subsidiary, or a fiduciary of the plan when acting in a fiduciary capacity pursuant to the plan.

For purposes of this subdivision, shares beneficially owned by a plan described in clause (2), or by a fiduciary of a plan described in clause (2) pursuant to the plan, are not deemed to be beneficially owned by a person who is a fiduciary of the plan.

Subd. 50. Market value. "Market value," when used in reference to shares or other property of any corporation, means the following:

(1) in the case of shares, the average closing sale price of a share on the composite tape for New York Stock Exchange listed shares during the 30 trading days immediately preceding the date in question or, with respect to the references in section 302A.553, subdivision 3, if a person or persons selling the shares have commenced a tender offer or have announced an intention to seek control of the corporation, during the 30 trading days preceding the earlier of the commencement of the tender offer or the making of the announcement, or, if the shares are not quoted on the composite tape or not listed on the New York Stock Exchange, on the principal United States securities exchange registered under the Securities Exchange Act of 1934 on which the shares are listed, or, if the shares are not listed on any such exchange, on the NASDAQ National Market, or, if the shares are not quoted on the NASDAQ National Market, on the NASDAQ Small Cap Market, or any system then in use, or, with respect to the reference in section 302A.553, subdivision 3, if the person or persons selling the shares shall have commenced a tender offer or have announced an intention to seek control of the corporation, during the 30 trading days preceding the earlier of the commencement of the tender offer or the making of the announcement, provided that if no quotation is available, the market value is the fair market value on the date in question of the shares as determined in good faith by the board of the corporation;

(2) in the case of property other than cash or shares, the fair market value of the property on the date in question as determined in good faith by the board of the corporation.

Subd. 51. Share acquisition date. "Share acquisition date," with respect to any person and any issuing public corporation, means the date that the person first becomes an interested shareholder of the issuing public corporation; provided, however, that in the event a person becomes, on one or more dates, an interested shareholder of the issuing public corporation, but thereafter ceases to be an interested shareholder of the issuing public corporation, and subsequently again becomes an interested shareholder, "share acquisition date," with respect to that person means the date on which the person most recently became an interested shareholder of the issuing public corporation.

Subd. 52. Offeror. "Offeror" means a person who makes or in any way participates in making a takeover offer. Offeror does not include a bank or broker-dealer loaning funds to an offeror in the ordinary course of its business or a bank, broker-dealer, attorney, accountant, consultant, employee, or other person furnishing information or advice to or performing ministerial duties for an offeror and not otherwise participating in the takeover offer. When two or more persons act as a partnership, limited partnership, syndicate, or other group pursuant to any agreement, arrangement, relationship, understanding, or otherwise, whether or not in writing, for the purpose of acquiring, owning, or voting shares of a target company, all members of the partnership, syndicate, or other group constitute "a person."

Subd. 53. Takeover offer. (a) "Takeover offer" means an offer to acquire shares of an issuing public corporation from a shareholder pursuant to a tender offer or request or invitation for tenders, if, after the acquisition of all shares acquired pursuant to the offer:

(1) the offeror would be directly or indirectly a beneficial owner of more than ten percent of any class or series of the outstanding shares of the issuing public corporation and was directly or indirectly the beneficial owner of ten percent or less of that class or series of the outstanding shares of the issuing public corporation before commencement of the offer; or

(2) the beneficial ownership by the offeror of any class or series of the outstanding shares of the issuing public corporation would be increased by more than ten percent of that class or series and the offeror was directly or indirectly the beneficial owner of ten percent or more of any class or series of the outstanding shares of the issuing public corporation before commencement of the offer.

(b) Takeover offer does not include:

(1) an offer in connection with the acquisition of a share which, together with all other acquisitions by the offeror of shares of the same class or series of shares of the issuer, would not result in the offeror having acquired more than two percent of that class or series during the preceding 12-month period;

(2) an offer by the issuer to acquire its own shares unless the offer is made during the pendency of a takeover offer by a person who is not an associate or affiliate of the issuer;

(3) an offer in which the issuing public corporation is an insurance company subject to regulation by the commissioner of commerce, a financial institution regulated by the commissioner, or a public service utility subject to regulation by the public utilities commission.

Subd. 54. Division or combination. "Division" or "combination" means dividing or combining shares of a class or series, whether issued or unissued, into a greater or lesser number of shares of the same class or series.

Subd. 55. Acquiring organization. "Acquiring organization" means a corporation, foreign corporation, or domestic or foreign limited liability company that acquires in an exchange the shares of a corporation or foreign corporation or the membership interests of a domestic or foreign limited liability company.

Subd. 56. Constituent organization. "Constituent organization" means a corporation, foreign corporation, limited liability company or foreign limited liability company that:

(1) in a merger is either the surviving organization or an organization that is merged into the surviving organization; or

(2) in an exchange is either the acquiring organization or

an organization whose securities are acquired by the acquiring organization.

Subd. 57. Owners. "Owners" means shareholders in the case of a corporation or foreign corporation and members in the case of a limited liability company.

Subd. 58. Ownership interests. "Ownership interests" means shares in the case of a corporation or foreign corporation and membership interests in the case of a domestic or foreign limited liability company.

Subd. 59. Surviving organization. "Surviving organization" means the corporation or foreign corporation or domestic or foreign limited liability company resulting from a merger.

302A.101 Purposes

A corporation may be incorporated under this chapter for any business purpose or purposes, unless some other statute of this state requires incorporation for any of those purposes under a different law. Unless otherwise provided in its articles, a corporation has general business purposes.

302A.105 Incorporators

One or more natural persons of at least 18 years of age may act as incorporators of a corporation by filing with the secretary of state articles of incorporation for the corporation.

302A.111 Articles

Subdivision 1. Required provisions. The articles of incorporation shall contain:

(a) The name of the corporation;

(b) The address of the registered office of the corporation and the name of its registered agent, if any, at that address;

(c) The aggregate number of shares that the corporation has authority to issue; and

(d) The name and address of each incorporator.

Subd. 2. Statutory provisions that may be modified only in articles. The following provisions govern a corporation unless modified in the articles:

(a) A corporation has general business purposes (section 302A.101);

(b) A corporation has perpetual existence and certain powers (section 302A.161);

(c) The power to adopt, amend, or repeal the bylaws is vested in the board (section 302A.181);

(d) A corporation must allow cumulative voting for directors (section 302A.215);

(e) The affirmative vote of a majority of directors present is required for an action of the board (section 302A.237);

(f) A written action by the board taken without a meeting must be signed by all directors (section 302A.239);

(g) The board may authorize the issuance of securities and rights to purchase securities (section 302A.401, subdivision 1);

(h) All shares are common shares entitled to vote and are of one class and one series (section 302A.401, subdivision 2, clauses (a) and (b));

(i) All shares have equal rights and preferences in all matters not otherwise provided for by the board (section 302A.401, subdivision 2, clause (b));

(j) The par value of shares is fixed at one cent per share for certain purposes and may be fixed by the board for certain other purposes (section 302A.401, subdivision 2, clause (c));

(k) The board or the shareholders may issue shares for any consideration or for no consideration to effectuate share dividends, divisions, or combinations, and determine the value of nonmonetary consideration (section 302A.405, subdivision 1);

(l) Shares of a class or series must not be issued to holders of shares of another class or series to effectuate share dividends, divisions, or combinations, unless authorized by a majority of the voting power of the shares of the same class or series as the shares to be issued (section 302A.405, subdivision 1);

(m) A corporation may issue rights to purchase securities whose terms, provisions, and conditions are fixed by the board (section 302A.409);

(n) A shareholder has certain preemptive rights, unless otherwise provided by the board (section 302A.413);

(o) The affirmative vote of the holders of a majority of the voting power of the shares present and entitled to vote at a duly held meeting is required for an action of the shareholders, except where this chapter requires the affirmative vote of a majority of the voting power of all shares entitled to vote (section 302A.437, subdivision 1);

(p) Shares of a corporation acquired by the corporation may be reissued (section 302A.553, subdivision 1);

(q) Each share has one vote unless otherwise provided in the terms of the share (section 302A.445, subdivision 3);

(r) A corporation may issue shares for a consideration less than the par value, if any, of the shares (section 302A.405, subdivision 2); and

(s) The board may effect share dividends, divisions, and combinations under certain circumstances without shareholder approval (section 302A.402).

Subd. 3. Statutory provisions that may be modified either in articles or in bylaws. The following provisions govern a corporation unless modified either in the articles or in the bylaws:

(a) Directors serve for an indefinite term that expires at the next regular meeting of shareholders (section 302A.207);

(b) The compensation of directors is fixed by the board (section 302A.211);

(c) A certain method must be used for removal of directors (section 302A.223);

(d) A certain method must be used for filling board vacancies (section 302A.225);

(e) If the board fails to select a place for a board meeting, it must be held at the principal executive office (section 302A.231, subdivision 1);

(f) The notice of a board meeting need not state the purpose of the meeting (section 302A.231, subdivision 3);

(g) A majority of the board is a quorum for a board meeting (section 302A.235);

(h) A committee shall consist of one or more persons, who need not be directors, appointed by affirmative vote of a majority of the directors present (section 302A.241, subdivision 2);

(i) The board may establish a special litigation committee (section 302A.241);

(j) The chief executive officer and chief financial officer have specified duties, until the board determines otherwise (section 302A.305);

(k) Officers may delegate some or all of their duties and powers, if not prohibited by the board from doing so (section 302A.351);

(l) The board may establish uncertificated shares (section 302A.417, subdivision 7);

(m) Regular meetings of shareholders need not be held, unless demanded by a shareholder under certain conditions (section 302A.431);

(n) In all instances where a specific minimum notice period has not otherwise been fixed by law, not less than ten-days notice is required for a meeting of shareholders (section 302A.435, subdivision 2);

(o) The number of shares required for a quorum at a shareholders' meeting is a majority of the voting power of the shares entitled to vote at the meeting (section 302A.443);

(p) The board may fix a date up to 60 days before the date of a shareholders' meeting as the date for the determination of the holders of shares entitled to notice of and entitled to vote at the meeting (section 302A.445, subdivision 1);

(q) Indemnification of certain persons is required (section 302A.521); and

(r) The board may authorize, and the corporation may make, distributions not prohibited, limited, or restricted by an agreement (section 302A.551, subdivision 1).

Subd. 4. Optional provisions; specific subjects. The provisions in paragraphs (a), (g), (q), (r), and (u) may be included in the articles.

The provisions in paragraphs (b) to (f), (h) to (p), (s), and (t) may be included either in the articles or the bylaws:

(a) The members of the first board may be named in the articles (section 302A.201, subdivision 1);

(b) A manner for increasing or decreasing the number of directors may be provided (section 302A.203);

(c) Additional qualifications for directors may be imposed (section 302A.205);

(d) Directors may be classified (section 302A.213);

(e) The day or date, time, and place of board meetings may be fixed (section 302A.231, subdivision 1);

(f) Absent directors may be permitted to give written consent or opposition to a proposal (section 302A.233);

(g) A larger than majority vote may be required for board action (section 302A.237);

(h) Authority to sign and deliver certain documents may be delegated to an officer or agent of the corporation other than the chief executive officer (section 302A.305, subdivision 2);

(i) Additional officers may be designated (section 302A.311);

(j) Additional powers, rights, duties, and responsibilities may be given to officers (section 302A.311);

(k) A method for filling vacant offices may be specified (section 302A.341, subdivision 3);

(l) A certain officer or agent may be authorized to sign share certificates (section 302A.417, subdivision 2);

(m) The transfer or registration of transfer of securities may be restricted (section 302A.429);

(n) The day or date, time, and place of regular shareholder meetings may be fixed (section 302A.431, subdivision 3);

(o) Certain persons may be authorized to call special meetings of shareholders (section 302A.433, subdivision 1);

(p) Notices of shareholder meetings may be required to contain certain information (section 302A.435, subdivision 3);

(q) A larger than majority vote may be required for shareholder action (section 302A.437);

(r) Voting rights may be granted in or pursuant to the articles to persons who are not shareholders (section 302A.445, subdivision 4);

(s) Corporate actions giving rise to dissenter rights may be designated (section 302A.471, subdivision 1, clause (e));

(t) The rights and priorities of persons to receive distributions may be established (section 302A.551); and

(u) A director's personal liability to the corporation or its shareholders for monetary damages for breach of fiduciary duty as a director may be eliminated or limited in the articles (section 302A.251, subdivision 4).

Nothing in this subdivision limits the right of the board, by resolution, to take an action that may be included in the bylaws under this subdivision without including it in the bylaws, unless it is required to be included in the bylaws by another provision of this chapter.

Subd. 5. Optional provisions: generally. The articles may contain other provisions not inconsistent with section 302A.201 or any other provision of law relating to the management of the business or the regulation of the affairs of the corporation.

Subd. 6. Powers need not be stated. It is not necessary to set forth in the articles any of the corporate powers granted by this chapter.

302A.121 Registered office; registered agent

Subdivision 1. Registered office. A corporation shall continuously maintain a registered office in this state. A registered office need not be the same as the principal place of business or the principal executive office of the corporation. If the current registered office address listed in the records of the secretary of state is not in compliance with section 302A.011, subdivision 3, the corporation must provide a new registered office address that is in compliance. A fee may not be charged if the registered office address is being changed only to bring the address into compliance. The new registered office address must have been approved by the board of directors.

Subd. 2. Registered agent. A corporation may designate in its articles a registered agent. The registered agent may be a natural person residing in this state, a domestic corporation, or limited liability company, or a foreign corporation or foreign limited liability company authorized to transact business in this state. The registered agent must maintain a business office that is identical with the registered office.

302A.123 Change of registered office or registered agent; change of name of registered agent

Subdivision 1. Statement. A corporation may change its registered office, designate or change its registered agent, or state a change in the name of its registered agent, by filing with the secretary of state a statement containing:

(a) The name of the corporation;

(b) If the address of its registered office is to be changed, the new address of its registered office;

(c) If its registered agent is to be designated or changed, the name of its new registered agent;

(d) If the name of its registered agent is to be changed, the name of its registered agent as changed;

(e) A statement that the address of its registered office and the address of the business office of its registered agent, as changed, will be identical; and

(f) A statement that the change of registered office or registered agent was authorized by resolution approved by the affirmative vote of a majority of the directors present.

Subd. 2. Resignation of agent. A registered agent of a corporation may resign by filing with the secretary of state a signed written notice of resignation, including a statement that a signed copy of the notice has been given to the corporation at its principal executive office or to a legal representative of the corporation. The appointment of the agent terminates 30 days after the notice is filed with the secretary of state.

Subd. 3. Change of business address or name of agent. If the business address or name of a registered agent changes, the agent shall change the address of the registered office or the name of the registered agent, as the case may be, of each corporation represented by that agent by filing with the secretary of state a statement as required in subdivision 1, except that it need be signed only by the registered agent, need not be responsive to clause (f), and must state that a copy of the statement has been mailed to each of those corporations or to the legal representative of each of those corporations.

302A.131 Amendment of articles

The articles of a corporation may be amended at any time to include or modify any provision that is required or permitted to appear in the articles or to omit any provision not required to be included in the articles, except that when articles are amended to restate them, the name and address of each incorporator may be omitted. Unless otherwise provided in this chapter, the articles may be amended or modified only in accordance with sections 302A.133 to 302A.139. An amendment which merely restates the then-existing articles of incorporation, as amended, is not an amendment for the purposes of section 302A.215, subdivision 2, or 302A.413, subdivision 9.

302A.133 Procedure for amendment when no shares are outstanding

Before the issuance of shares by a corporation, the articles may be amended pursuant to section 302A.171 by the incorporators or by the board. The articles may also be amended by the board to change or cancel a statement pursuant to section 302A.401, subdivision 3, establishing or fixing the rights and preferences of a class or series of shares before the issuance of any shares of that class or series or at any subsequent time that no shares of that class or series are outstanding by filing articles of amendment or a statement of cancellation, as appropriate, with the secretary of state. If a statement filed pursuant to section 302A.401, subdivision 3, is canceled, the shares of the class and series originally covered by the statement have the status of authorized but unissued, undesignated shares, unless the articles otherwise provide. If the articles provide that the canceled shares may not be reissued, the statement of cancellation must include the information specified by section 302A.553, subdivision 2.

302A.135 Procedure for amendment after issuance of shares

Subdivision 1. Manner of amendment. Except as otherwise set forth in section 302A.133, after the issuance of shares by the corporation, the articles may be amended in the manner set forth in this section.

Subd. 2. Submission to shareholders. A resolution approved by the affirmative vote of a majority of the directors present, or proposed by a shareholder or shareholders holding three percent or more of the voting power of the shares entitled to vote, that sets forth the proposed amendment shall be submitted to a vote at the next regular or special meeting of the shareholders of which notice has not yet been given but still can be timely given. Any number of amendments may be submitted to the shareholders and voted upon at one meeting, but the same or substantially the same amendment proposed by a shareholder or shareholders need not be submitted to the shareholders or be voted upon at more than one meeting during a 15-month period, except that if a corporation is registered or reporting under the federal securities laws, the provisions of this sentence do not apply to the extent that those provisions are in conflict with the federal securities laws or rules adopted under those laws. The resolution may amend the articles in their entirety to restate and supersede the original articles and all amendments to them.

Subd. 3. Notice. Written notice of the shareholders' meeting setting forth the substance of the proposed amendment shall be given to each shareholder entitled to vote in the manner provided in section 302A.435 for the giving of notice of meetings of shareholders.

Subd. 4. Approval by shareholders. (a) The proposed amendment is adopted when approved by the affirmative vote of the shareholders required by section 302A.437, except as provided in paragraphs (b) and (c) and subdivision 5.

(b) For a closely held corporation, if the articles provide for a specified proportion or number equal to or larger than the majority necessary to transact a specified type of business at a meeting, or if it is proposed to amend the articles to provide for a specified proportion or number equal to or larger than the majority necessary to transact a specified type of business at a meeting, the affirmative vote necessary to add the provision to, or to amend an existing provision in, the articles is the larger of:

(1) the specified proportion or number or, in the absence of a specific provision, the affirmative vote necessary to transact the type of business described in the proposed amendment at a meeting immediately before the effectiveness of the proposed amendment; or

(2) the specified proportion or number that would, upon effectiveness of the proposed amendment, be necessary to transact the specified type of business at a meeting.

(c) For corporations other than closely held corporations, if the articles provide for a larger proportion or number to transact a specified type of business at a meeting, the affirmative vote of that larger proportion or number is necessary to amend the articles to decrease the proportion or number necessary to transact the business.

Subd. 5. Certain restatements. An amendment that merely restates the existing articles, as amended, may be authorized by a resolution approved by the board and may, but need not, be submitted to and approved by the shareholders as provided in subdivisions 2, 3, and 4.

302A.137 Class or series voting on amendments

The holders of the outstanding shares of a class or series are entitled to vote as a class or series upon a proposed amendment, whether or not entitled to vote thereon by the provisions of the articles, if the amendment would:

(a) Increase or decrease the aggregate number of authorized shares of the class or series;

(b) Effect an exchange, reclassification, or cancellation of all or part of the shares of the class or series;

(c) Effect an exchange, or create a right of exchange, of all or any part of the shares of another class or series for the shares of the class or series;

(d) Change the rights or preferences of the shares of the class or series;

(e) Change the shares of the class or series, whether with or without par value, into the same or a different number of shares, either with or without par value, of another class or series;

(f) Create a new class or series of shares having rights and preferences prior and superior to the shares of that class or series, or increase the rights and preferences or the number of authorized shares, of a class or series having rights and preferences prior or superior to the shares of that class or series;

(g) Divide the shares of the class into series and determine the designation of each series and the variations in the relative rights and preferences between the shares of each series, or authorize the board to do so;

(h) Limit or deny any existing preemptive rights of the shares of the class or series; or

(i) Cancel or otherwise affect distributions on the shares of the class or series that have accrued but have not been declared.

302A.139 Articles of amendment

When an amendment has been adopted, articles of amendment shall be prepared that contain:
(a) The name of the corporation;
(b) The amendment adopted;
(c) With respect to an amendment restating the articles, a statement that the amendment restating the articles correctly sets forth without change the corresponding provisions of the articles as previously amended if the amendment was approved only by the board;
(d) If the amendment provides for but does not establish the manner for effecting an exchange, reclassification, division, combination, or cancellation of issued shares, a statement of the manner in which it will be effected; and
(e) A statement that the amendment has been adopted pursuant to this chapter.

302A.151 Filing articles

Articles of incorporation and articles of amendment shall be filed with the secretary of state.

302A.161 Powers

Subdivision 1. Generally; limitations. A corporation has the powers set forth in this section, subject to any limitations provided in any other statute of this state or in its articles.
Subd. 2. Duration. A corporation has perpetual duration.
Subd. 3. Legal capacity. A corporation may sue and be sued, complain and defend and participate as a party or otherwise in any legal, administrative, or arbitration proceeding, in its corporate name.
Subd. 4. Property ownership. A corporation may purchase, lease, or otherwise acquire, own, hold, improve, use, and otherwise deal in and with, real or personal property, or any interest therein, wherever situated.
Subd. 5. Property disposition. A corporation may sell, convey, mortgage, create a security interest in, lease, exchange, transfer, or otherwise dispose of all or any part of its real or personal property, or any interest therein, wherever situated.
Subd. 6. Trading in securities; obligations. A corporation may purchase, subscribe for, or otherwise acquire, own, hold, vote, use, employ, sell, exchange, mortgage, lend, create a security interest in, or otherwise dispose of and otherwise use and deal in and with, securities or other interests in, or obligations of, a person or direct or indirect obligations of any domestic or foreign government or instrumentality thereof.
Subd. 7. Contracts; mortgages. A corporation may make contracts and incur liabilities, borrow money, issue its securities, and secure any of its obligations by mortgage of or creation of a security interest in all or any of its property, franchises and income.
Subd. 8. Investment. A corporation may invest and reinvest its funds.
Subd. 9. Holding property as security. A corporation may take and hold real and personal property, whether or not of a kind sold or otherwise dealt in by the corporation, as security for the payment of money loaned, advanced, or invested.
Subd. 10. Location. A corporation may conduct its business, carry on its operations, have offices, and exercise the powers granted by this chapter anywhere in the universe.
Subd. 11. Donations. A corporation may make donations, irrespective of corporate benefit, for the public welfare; for social, community, charitable, religious, educational, scientific, civic, literary, and testing for public safety purposes, and for similar or related purposes; for the purpose of fostering national or international amateur sports competition; and for the prevention of cruelty to children and animals.
Subd. 12. Pensions; benefits. A corporation may pay pensions, retirement allowances, and compensation for past services to and for the benefit of, and establish, maintain, continue, and carry out, wholly or partially at the expense of the corporation, employee or incentive benefit plans, trusts, and provisions to or for the benefit of, any or all of its and its related organizations' officers, managers, directors, governors, employees, and agents and, in the case of a related organization that is a limited liability company, members who provide services to the limited liability company, and the families, dependents, and beneficiaries of any of them. It may indemnify and purchase and maintain insurance for and on behalf of a fiduciary of any of these employee benefit and incentive plans, trusts, and provisions.
Subd. 13. Participating in management. A corporation may participate in any capacity in the promotion, organization, ownership, management, and operation of any organization or in any transaction, undertaking, or arrangement that the participating corporation would have power to conduct by itself, whether or not the participation involves sharing or delegation of control with or to others.
Subd. 14. Insurance. A corporation may provide for its benefit life insurance and other insurance with respect to the services of any or all of its officers, directors, employees, and agents, or on the life of a shareholder for the purpose of acquiring at the death of the shareholder any or all shares in the corporation owned by the shareholder.
Subd. 15. Corporate seal. A corporation may have, alter at pleasure, and use a corporate seal as provided in section 302A.163.

Subd. 16. Bylaws. A corporation may adopt, amend, and repeal bylaws relating to the management of the business or the regulation of the affairs of the corporation as provided in section 302A.181.

Subd. 17. Committees. A corporation may establish committees of the board of directors, elect or appoint persons to the committees, and define their duties as provided in section 302A.241 and fix their compensation.

Subd. 18. Officers; employees; agents. A corporation may elect or appoint officers, employees, and agents of the corporation, and define their duties as provided in sections 302A.301 to 302A.361 and fix their compensation.

Subd. 19. Securities. A corporation may issue securities and rights to purchase securities as provided in sections 302A.401 to 302A.425.

Subd. 20. Loans; guaranties; sureties. A corporation may lend money to, guarantee an obligation of, become a surety for, or otherwise financially assist persons as provided in section 302A.501.

Subd. 21. Advances. A corporation may make advances to its directors, officers, and employees and those of its subsidiaries as provided in section 302A.505.

Subd. 22. Indemnification. A corporation shall indemnify those persons identified in section 302A.521 against certain expenses and liabilities only as provided in section 302A.521 and may indemnify other persons.

Subd. 23. Assumed names. A corporation may conduct all or part of its business under one or more assumed names as provided in sections 333.001 to 333.06.

Subd. 24. Other powers. A corporation may have and exercise all other powers necessary or convenient to effect any or all of the business purposes for which the corporation is incorporated.

302A.163 Corporate seal

Subdivision 1. Seal not required. A corporation may, but need not, have a corporate seal, and the use or nonuse of a corporate seal does not affect the validity, recordability, or enforceability of a document or act. If a corporation has a corporate seal, the use of the seal by the corporation on a document is not necessary.

Subd. 2. Required words; use. If a corporation has a corporate seal, the seal may consist of a mechanical imprinting device, or a rubber stamp with a facsimile of the seal affixed thereon, or a facsimile or reproduction of either. The seal need include only the word "Seal," but it may also include a part or all of the name of the corporation and a combination, derivation, or abbreviation of either or both of the phrases "a Minnesota Corporation" and "Corporate Seal." If a corporate seal is used, it or a facsimile of it may be affixed, engraved, printed, placed, stamped with indelible ink, or in any other manner reproduced on any document.

302A.171 Organization

Subdivision 1. Role of incorporators. If the first board is not named in the articles, the incorporators may elect the first board or may act as directors with all of the powers, rights, duties, and liabilities of directors, until directors are elected or until shares are issued, whichever occurs first.

Subd. 2. Meeting. After the filing of articles of incorporation, the incorporators or the directors named in the articles shall either hold an organizational meeting at the call of a majority of the incorporators or of the directors named in the articles, or take written action, for the purposes of transacting business and taking actions necessary or appropriate to complete the organization of the corporation, including, without limitation, amending the articles, electing directors, adopting bylaws, electing officers, adopting banking resolutions, authorizing or ratifying the purchase, lease, or other acquisition of suitable space, furniture, furnishings, supplies, and materials, approving a corporate seal, approving forms of certificates for shares of the corporation, adopting a fiscal year for the corporation, accepting subscriptions for and issuing shares of the corporation, and making any appropriate tax elections. If a meeting is held, the person or persons calling the meeting shall give at least three days' notice of the meeting to each incorporator or director named, stating the date, time, and place of the meeting. Incorporators and directors may waive notice of an organizational meeting in the same manner that a director may waive notice of meetings of the board pursuant to section 302A.231, subdivision 5.

302A.181 Bylaws

Subdivision 1. Generally. A corporation may, but need not, have bylaws. Bylaws may contain any provision relating to the management of the business or the regulation of the affairs of the corporation not inconsistent with section 302A.201 or any other provision of law or the articles.

Subd. 2. Power of board. Initial bylaws may be adopted pursuant to section 302A.171 by the incorporators or by the first board. Unless reserved by the articles to the shareholders, the power to adopt, amend, or repeal the bylaws is vested in the board. The power of the board is subject to the power of the shareholders, exercisable in the manner provided in subdivision 3, to adopt, amend, or repeal bylaws adopted, amended, or repealed by the board. After the adoption of the initial bylaws, the board shall not adopt, amend, or repeal a bylaw fixing a quorum for meetings of shareholders, prescribing procedures for removing directors or filling vacancies in the board, or fixing the number of directors or their classifications, qualifications, or terms of office, but may adopt or amend a bylaw to increase the number of directors.

Subd. 3. Power of shareholders; procedure. If a shareholder or shareholders holding three percent or more of the voting power of the shares entitled to vote propose a resolution for action by the shareholders to adopt, amend, or repeal bylaws adopted, amended, or repealed by the board and the resolution sets forth the provision or provisions proposed for adoption, amendment, or repeal, the limitations and procedures for submitting, considering, and adopting the resolution are the same as provided in section 302A.135, subdivisions 2 to 4, for amendment of the articles.

302A.201 Board

Subdivision 1. Board to manage. The business and affairs of a corporation shall be managed by or under the direction of a board, subject to the provisions of subdivision 2 and section 302A.457. The members of the first board may be named in the articles or elected by the incorporators pursuant to section 302A.171 or by the shareholders.

Subd. 2. Shareholder management. The holders of the shares entitled to vote for directors of the corporation may, by unanimous affirmative vote, take any action that this chapter requires or permits the board to take. As to an action taken by the shareholders in that manner:

(a) The directors have no duties, liabilities, or responsibilities as directors under this chapter with respect to or arising from the action;

(b) The shareholders collectively and individually have all of the duties, liabilities, and responsibilities of directors under this chapter with respect to and arising from the action;

(c) If the action relates to a matter required or permitted by this chapter or by any other law to be approved or adopted by the board, either with or without approval or adoption by the shareholders, the action is deemed to have been approved or adopted by the board; and

(d) A requirement that an instrument filed with a governmental agency contain a statement that the action has been approved and adopted by the board is satisfied by a statement that the shareholders have taken the action under this subdivision.

302A.235 Quorum

A majority, or a larger or smaller proportion or number provided in the articles or bylaws, of the directors currently holding office is a quorum for the transaction of business. In the absence of a quorum, a majority of the directors present may adjourn a meeting from time to time until a quorum is present. If a quorum is present when a duly called or held meeting is convened, the directors present may continue to transact business until adjournment, even though the withdrawal of a number of directors originally present leaves less than the proportion or number otherwise required for a quorum.

302A.237 Act of the board

The board shall take action by the affirmative vote of the greater of (1) a majority of directors present at a duly held meeting at the time the action is taken, or (2) a majority of the minimum proportion or number of directors that would constitute a quorum for the transaction of business at the meeting, except where this chapter or the articles require the affirmative vote of a larger proportion or number. If the articles require a larger proportion or number than is required by this chapter for a particular action, the articles shall control.

302A.239 Action without meeting

Subdivision 1. Method. An action required or permitted to be taken at a board meeting may be taken by written action signed by all of the directors. If the articles so provide, any action, other than an action requiring shareholder approval, may be taken by written action signed by the number of directors that would be required to take the same action at a meeting of the board at which all directors were present.

Subd. 2. Effective time. The written action is effective when signed by the required number of directors, unless a different effective time is provided in the written action.

Subd. 3. Notice; liability. When written action is permitted to be taken by less than all directors, all directors shall be notified immediately of its text and effective date. Failure to provide the notice does not invalidate the written action. A director who does not sign or consent to the written action has no liability for the action or actions taken thereby.

302A.301 Officers required

A corporation shall have one or more natural persons exercising the functions of the offices, however designated, of chief executive officer and chief financial officer.

302A.401 Authorized shares

Subdivision 1. Board may authorize. Subject to any restrictions in the articles, a corporation may issue securities and rights to purchase securities only when authorized by the board.

Subd. 2. Terms of shares. All the shares of a corporation:

(a) Shall be of one class and one series, unless the articles establish, or authorize the board to establish, more than one class or series;

(b) Shall be common shares entitled to vote and shall have equal rights and preferences in all matters not otherwise provided for by the board, unless and to the extent that the articles have fixed the relative rights and preferences of different classes and series; and

(c) Shall have, unless a different par value is specified in the articles, a par value of one cent per share, solely for the purpose of a statute or rule imposing a tax or fee based upon the capitalization of a corporation, and a par value fixed by the board for the purpose of a statute or rule requiring the shares of the corporation to have a par value.

Subd. 3. Procedure for fixing terms. (a) Subject to any restrictions in the articles, the power granted in subdivision 2 may be exercised by a resolution or resolutions approved by the affirmative vote of the directors required by section 302A.237 establishing a class or series, setting forth the designation of the class or series, and fixing the relative rights and preferences of the class or series. Any of the rights and preferences of a class or series established in the articles or by resolution of the directors:

(1) may be made dependent upon facts ascertainable outside the articles, or outside the resolution or resolutions establishing the class or series, provided that the manner in which the facts operate upon the rights and preferences of the class or series is clearly and expressly set forth in the articles or in the resolution or resolutions establishing the class or series; and

(2) may incorporate by reference some or all of the terms of any agreements, contracts, or other arrangements entered into by the issuing corporation in connection with the establishment of the class or series if the corporation retains at its principal executive office a copy of the agreements, contracts, or other arrangements or the portions incorporated by reference.

(b) A statement setting forth the name of the corporation and the text of the resolution and certifying the adoption of the resolution and the date of adoption shall be filed with the secretary of state before the issuance of any shares for which the resolution creates rights or preferences not set forth in the articles; provided, however, where the shareholders have received notice of the creation of shares with rights or preferences not set forth in the articles before the issuance of the shares, the statement may be filed any time within one year after the issuance of the shares. The resolution is effective when the statement has been filed with the secretary of state; or, if it is not required to be filed with the secretary of state before the issuance of shares, on the date of its adoption by the directors.

(c) A statement filed with the secretary of state in accordance with paragraph (b) is not considered an amendment of the articles for purposes of sections 302A.137 and 302A.471.

Subd. 4. Specific terms. Without limiting the authority granted in this section, a corporation may issue shares of a class or series:

(a) Subject to the right of the corporation to redeem any of those shares at the price fixed for their redemption by the articles or by the board or at a price determined in the manner specified by the articles or by the board;

(b) Entitling the shareholders to cumulative, partially cumulative, or noncumulative distributions in the amounts fixed by the articles or by the board or in amounts determined in the manner specified by the articles or by the board;

(c) Having preference over any class or series of shares for the payment of distributions of any or all kinds;

(d) Convertible into shares of any other class or any series of the same or another class on the terms fixed by the articles or by the board or on terms determined in the manner specified by the articles or by the board; or

(e) Having full, partial, or no voting rights, except as provided in section 302A.137.

302A.402 Share dividends, divisions, and combinations

Subdivision 1. Power to effect. A corporation may effect a share dividend or a division or combination of its shares as provided in this section.

Subd. 2. When shareholder approval required; filing of articles of amendment. (a) Articles of amendment must be adopted by the board and the shareholders under sections 302A.135 and 302A.137 to effect a division or combination if, as a result of the proposed division or combination:

(1) the rights or preferences of the holders of outstanding shares of any class or series will be adversely affected; or

(2) the percentage of authorized shares of any class or series remaining unissued after the division or combination will exceed the percentage of authorized shares of that class or series that were unissued before the division or combination.

(b) If a division or combination is effected under this subdivision, articles of amendment must be prepared that contain the information required by section 302A.139.

Subd. 3. By action of board alone; filing of articles of amendment. (a) Subject to the restrictions provided in subdivision 2 or any provision in the articles that states that section 302A.402, subdivision 3, does not apply, a share dividend, division, or combination may be effected by action of the board alone, without the approval of shareholders under sections 302A.135 and 302A.137. In effecting a division or combination under this subdivision, the board may amend the articles to increase or decrease the par value of shares, increase or decrease the number of authorized shares, and make any other change necessary or appropriate to assure that the rights or preferences of the holders of outstanding shares of any class or series will not be adversely affected by the division or combination.

(b) If a division or combination that includes an amendment of the articles is effected under this subdivision, then articles of amendment must be prepared that contain the information required by section 302A.139 and a statement that the amendment will not adversely affect the rights or preferences of the holders of outstanding shares of any class or series and will not result in the percentage of authorized shares of any class or series that remains unissued after the division or combination exceeding the percentage of authorized shares of that class or series that were unissued before the division or combination.

Subd. 4. Changes in voting rights; fractional shares. For purposes of this section, an increase or decrease in the relative voting rights of the shares that are the subject of the division or combination that arises solely from the increase or decrease in the number of shares outstanding is not an adverse effect on the outstanding shares of any class or series and any increase in the percentage of authorized shares remaining unissued arising solely from the elimination of fractional shares under section 302A.423 must be disregarded.

302A.403 Subscriptions for shares

Subdivision 1. Signed writing. A subscription for shares, whether made before or after the incorporation of a corporation, is not enforceable against the subscriber unless it is in writing and signed by the subscriber.

Subd. 2. Irrevocable period. Unless otherwise provided in the subscription agreement, or unless all of the subscribers and, if in existence, the corporation consent to a shorter or longer period, a subscription for shares is irrevocable for a period of six months.

Subd. 3. Payment; installments. A subscription for shares, whether made before or after the incorporation of a corporation, shall be paid in full at the time or times, or in the installments, if any, specified in the subscription agreement. In the absence of a provision in the subscription agreement specifying the time at which the subscription is to be paid, the subscription shall be paid at the time or times determined by the board, but a call made by the board for payment on subscriptions shall be uniform for all shares of the same class or for all shares of the same series.

Subd. 4. Method of collection; cancellation or sale for account of subscriber. (a) Unless otherwise provided in the subscription agreement, in the event of default in the payment of an installment or call when due, the corporation may proceed to collect the amount due in the same manner as a debt due the corporation.

(b) If the amount due on a subscription for shares remains unpaid for a period of 20 days after written notice of demand for payment has been given to the delinquent subscriber, the shares subscribed for may be offered for sale by the corporation for a price in money equaling or exceeding the sum of the full balance owed by the delinquent subscriber plus the expenses incidental to the sale. If the shares subscribed for are sold pursuant to this paragraph, the corporation shall pay to the delinquent subscriber or to the delinquent subscriber's legal representative the lesser of (i) the excess of net proceeds realized by the corporation over the sum of the amount owed by the delinquent subscriber plus the expenses incidental to the sale, and (ii) the amount actually paid by the delinquent subscriber. If the shares subscribed for are not sold pursuant to this paragraph, the corporation may collect the amount due in the same manner as a debt due the corporation or cancel the subscription in accordance with paragraph (c).

(c) If the amount due on a subscription for shares remains unpaid for a period of 20 days after written notice of demand for payment has been given to the delinquent subscriber and the shares subscribed for by the delinquent subscriber have not been sold pursuant to paragraph (b), the corporation may cancel the subscription, in which event the shares subscribed for must be restored to the status of authorized but unissued shares, the corporation may retain the portion of the subscription price actually paid that does not exceed ten percent of the subscription price, and the corporation shall refund to the delinquent subscriber or the delinquent subscriber's legal representative that portion of the subscription price actually paid which exceeds ten percent of the subscription price.

302A.405 Consideration for shares; value and payment; liability

Subdivision 1. Consideration; procedure. Subject to any restrictions in the articles:

(a) Shares may be issued for any consideration, including, without limitation, money or other tangible or intangible property received by the corporation or to be received by the corporation under a written agreement, or services rendered to the corporation or to be rendered to the corporation, as authorized by resolution approved by the affirmative vote of the directors required by section 302A.237, or, if provided for in the articles, approved by the affirmative vote of the shareholders required by section 302A.437, establishing a price in money or other consideration, or a minimum price, or a general formula or method by which the price will be determined; and

(b) A corporation may, without any new or additional consideration, issue its own shares in exchange for or in conversion of its outstanding shares, or, subject to authorization of share dividends, divisions, and combinations according to section 302A.402, issue its own shares pro rata to its shareholders or the shareholders of one or more classes or series, to effectuate share dividends, divisions, or combinations. No shares of a class or series, shares of which are then outstanding, shall be issued to the holders of shares of another class or series (except in exchange for or in conversion of outstanding shares of the other class or series), unless the issuance either is expressly provided for in the articles or is approved at a meeting by the affirmative vote of the holders of a majority of the voting power of all shares of the same class or series as the shares to be issued.

Subd. 2. Value; liability. The determinations of the board or the shareholders as to the amount or fair value or the fairness to the corporation of the consideration received or to be received by the corporation for its shares or the terms of payment, as well as the agreement to issue shares for that consideration, are presumed to be proper if they are made in good faith and on the basis of accounting methods, or a fair valuation or other method, reasonable in the circumstances, and, unless otherwise required by the articles, the consideration may be less than the par value, if any, of the shares. Directors or shareholders who are present and entitled to vote, and who, intentionally or without reasonable investigation, fail to vote against approving an issue of shares for a consideration that is unfair to the corporation, or overvalue property or services received or to be received by the corporation as consideration for shares issued, are jointly and severally liable to the corporation for the benefit of the then shareholders who did not consent to and are damaged by the action, to the extent of the damages of those shareholders. A director or shareholder against whom a claim is asserted pursuant to this subdivision, except in case of knowing participation in a deliberate fraud, is entitled to contribution on an equitable basis from other directors or shareholders who are liable under this section.

Subd. 3. Payment; liability; contribution; statute of limitations. (a) A corporation shall issue only shares that are nonassessable or that are assessable but are issued with the unanimous consent of the shareholders. "Nonassessable" shares are shares for which the agreed consideration has been fully paid, delivered, or rendered to the corporation. Consideration in the form of a promissory note, a check, or a written agreement to transfer property to a corporation in the future is fully paid when the note, check, or written agreement is delivered to the corporation, and consideration in the form of services to be rendered to the corporation is fully paid when the issuance of the shares is authorized or approved pursuant to subdivision 1, paragraph (a).

(b) If shares are issued in violation of paragraph (a), the following persons are jointly and severally liable to the corporation for the difference between the agreed consideration for the shares and the consideration actually received by the corporation:

(1) A director or shareholder who was present and entitled to vote but who failed to vote against the issuance of the shares knowing of the violation;

(2) The person to whom the shares were issued; and

(3) A successor or transferee of the interest in the corporation of a person described in clause (1) or (2), including a purchaser of shares, a subsequent assignee, successor, or transferee, a pledgee, a holder of any other security interest in the assets of the corporation or shares granted by the person described in clause (1) or (2), or a legal representative of or for the person or estate of the person, which successor, transferee, purchaser, assignee, pledgee, holder, or representative acquired the interest knowing of the violation.

(c) (1) A pledgee or holder of any other security interest in all or any shares that have been issued in violation of paragraph (a) is not liable under paragraph (b) if all those shares are surrendered to the corporation. The surrender does not impair any rights of the pledgee or holder of any other security interest against the pledgor or person granting the security interest.

(2) A pledgee, holder of any other security interest, or legal representative is liable under paragraph (b) only in that capacity. The liability of the person under paragraph (b) is limited to the assets held in that capacity for the person or estate of the person described in clause (1) or (2) of paragraph (b).

(3) Each person liable under paragraph (b) has a full right of contribution on an equitable basis from all other persons liable under paragraph (b) for the same transaction.

(4) An action shall not be maintained against a person under paragraph (b) unless commenced within two years from the date on which shares are issued in violation of paragraph (a).

302A.409 Rights to purchase

Subdivision 1. Definition. "Right to purchase" means the right, however designated, pursuant to the terms of a security or agreement, entitling a person to subscribe to, purchase, or acquire securities of a corporation, whether by the exchange or conversion of other securities, or by the exercise of options, warrants, or other rights, or otherwise, but excluding preemptive rights.

Subd. 2. Transferability; separability. Rights to purchase may be either transferable or nontransferable and either separable or inseparable from other securities of the corporation, as the board may determine under this section.

Subd. 3. Issuance permitted. A corporation may issue rights to purchase after the terms, provisions, and conditions of the rights to purchase to be issued, including the conversion basis or the price at which securities may be purchased or subscribed for, are fixed by the board, or by an officer pursuant to board authorization, subject to any restrictions in the articles. Notwithstanding any provision of this chapter, a corporation may issue rights to purchase or amend the instrument or agreement fixing the terms, provisions, and conditions of the rights to purchase to include terms and conditions that prevent the holder of a specified percentage of the outstanding shares of the corporation, including subsequent transferees of the holder, from exercising those rights to purchase.

Subd. 4. Terms set forth. The instrument evidencing the right to purchase or, if no instrument exists, a written agreement, shall set forth in full, summarize, or incorporate by reference all the terms, provisions, and conditions applicable to the right to purchase.

302A.425 Liability of subscribers and shareholders with respect to shares

A subscriber for shares or a shareholder of a corporation is under no obligation to the corporation or its creditors with respect to the shares subscribed for or owned, except to pay to the corporation the full consideration for which the shares are issued or to be issued.

302A.429 Restriction on transfer or registration of securities

Subdivision 1. How imposed. A restriction on the transfer or registration of transfer of securities of a corporation may be imposed in the articles, in the bylaws, by a resolution adopted by the shareholders, or by an agreement among or other written action by a number of shareholders or holders of other securities or among them and the corporation. A restriction is not binding with respect to securities issued prior to the adoption of the restriction, unless the holders of those securities are parties to the agreement or voted in favor of the restriction.

Subd. 2. Restrictions permitted. A written restriction on the transfer or registration of transfer of securities of a corporation that is not manifestly unreasonable under the circumstances and is either: (1) noted conspicuously on the face or back of the certificate; or (2) included in information sent to the holders of uncertificated shares in accordance with section 302A.417, subdivision 7, may be enforced against the holder of the restricted securities or a successor or transferee of the holder, including a pledgee or a legal representative. Unless noted conspicuously on the face or back of the certificate or included in information sent to the holders of uncertificated shares in accordance with section 302A.417, subdivision 7, a restriction, even though permitted by this section, is ineffective against a person without knowledge of the restriction. A restriction under this section is deemed to be noted conspicuously and is effective if the existence of the restriction is stated on the certificate and reference is made to a separate document creating or describing the restriction.

302A.701 Methods of dissolution

A corporation may be dissolved:
(a) By the incorporators pursuant to section 302A.711;
(b) By the shareholders pursuant to sections 302A.721 to 302A.7291;
(c) By order of a court pursuant to sections 302A.741 to 302A.765; or
(d) By the secretary of state according to section 302A.821.

302A.711 Voluntary dissolution by incorporators or directors

Subdivision 1. Manner. A corporation that has not issued shares may be dissolved by the incorporators or directors in the manner set forth in this section.

Subd. 2. Articles of dissolution. (a) A majority of the incorporators or directors shall sign articles of dissolution containing:
(1) The name of the corporation;
(2) The date of incorporation;
(3) A statement that shares have not been issued;
(4) A statement that all consideration received from subscribers for shares to be issued, less expenses incurred in the organization of the corporation, has been returned to the subscribers; and
(5) A statement that no debts remain unpaid.
(b) The articles of dissolution shall be filed with the secretary of state.

Subd. 3. Effective date. When the articles of dissolution have been filed with the secretary of state, the corporation is dissolved.

Subd. 4. Certificate. The secretary of state shall issue to the dissolved corporation or its legal representative a certificate of dissolution that contains:
(a) The name of the corporation;
(b) The date and time the articles of dissolution were filed with the secretary of state; and
(c) A statement that the corporation is dissolved.

302A.721 Voluntary dissolution by shareholders

Subdivision 1. Manner. A corporation may be dissolved by the shareholders when authorized in the manner set forth in this section.

Subd. 2. Notice; approval. (a) Written notice shall be given to each shareholder, whether or not entitled to vote at a meeting of shareholders, within the time and in the manner provided in section 302A.435 for notice of meetings of shareholders and, whether the meeting is a regular or a special meeting, shall state that a purpose of the meeting is to consider dissolving the corporation.

(b) The proposed dissolution shall be submitted for approval at a meeting of shareholders. If the proposed dissolution is approved at a meeting by the affirmative vote of the holders of a majority of the voting power of all shares entitled to vote, the dissolution shall be commenced.

302A.723 Filing notice of intent to dissolve; effect

Subdivision 1. Contents. If dissolution of the corporation is approved pursuant to section 302A.721, subdivision 2, the corporation shall file with the secretary of state a notice of intent to dissolve. The notice shall contain:
(a) The name of the corporation;
(b) The date and place of the meeting at which the resolution was approved pursuant to section 302A.721, subdivision 2; and
(c) A statement that the requisite vote of the shareholders was received, or that all shareholders entitled to vote signed

a written action.

Subd. 2. Winding up. When the notice of intent to dissolve has been filed with the secretary of state, and subject to section 302A.731, the corporation shall cease to carry on its business, except to the extent necessary for the winding up of the corporation. The shareholders shall retain the right to revoke the dissolution proceedings in accordance with section 302A.731 and the right to remove directors or fill vacancies on the board. The corporate existence continues to the extent necessary to wind up the affairs of the corporation until the dissolution proceedings are revoked or articles of dissolution are filed with the secretary of state.

Subd. 3. Remedies continued. The filing with the secretary of state of a notice of intent to dissolve does not affect any remedy in favor of the corporation or any remedy against it or its directors, officers, or shareholders in those capacities, except as provided in sections 302A.727, 302A.7291, and 302A.781.

302A.725 Procedure in dissolution

Subdivision 1. Collection; payment. When a notice of intent to dissolve has been filed with the secretary of state, the board, or the officers acting under the direction of the board, shall proceed as soon as possible:

(a) To collect or make provision for the collection of all known debts due or owing to the corporation, including unpaid subscriptions for shares;

(b) Except as provided in sections 302A.727, 302A.7291, and 302A.781, to pay or make provision for the payment of all known debts, obligations, and liabilities of the corporation according to their priorities; and

(c) To give notice to creditors and claimants under section 302A.727 or to proceed under section 302A.7291.

Subd. 2. Transfer of assets. Notwithstanding the provisions of section 302A.661, when a notice of intent to dissolve has been filed with the secretary of state, the directors may sell, lease, transfer, or otherwise dispose of all or substantially all of the property and assets of a dissolving corporation without a vote of the shareholders.

Subd. 3. Distribution to shareholders. All tangible or intangible property, including money, remaining after the discharge of, or after making adequate provision for the discharge of, the debts, obligations, and liabilities of the corporation shall be distributed to the shareholders in accordance with section 302A.551, subdivision 4.

302A.727 Dissolution procedure for corporations that give notice to creditors and claimants

Subdivision 1. When permitted; how given. When a notice of intent to dissolve has been filed with the secretary of state, the corporation may give notice of the filing to each creditor of and claimant against the corporation known or unknown, present or future, and contingent or noncontingent. If notice to creditors and claimants is given, it must be given by publishing the notice once each week for four successive weeks in a legal newspaper in the county or counties where the registered office and the principal executive office of the corporation are located and by giving written notice to known creditors and claimants pursuant to section 302A.011, subdivision 17.

Subd. 2. Contents. The notice to creditors and claimants shall contain:

(a) A statement that the corporation is in the process of dissolving;

(b) A statement that the corporation has filed with the secretary of state a notice of intent to dissolve;

(c) The date of filing the notice of intent to dissolve;

(d) The address of the office to which written claims against the corporation must be presented; and

(e) The date by which all the claims must be received, which shall be the later of 90 days after published notice or, with respect to a particular known creditor or claimant, 90 days after the date on which written notice was given to that creditor or claimant. Published notice is deemed given on the date of first publication for the purpose of determining this date.

Subd. 3. Claims against corporations that give notice.

(a) A corporation that gives notice to creditors and claimants has 30 days from the receipt of each claim filed according to the procedures set forth by the corporation on or before the date set forth in the notice to accept or reject the claim by giving written notice to the person submitting it; a claim not expressly rejected in this manner is deemed accepted.

(b) A creditor or claimant to whom notice is given and whose claim is rejected by the corporation has 60 days from the date of rejection, 180 days from the date the corporation filed with the secretary of state the notice of intent to dissolve, or 90 days after the date on which notice was given to the creditor or claimant, whichever is longer, to pursue any other remedies with respect to the claim.

(c) A creditor or claimant to whom notice is given who fails to file a claim according to the procedures set forth by the corporation on or before the date set forth in the notice is barred from suing on that claim or otherwise realizing upon or enforcing it, except as provided in section 302A.781.

(d) A creditor or claimant whose claim is rejected by the corporation under paragraph (b) is barred from suing on that claim or otherwise realizing upon or enforcing it, if the creditor or claimant does not initiate legal, administrative, or arbitration proceedings with respect to the claim within the time provided in paragraph (b).

Subd. 4. Articles of dissolution; when filed. Articles of dissolution for a corporation that has given notice to creditors and claimants under this section must be filed with the secretary of state after:

(1) the 90-day period in subdivision 2, paragraph (e), has expired and the payment of claims of all creditors and claimants filing a claim within that period has been made or provided for; or

(2) the longest of the periods described in subdivision 3, paragraph (b), has expired and there are no pending legal, administrative, or arbitration proceedings by or against the corporation commenced within the time provided in subdivision 3, paragraph (b).

Subd. 5. Contents of articles. The articles of dissolution must state:

(1) the last date on which the notice was given and: (i) that the payment of all creditors and claimants filing a claim within the 90-day period in subdivision 2, paragraph (e), has been made or provided for; or (ii) the date on which the longest of the periods described in subdivision 3, paragraph (b), expired;

(2) that the remaining property, assets, and claims of the corporation have been distributed among its shareholders in

accordance with section 302A.551, subdivision 4, or that adequate provision has been made for that distribution; and

(3) that there are no pending legal, administrative, or arbitration proceedings by or against the corporation commenced within the time provided in subdivision 3, paragraph (b), or that adequate provision has been made for the satisfaction of any judgment, order, or decree that may be entered against it in a pending proceeding.

302A.7291 Dissolution procedure for corporations that do not give notice

Subdivision 1. Articles of dissolution; when filed. Articles of dissolution for a corporation that has not given notice to creditors and claimants in the manner provided in section 302A.727 must be filed with the secretary of state after:

(1) the payment of claims of all known creditors and claimants has been made or provided for; or

(2) at least two years have elapsed from the date of filing the notice of intent to dissolve.

Subd. 2. Contents of articles. The articles of dissolution must state:

(1) if articles of dissolution are being filed pursuant to subdivision 1, clause (1), that all known debts, obligations, and liabilities of the corporation have been paid and discharged or that adequate provision has been made for payment or discharge;

(2) that the remaining property, assets, and claims of the corporation have been distributed among its shareholders in accordance with section 302A.551, subdivision 4, or that adequate provision has been made for that distribution; and

(3) that there are no pending legal, administrative, or arbitration proceedings by or against the corporation, or that adequate provision has been made for the satisfaction of any judgment, order, or decree that may be entered against it in a pending proceeding.

Subd. 3. Claims against corporations that do not give notice.

(a) If the corporation has paid or provided for all known creditors or claimants at the time articles of dissolution are filed, a creditor or claimant who does not file a claim or pursue a remedy in a legal, administrative, or arbitration proceeding within two years after the date of filing the notice of intent to dissolve is barred from suing on that claim or otherwise realizing upon or enforcing it.

(b) If the corporation has not paid or provided for all known creditors and claimants at the time articles of dissolution are filed, a person who does not file a claim or pursue a remedy in a legal, administrative, or arbitration proceeding within two years after the date of filing the notice of intent to dissolve is barred from suing on that claim or otherwise realizing upon or enforcing it, except as provided in section 302A.781.

302A.821 Minnesota corporate registration.

Subdivision 1. MS 1998 Renumbered subd 2
Subdivision 1. Annual registration form. Each calendar year beginning in the calendar year following the calendar year in which a corporation incorporates, the secretary of state must mail by first class mail an annual registration form to the registered office of each corporation as shown on the records of the secretary of state. The form must include the following notice: "NOTICE: Failure to file this form by December 31 of this year will result in this corporation losing its good standing without further notice from the secretary of state."
Subd. 2. MS 1998 Renumbered subd 3
Subd. 2. Information required. A domestic corporation shall file with the secretary of state a registration by December 31 each calendar year containing:

(a) the name of the corporation;

(b) the address of its principal executive office, if different from the registered office address;

(c) the address of its registered office and the name of the registered agent, if any;

(d) the state of incorporation; and

(e) the name and business address of the officer or other person exercising the principal functions of the chief executive officer of the corporation.

Subd. 3. MS 1998 Repealed by amendment, 2000 c 395 s 5
Subd. 3. Information public. The information required by subdivision 2 is public data. Chapter 13 does not apply to this information.
Subd. 4. MS 1998 Repealed by amendment, 2000 c 395 s 5
Subd. 4. Penalty. (a) A corporation that has failed to file a registration pursuant to the requirements of subdivision 2 must be dissolved by the secretary of state as described in paragraph (b).

(b) If the corporation has not filed the registration for three consecutive calendar years, the secretary of state shall send by forwardable United States mail to the registered office of the corporation a postcard notifying the corporation that the corporation will be dissolved if no registration is filed with a $25 fee pursuant to this section by the beginning of the following calendar year. The secretary of state shall annually inform the attorney general and the commissioner of revenue of the methods by which the names of corporations dissolved under this section during the preceding year may be determined. The secretary of state must also make available in an electronic format the names of the dissolved corporations. A corporation dissolved in this manner is not entitled to the benefits of section 302A.781. The liability, if any, of the shareholders of a corporation dissolved in this manner shall be determined and limited in accordance with section 302A.557, except that the shareholders shall have no liability to any director of the corporation under section 302A.559, subdivision 2.
Subd. 5. Renumbered subd 4
Subd. 6. Repealed by amendment, 2000 c 395 s 5

CHAPTER 319B
PROFESSIONAL FIRMS

319B.02 Definitions

Subdivision 1. Scope. For the purposes of sections 319B.01 to 319B.12, the terms defined in this section have the meanings given them.
Subd. 2. Board. "Board" means an agency of the state of Minnesota which has jurisdiction to grant a license to furnish professional services of a category within subdivision 19, except that in the case of a professional firm that provides legal services, "board" means the board of professional responsibility.
Subd. 3. Certificate of authority. "Certificate of authority" means:

(1) with respect to a foreign firm that is a corporation, the certificate of authority required under sections 303.01 to

303.24 and any notice filed under section 303.115 in connection with that certificate; and

(2) with respect to a foreign firm that is a limited liability company, the certificate of authority required under sections 322B.905 to 322B.955 and any notice filed under section 322B.92, clause (3), in connection with that certificate.

Subd. 4. Disqualified. "Disqualified" means to have a license to provide pertinent professional services:

(1) suspended, unless by its terms the suspension will automatically end less than 90 days after it takes effect; or

(2) revoked.

The disqualification occurs when the suspension or revocation first takes effect.

Subd. 5. Firm. "Firm" includes a corporation, limited liability company, and limited liability partnership, wherever incorporated, organized, or registered.

Subd. 6. Foreign firm. "Foreign firm" means a corporation incorporated, limited liability company organized, or limited liability partnership registered under the laws of a state other than Minnesota.

Subd. 7. Foreign professional firm. "Foreign professional firm" means a foreign firm that has in effect an election under section 319B.04, subdivision 2.

Subd. 8. Generally applicable governing law. "Generally applicable governing law" of a firm means:

(1) with respect to a firm that is a corporation, the state statute under which the corporation is incorporated;

(2) with respect to a firm that is a limited liability company, the state statute under which the limited liability company is organized; and

(3) with respect to a firm that is a limited liability partnership, the state statute under which the limited liability partnership obtains its status as a limited liability partnership;

plus any other law that is generally relevant to the structure, governance, operations, or other internal affairs of the firm.

Subd. 9. Governance authority. "Governance authority" means the authority and responsibility to:

(1) determine important policies for a professional firm;

(2) superintend the professional firm's overall operations; and

(3) maintain general, active management of and ultimate control over all matters involving professional judgment.

Subd. 9a. License. "License" includes any license, certificate, registration, or other authority referred to in subdivision 17 or 19.

Subd. 10. Minnesota firm. "Minnesota firm" includes a corporation organized under chapter 302A or 317A, limited liability company organized under chapter 322B, limited liability partnership registered under section 323.44, and limited liability partnership that has an effective statement of qualification under section 323A.10-01.

Subd. 11. Minnesota professional firm. "Minnesota professional firm" means a Minnesota firm that has in effect an election under section 319B.03, subdivision 2.

Subd. 12. Organizational document. "Organizational document" means:

(1) with respect to a corporation organized under chapter 302A or 317A, that corporation's articles of incorporation;

(2) with respect to a limited liability company organized under chapter 322B, that limited liability company's articles of organization;

(3) with respect to a limited liability partnership registered under section 323.44, that limited liability partnership's registration and any notice filed under section 323.44, subdivision 9, in connection with that registration; and

(4) with respect to a limited liability partnership that has an effective statement of qualification under section 323A.10-01, that statement of qualification.

Subd. 13. Owner. "Owner" means:

(1) with respect to a professional firm that is a corporation, except a nonprofit corporation, an owner of shares in the corporation;

(2) with respect to a professional firm that is a limited liability company, a member in the limited liability company; and

(3) with respect to a professional firm that is a limited liability partnership, a partner in the limited liability partnership.

Subd. 14. Ownership interest. "Ownership interest" means:

(1) with respect to a professional firm that is a corporation, except a nonprofit corporation, shares in the corporation;

(2) with respect to a professional firm that is a limited liability company, a membership interest in the limited liability company; and

(3) with respect to a professional firm that is a limited liability partnership, a partnership interest.

Subd. 15. Partial right. "Partial right" means a right in or with respect to an ownership interest where the right is by itself insufficient to make the right's holder an owner.

Subd. 16. Pertinent professional services. "Pertinent professional services" means, with respect to a professional firm, the category or categories of professional services specified by the firm in its election under section 319B.03, subdivision 2, or 319B.04, subdivision 2.

Subd. 17. Professional. "Professional" means a natural person who is licensed by the laws of the state of Minnesota or similar laws of another state to furnish one or more of the categories of professional services listed in subdivision 19. Professional includes a natural person who is licensed or otherwise authorized to practice law under the laws of a foreign nation.

Subd. 18. Professional firm. "Professional firm" means both Minnesota professional firms and foreign professional firms.

Subd. 19. Professional services. "Professional services" means services of the type required or permitted to be furnished by a professional under a license, registration, or certificate issued by the state of Minnesota to practice medicine and surgery under sections 147.01 to 147.22, as a physician assistant pursuant to sections 147A.01 to 147A.27, chiropractic under sections 148.01 to 148.105, registered nursing under sections 148.171 to 148.285, optometry under sections 148.52 to 148.62, psychology under sections 148.88 to 148.98, dentistry and dental hygiene under sections 150A.01 to 150A.12, pharmacy under sections 151.01 to 151.40, podiatric medicine under sections 153.01 to 153.25, veterinary medicine under sections 156.001 to 156.14, architecture, engineering, surveying, landscape architecture, geoscience, and certified interior design under sections 326.02 to 326.15, accountancy under sections 326.17 to 326.229, or law under sections 481.01 to 481.17, or under a license or certificate issued by another state under similar laws. Professional services includes services of the type required to be furnished by a professional pursuant to a license or other authority to practice law under the laws of a foreign nation.

Subd. 20. State. "State" means a state of the United States and the District of Columbia.

Subd. 21. Statement of foreign qualification. "Statement of foreign qualification" means:

(1) with respect to a foreign firm that is a limited liability partnership and has filed a statement of qualification under section 323.49, that statement of qualification and any notice filed under section 323.49, subdivision 9; and

(2) with respect to a limited liability partnership that has an effective statement of foreign qualification under section 323A.11-02, that statement of foreign qualification.

Subd. 22. Update. "Update" means:

(1) with respect to a Minnesota professional firm that is either a Minnesota corporation or a Minnesota limited liability company, amend the organizational document;

(2) with respect to a Minnesota professional firm that is a Minnesota limited liability partnership registered under section 323.44, file a notice under section 323.44, subdivision 9, in connection with the Minnesota limited liability partnership's registration;

(3) with respect to a foreign professional firm that is a foreign corporation, file a notice under section 303.115 in connection with the foreign corporation's certificate of authority;

(4) with respect to a foreign firm that is a limited liability company, file a notice under section 322B.92, clause (3), in connection with the foreign limited liability company's certificate of authority;

(5) with respect to a foreign professional firm that is a foreign limited liability partnership and has filed a statement of qualification under section 323.49, file a notice under section 323.49, subdivision 9, in connection with that statement of qualification;

(6) with respect to a Minnesota professional firm that is a limited liability partnership and has an effective statement of qualification under section 323A.10-01, amend that statement of qualification; and

(7) with respect to a foreign professional firm that is a limited liability partnership and has an effective statement of foreign qualification under section 323A.11-02, amend that statement of foreign qualification.

319B.05 Firm name

Subdivision 1. No implication of superiority. The name of a professional firm must not imply or be used to imply superiority.

Subd. 2. Required name endings. The name of a professional firm must end:

(1) in the case of a corporation, with any one of the following phrases, words, or abbreviations: "Professional Corporation"; "Professional Service Corporation"; "Service Corporation"; "Professional Association"; "Chartered"; "Limited"; "P.C."; "P.S.C."; "S.C."; "P.A."; or "Ltd.";

(2) in the case of a limited liability company, with any one of the following phrases or abbreviations: "Professional Limited Liability Company"; "Limited Liability Company"; "P.L.L.C."; "P.L.C."; or "L.L.C."; or

(3) in the case of a limited liability partnership, with any one of the following phrases or abbreviations: "Professional Limited Liability Partnership"; "Limited Liability Partnership"; "P.L.L.P."; or "L.L.P."

A permitted abbreviation may include or omit periods.

319B.06 Furnishing services

Subdivision 1. Categories of service. (a) A professional firm may provide professional services within Minnesota in one of the categories listed in section 319B.02, subdivision 19, if:

(1) the professional firm's election under section 319B.03, subdivision 2, or 319B.04, subdivision 2, specifies that category; and

(2) each of the professional firm's owners meet the requirements of section 319B.07 with regard to that category.

(b) A professional firm may provide professional services within Minnesota in more than one of the categories listed in section 319B.02, subdivision 19, if:

(1) the professional firm's election under section 319B.03, subdivision 2, or 319B.04, subdivision 2, specifies those categories;

(2) each of the professional firm's owners meet the requirements of section 319B.07 with regard to at least one of those categories; and

(3) the relevant licensing statutes, as listed in section 319B.02, subdivision 19, or rules in effect under those statutes, specifically authorize those categories of services to be practiced in combination.

(c) A professional firm may exercise any powers accorded it by its generally applicable governing law, so long as the professional firm exercises those powers solely to provide the pertinent professional services or to accomplish tasks ancillary to providing those services.

(d) A professional firm may not conduct any other business or provide any other services beyond those authorized in this subdivision, either within or outside of Minnesota.

(e) A professional firm may not adopt, implement, or follow a policy, procedure, or practice that would give a board grounds for disciplinary action against a professional who follows, agrees to, or acquiesces in the policy, procedure, or practice.

Subd. 2. Manner of furnishing services. (a) A professional firm may furnish professional services within Minnesota only through professionals licensed or otherwise authorized by the state of Minnesota to furnish the pertinent professional services. Firm owners who are properly licensed professionals may provide professional services on a professional firm's behalf, and a professional firm may also hire or retain properly licensed professionals as employees, nonemployee agents, or independent contractors to furnish professional services on the professional firm's behalf.

(b) If a professional firm is authorized under subdivision 1, paragraph (b), to furnish more than one category of professional services, a professional furnishing professional services on behalf of the professional firm is required to be licensed or authorized only with respect to the category or categories of services which the professional actually furnishes.

Subd. 3. Relationship to person served. (a) Sections 319B.01 to 319B.12 do not alter any law applicable to the relationship between a person furnishing professional services and a person receiving the professional services, including liability arising out of the professional services and the confidential relationship and privilege of communications between the person furnishing professional services and the person receiving the professional services.

(b) Sections 319B.01 to 319B.12 do not alter any law applicable to the relationship between a professional firm furnishing professional services and a person receiving the professional services, including liability arising out of the professional services and the confidential relationship and privilege of communications between the professional firm furnishing professional services and the person receiving the professional services.

(c) Whether a professional firm's owners and persons who control, manage, or act for the firm are personally liable for the firm's debts and obligations is determined according to the firm's generally applicable governing law.

CHAPTER 333
ASSUMED NAMES, INSIGNIA, AND MARKS

333.001 Definitions

Subdivision 1. Scope. As used in sections 333.001 to 333.06, the following terms shall have the meanings given, unless the context clearly indicates that a different meaning is intended.

Subd. 2. Person. "Person" means one or more natural persons; a limited liability company, whether domestic or foreign; a registered limited liability partnership, whether domestic or foreign; a partnership; a limited partnership; a corporation, including a foreign, domestic, or nonprofit corporation; a trust; or any other business organization.

Subd. 3. True name. "True name" means the true full name of the natural person, if a proprietorship; the true full name of each partner, if a partnership; the full corporate name as stated in its articles, if a corporation; the full name of the limited liability company as stated in its articles of organization or certificate of authority; the full name of the limited partnership, if a limited partnership; the full name of the registered limited liability partnership; the true full name of at least one trustee, if a trust; or the true full name of at least one beneficial owner, if any other form of business organization.

Subd. 4. Address. "Address" means the full residential address of each natural person, trustee or beneficial owner, limited liability company, whether domestic or foreign, registered limited liability partnership, whether domestic or foreign, or corporation, included in subdivision 3, and the address of the principal place in Minnesota where the business is conducted or transacted.

Subd. 5. Executed. "Executed" means signed.

Subd. 6. Signed. (a) "Signed" means that the signature of a person has been written on a document, as provided in section 645.44, subdivision 14, and, with respect to a document required by this chapter to be filed with the secretary of state, means that the document has been signed by a person authorized to do so by the organizational documents, bylaws, agreements, or by a resolution approved by the ultimately responsible managing entity for the business organization.

(b) A signature on a document may be a facsimile affixed, engraved, printed, placed, stamped with indelible ink, transmitted by facsimile or electronically, or in any other manner reproduced on the document.

Subd. 7. Filed with the secretary of state. "Filed with the secretary of state" means that a document meeting the applicable requirements of this chapter, signed and accompanied by the required filing fee, has been delivered to the secretary of state of this state. The secretary of state shall endorse on the document the word "Filed" and the month, day, and year of filing, record the document in the office of the secretary of state, and return a document to the person who delivered it for filing.

333.01 Commercial assumed names

Subdivision 1. Certificate. No person shall hereafter carry on or conduct or transact a commercial business in this state under any designation, name, or style, which does not set forth the true name of every person interested in such business unless such person shall file in the office of the secretary of state, a certificate setting forth the name and business address under which the business is conducted or transacted, or is to be conducted or transacted, and the true name of each person conducting or transacting the same, with the address of such person. The name of the business must not include any of the following phrases or their abbreviations: corporation, incorporated, limited, chartered, professional association, cooperative, limited partnership, limited liability company, professional limited liability company, limited liability partnership, or professional limited liability partnership, except to the extent that an entity filing a certificate would be authorized to use the phrase or abbreviation. The certificate shall be executed by one of the persons conducting, or intending to conduct, the business. The certificate shall be published after it has been filed with the secretary of state in a qualified newspaper in the county in which the person has a principal or registered office for two successive issues.

Subd. 2. Intentional misrepresentation prohibited. No person shall use an assumed or fictitious name in the conduct of its business to intentionally misrepresent its geographic origin or location.

333.02 Filing of certificate

Persons conducting or transacting any business under any designation, name, or style referred to in section 333.01 shall, before commencing such business, file such certificate and shall publish the certificate in the manner prescribed in section 333.01.

333.065 Penalty for violation

A person who violates any provision of sections 333.01 to 333.06 is subject to the penalties and remedies provided in section 8.31.

The relief provided in this section is in addition to the remedies or penalties otherwise available.

333.28 Identical or similar marks; liability for misuse

Subject to the provisions of section 333.30 any person who shall (a) use without the consent of the registrant any mark on or in connection with rendering of services, selling, offering for sale, or advertising of any goods or services, which mark is identical to or so similar to the registered mark as to be likely to cause confusion or mistake on the part of a purchaser of the goods or services or to deceive such a purchaser as to the source or origin of the goods or services; or (b) reproduce, counterfeit, copy or colorably imitate any such mark and apply such reproduction, counterfeit, copy or colorable imitation to labels, signs, prints, packages, wrappers, receptacles, or advertisements intended to be used upon or in conjunction with the sale or other distribution of such goods or the sale or rendering of services: shall be liable to a civil action by the owner of such registered mark for any or all of the remedies provided in section 333.29, except that under subsection (b) hereof the registrant shall not be entitled to recover profits or damages unless the acts have been committed with knowledge that such mark is intended to be used to cause confusion or mistake or to deceive.

Appendix B
Checklists

The following checklists include all steps necessary to form a simple for-profit corporation; conduct a meeting of directors, and to form a professional firm in Minnesota.

Checklist for Forming a Minnesota For-Profit Corporation

- ❐ Decide on corporate name
- ❐ Prepare and file Articles of Incorporation
- ❐ Send for Federal Employer Identification Number (IRS Form SS-4)
- ❐ Prepare Shareholders' Agreement, if necessary
- ❐ Meet with accountant to discuss capitalization and tax planning
- ❐ If necessary, meet with securities lawyer regarding stock sales
- ❐ Obtain corporate seal if needed and ring binder for minutes
- ❐ Hold organizational meeting
    - ❐ Complete Bylaws, Waiver, Minutes, Offers to Purchase Stock
    - ❐ Sign all documents and place in minute book
- ❐ Issue stock certificates
    - ❐ Be sure consideration is paid
    - ❐ Complete Bill of Sale if property is traded for stock
    - ❐ Fill in Transfer ledger
- ❐ If assumed name is to be used, file **CERTIFICATE OF ASSUMED NAME**
- ❐ Get city or county licenses, if needed
- ❐ Open Bank account
- ❐ For S corporation status, file Form 2553

Checklist for Agenda for Meeting of Directors

- ❐ Send written notice to each director with
    - ❐ Date
    - ❐ Time (from when to when)
    - ❐ Location of Meeting
- ❐ Attach agenda with at least the following items
    - ❐ Call to order (by whom)
    - ❐ Roll call of members (list who is present and who is absent)
    - ❐ Approval of Minutes
    - ❐ Old business (even if you think there is none, include it in case some else does.
    - ❐ Reports
        - ❐ List each one and attach it to the notice, such as financials and all other reports essential to your operation.
        - ❐ Some reports may be identified on the agenda but given only verbally at the meeting
        - ❐ Indicate about how long it will take to present and discuss each report
    - ❐ Action required (list each item that will be discussed and voted upon and amount of time you anticipate will be spent on each item)
    - ❐ New business (to be discussed at the meeting but not identified on the notice) note amount of time allotted at the meeting to this item(s)
    - ❐ Adjournment (include time and if appropriate, the date. Some meetings take place over more than one day)

Checklist for Forming a Professional Firm in Minnesota

- ❒ Identify the names of each professional who will be a shareholder
- ❒ Contact each person's Minnesota Board of Licensure to determine if he or she is currently licensed and in good standing
- ❒ Decide on the name of the firm
- ❒ Prepare and file the Articles of Incorporation
- ❒ Obtain Federal Employer Identification Number (SS-4 Form)
- ❒ Prepare Shareholder Agreement, if appropriate
- ❒ Meet with accountant to discuss capitalization and tax planning
- ❒ If appropriate, meet with lawyer
- ❒ Obtain corporate seal if wanted
- ❒ Acquire ring binder for minutes
- ❒ Hold organizational Meeting
    - ❒ Complete Bylaws, Waiver, Minutes
- ❒ Issue stock certificates
    - ❒ Be sure consideration is paid
    - ❒ Complete Bill of Sale if property is traded for stock
    - ❒ Fill in transfer ledger
- ❒ If assumed name is to be used, file CERTIFICATE OF ASSUMED NAME
- ❒ Open Bank account
- ❒ For S corporation status, file Form 2553

Appendix C
Corporate Name
Availability

Much emotion can be attached to the name under which you do business. You can sink a fair amount of time, energy and money can into stationery, brochures and products. So it is critical that you start off with a name you want and that passes muster with the Minnesota Secretary of State. This appendix has definitions and examples of words that the Secretary has determined do and do not work.

Office of the Minnesota Secretary of State

NAME AVAILABILITY

This document provides information about "distinguishable upon the records of the Secretary of State" as used in *Minnesota Statutes Chapters 302A, 303, 308A, 317A, 322A, 322B, 323, 323A and 333*. It also explains limitations on certain words and numbers that may be used in a business name. The registration of a business name with the Office of the Secretary of State advises the public that a particular name is registered to individuals or a particular entity. Registration of a name does **not** grant rights to or interests in that name nor does the Secretary of State have the power to determine or settle competing claims to a name under other statutes or under the common law, except as provided in *Minnesota Statutes Section 5.22*.

DEFINITIONS

1) Article of speech - any one of the words "a," "an," or "the."

2) Conjunction - a word or symbol that joins clauses, phrases or words together. Examples include "and", "or", "as", "because", "but", "+", "-", "/", "&".

3) Contraction - the shortened form of a word, such as "ass'n" for "association" and "nat'l" for national.

4) Abbreviation - the shortened form of a word or a recognized shortening of a word to an unrelated combination of letters. Examples include "Mister" to "Mr.", "pound" to "lb.", "Brothers" to "Bros."

5) Preposition - a word which expresses the relationship between a noun and another word. Examples are: "at", "by", "in", "up", "of", "to".

TWO NAMES WHICH ARE IDENTICAL EXCEPT FOR THE FOLLOWING ARE NOT DISTINGUISHABLE.

a) Corporate designations regardless of how many or where they appear in the name. These include Incorporated, Corporation, Company, Limited, Limited Liability Company, Professional Limited Liability Company, Professional Association, Service Corporation, Professional Service Corporation, Professional Corporation, Professional Limited Liability Partnership, Limited Partnership, Limited Liability Partnership, Limited Liability Limited Partnership and their abbreviations and Chartered.

Examples
Corporate Designations - Not Distinguishable

    Sunshine Service Corporation   Mooty and Mooty P.A.
    Sunshine Service Ltd.   Mooty and Mooty Inc.
    Sunshine Service Co.   Mooty and Mooty Limited
        Mooty and Mooty PLC

b)   The inclusion or omission of articles of speech, conjunctions, contractions, prepositions or punctuation.

Examples
Conjunctions - Not Distinguishable

    Mooty and Mooty P.A.   G and C Enterprises Co.
    Mooty, Mooty P.A.   G and C Enterprises Corporation
        G/C Enterprises Co.
        G.C. Enterprises Corporation
        G.C.'s Enterprises Inc.

Contractions - Not Distinguishable

    The Graphics Department Inc.   National Association of Novelists
    Graphics Dep't LLC   Nat'l Ass'n of Novelists Inc

Prepositions - Not Distinguishable

    A Galaxy of Homes Inc.   Widget Mfg of Saint Paul Inc.
    Galaxy Homes Inc.   Widget Mfg in St Paul Co
        Widget Mfg at St Paul Inc

c)   The use of a singular as opposed to the plural of a word.

Examples
Plural vs. Singular - Not Distinguishable

    Hill Market Inc
    Hills Markets Co.
    Hills Market Ltd.

d)   The abbreviation versus complete spelling of the word or different tenses or cases of the same word.

Examples
Abbreviations - Not Distinguishable

    Stop and Shop Ltd.   Mister Softy Inc.
    Stop 'N Shop Corp   Mr. Softie Corp.

    Saint Paul Shoe Co
    St. Paul Shoes Inc

Tenses - Not Distinguishable

    Advance Security Co.
    Advanced Security Corp.

e)   The spacing of words, the combination of commonly used two-word terms or the splitting of words usually found in compound form.

Examples
Spacing of Words - Not Distinguishable

    Mid Co Inc   Hilltop Stables Inc
    MidCo Inc   Hill Top Stables Inc

    Outbound Travel Co   North West Homes Inc
    Out Bound Travel Inc   Northwest Homes Co.

f)   An obvious misspelling or alternative spelling or a homonym.

Examples
Obvious misspellings - Not Distinguishable

    Concept Log Homes Inc   Professional Cleaners Co
    Concep Log Homes Inc   Proffessional Cleaners Company

    Respectful Cemetery Co.
    Respectful Cemetary Inc.

Alternative Spellings - Not Distinguishable

    Color My Hair, Inc.   Quick Stop Co.
    Colour My Hair, Co.   Quik Stop Inc.
                                          Kwik Stop Ltd.

Homonyms - Not Distinguishable

  Blue Moon Dust Co.   Hare Care Inc
  Blew Moon Dust Co.   Hair Care Co.

  Right Press Inc.
  Write Press Corporation

g) The use of a word or numerals (including roman) for the same number *i.e.* two versus 2 versus II.

Examples

Words vs. Numerals - Not Distinguishable

  Movie Madness Two Inc
  Movie Madness II Co.
  Movie Madness 2 LLC

The Secretary of State's Office does not discriminate on the basis of race, creed, color, sex, sexual orientation, national origin, age, marital status, disability, religion, reliance on public assistance or political opinions or affiliations in employment or the provision of services. This document can be made available in alternative formats, such as large print, Braille or audio tape, by calling (651)296-2803/Voice, or by looking at our Web site at www.sos.state.mn.us. For TTY communication, contact the Minnesota Relay Service at 1-800-627-3529 and ask them to place a call to (651)296-2803.

nameavai   Rev. 10/99

Appendix D
Fee Schedule

There is a charge for each document you need to file for your corporation with the Minnesota Secretary of State. This appendix contains a list of each type of document you may need to file and all of the current filing fees for each document. At the end of the list is the phone number for the Secretary of State's Business Services Division. The forms you will need are in Appendix E. Or, you can download the forms from the web at

> http//www.sos.state.mn.us/business/forms.html

Or you can order them from

> Secretary of State Business Services Division
> 180 State Office Building,
> 100 Constitution Avenue
> St. Paul, MN 55155-1299
> 651-296-2803

MINNESOTA SECRETARY OF STATE
BUSINESS SERVICES DIVISION
UPDATED FEE SCHEDULE

Effective January 1, 1999

MINNESOTA BUSINESS, PROFESSIONAL, FINANCIAL & INSURANCE CORPORATIONS
Chapter 302A, 300 and 319B

Incorporation	$135.00
Amendments	$35.00
Dissolution Filings	$35.00
Merger	$60.00
Reinstatement	$25.00
Name Reservation	$35.00
Annual Registration	No Fee

FOREIGN CORPORATIONS *Chapter 303*

Certificate of Authority	$200.00
Amendments	$50.00
Merger (per each qualified corporation)	$50.00
Non-Profit Certificate	$50.00
Reinstatement	$300.00
Annual Registration	$115.00
Withdrawal	$50.00

NONPROFIT CORPORATIONS *Chapter 317A*

Incorporation	$70.00
Amendments	$35.00
Dissolution Filings	$35.00
Merger	$35.00
Reinstatement	$25.00
Name Reservation	$35.00
Annual Registration	No Fee

MINNESOTA LIMITED LIABILITY COMPANIES
Chapter 322B

Articles of Organization	$135.00
Amendments	$35.00
Merger	$60.00
Reinstatment	$25.00
Termination	$35.00
Name Reservation	$35.00
Annual Registration	No Fee

FOREIGN LIMITED LIABILITY COMPANIES
Chapter 322B

Certificate of Authority	$185.00
Amendments	$35.00
Merger (per qualified company)	$35.00
Reinstatement	$25.00
Withdrawal	$35.00
Anual Registration	No Fee

MINNESOTA & FOREIGN LIMITED LIABILITY PARTNERSHIPS *Chapter 323, 323A*

Registration/Qualification/Renewal	$135.00
Withdrawal	No Fee
Termination	No Fee

PARTNERSHIP FILINGS *Chapter 323A*

All Filings	$135.00

ASSUMED NAMES *Chapter 333*

Registration	$25.00
Renewal	$25.00
Amendments	$25.00
Cancellation	No Fee

MINNESOTA LIMITED PARTNERSHIPS *Chapter 322A*

Registration	$100.00
Amendments	$50.00
Cancellation	$50.00
Name Reservation	$50.00

FOREIGN LIMITED PARTNERSHIPS *Chapter 322A*

Registration	$85.00
Amendments	$50.00
Cancellation	$50.00

CONSENT $35.00

TRADEMARK/SERVICE MARK *Chapter 333*

Registration	$50.00
Renewal	$25.00
Assignment	$15.00
Cancellation	No Fee

SERVICE OF PROCESS

Minnesota Entities	$35.00
Non-Minnesota Corporations	$50.00

ARTICLES OF CORRECTION $35.00

COOPERATIVES *Chapter 308A*

Incorporation	$60.00
Amendments	$35.00
Merger	$60.00

BUSINESS TRUSTS *Chapter 318*

Declaration of Trust	$150.00
Business Trust Amendment	$50.00

LEGAL NEWSPAPERS $25.00

EXPEDITED FEE $20.00
For immediate processing of transactions at the Office of the Secretary of State

If You Have Questions About The Fees Please Call (651)296-2803.

03950411 Rev. 03/01

APPENDIX E
BLANK FORMS

form 1: REQUEST FOR RESERVATION OF NAME 107

form 2: CONSENT TO THE USE OF A NAME 109

form 3: CERTIFICATE OF ASSUMED NAME 111

form 4: TRANSMITTAL LETTER (to Secretary of State) 113

form 5: ARTICLES OF INCORPORATION 115

form 6: AMENDMENT OF ARTICLES OF INCORPORATION 117

form 7: ARTICLES OF ORGANIZATION FOR A LIMITED LIABILITY COMPANY 118

form 8: LIMITED LIABILITY PARTNERSHIP STATEMENT OF QUALIFICATION 119

form 9: CERTIFICATE OF LIMITED PARTNERSHIP 121

form 10: APPLICATION FOR LEGAL NEWSPAPER STATUS 123

form 11: APPLICATION FOR EMPLOYER IDENTIFICATION NUMBER (IRS FORM SS-4) 125

form 12: WAIVER OF NOTICE OF ORGANIZATIONAL MEETING 129

form 13: MINUTES OF ORGANIZATIONAL MEETING OF INCORPORATORS AND DIRECTORS . . . 130

form 14: BYLAWS 133

form 15: BYLAWS (Professional Firms) 139

form 16: BANKING RESOLUTION 145

form 17: OFFER TO PURCHASE STOCK 147

form 18: RESOLUTION (TO REIMBURSE EXPENSES) 149

form 19: BILL OF SALE 151

form 20: ELECTION BY A SMALL BUSINESS CORPORATION (IRS FORM 2553) 153

form 21: RESOLUTION (Adopting S Corporation Status). 159

form 22: WAIVER OF NOTICE OF ANNUAL MEETING OF BOARD OF DIRECTORS 160

form 23: MINUTES OF ANNUAL MEETING OF BOARD OF DIRECTORS 161

form 24: WAIVER OF NOTICE OF ANNUAL MEETING OF SHAREHOLDERS. 162

form 25: MINUTES OF ANNUAL MEETING OF SHAREHOLDERS 163

form 26: WAIVER OF NOTICE OF SPECIAL MEETING OF BOARD OF DIRECTORS 164

form 27: MINUTES OF SPECIAL MEETING OF BOARD OF DIRECTORS. 165

form 28: WAIVER OF NOTICE OF SPECIAL MEETING OF SHAREHOLDERS. 166

form 29: MINUTES OF SPECIAL MEETING OF SHAREHOLDERS 167

form 30: ARTICLES OF DISSOLUTION (before Issuance of Stock) 169

form 31: CHANGE OF REGISTERED OFFICE/REGISTERED AGENT. 171

form 32: STOCK TRANSFER LEDGER 173

form 33: STOCK CERTIFICATE STUBS. 175

form 34: STOCK CERTIFICATES. 177

form 35: DOMESTIC CORPORATION ANNUAL REGISTRATION 187

form 36: APPLICATION FOR TRADEMARK, SERVICEMARK, CERTIFICATION MARK
OR COLLECTIVE MARK 189

form 37: SHAREHOLDER AGREEMENT 191

MINNESOTA SECRETARY OF STATE

form 1

REQUEST FOR RESERVATION OF NAME

I hereby request the Secretary of State to reserve the name listed below. I understand that the name reservation is valid for twelve months from the date on which it is filed and may be renewed for additional twelve month periods, pursuant to *Minnesota Statutes, Section 302A.117, 317A.117, or 322B.125.*

1. Desired Name: _____

2. Reserved For: _____
   (Note: if this name is reserved for an organization not yet formed, list the individual who will be signing the documents which will be submitted at the time of the organization of the business.)

   Located at: _____
   (Street Address)

   _____
   (City)   (State)   (Zip)

The applicant hereby states that the proposed nameholder is:

a. A person doing business in this state under that name or a deceptively similar name;
b. A person intending to form an entity under Chapter 302A, 317A, or 322B;
c. A domestic corporation, or limited liability company intending to change its name;
d. A foreign corporation, or foreign limited liability company intending to make application for a Certificate of Authority to transact business in this state;
e. A foreign corporation, or foreign limited liability company authorized to transact business in this state and intending to change its name;
f. A person intending to incorporate a foreign corporation, or foreign limited liability company and intending to have the foreign corporation, or foreign limited liability company make application for a Certificate of Authority to transact business in this state; or
g. A foreign corporation, or foreign limited liability company doing business under that name or a name deceptively similar to that name in a state other than Minnesota and not described in clauses d, e or f.

I certify that the foregoing is true and accurate and that I have the authority to sign this document on behalf of the proposed nameholder, and I further certify that I understand that by signing this reservation, I am subject to the penalties of perjury as set forth in section 609.48 as if I had signed this reservation under oath.

Signed: _____

Position: _____

Name and telephone number of contact person: _____ ( ) _____
Please print legibly

All of the information on this form is public and required in order to process this filing. Failure to provide the requested information will prevent the Office from approving or further processing this filing.

INSTRUCTIONS

1. Type or print with dark black ink.
2. Filing fee: $35.00.
3. Make check payable to Secretary of State.
4. Mail or bring completed forms to:

Secretary of State
Business Services Division
180 State Office Bldg., 100 Constitution Ave.
St. Paul, MN 55155-1299, (651)296-2803

nameres   Rev. 11/98

This page intentionally left blank.

form 2

STATE OF MINNESOTA
SECRETARY OF STATE
CONSENT TO THE USE OF A NAME

Please type or print in dark black ink for archival purposes.

Please complete this side if this office has a name already on file that is similar to the name you wish to register. If you are unable to locate the holder of the name already on file, see the reverse side of this form. **Submit this form to the office along with the original filing or amendment you wish to record.**

1. Name You Wish to Register: _____

2. Name Already on File: _____

Address: _____

PLEASE HAVE THIS PORTION COMPLETED BY THE HOLDER OF THE NAME ALREADY ON FILE:

I grant consent to register the name listed on line 1 to: _____
(list name of person or entity registering new name)

located at _____
(street)   (city)   (state)   (zip)

(Check one)   ____ unconditionally.
               ____ with the following conditions:* _____
               _____

*****NOTE:** Conditions must be privately enforced.

I certify that I am authorized to sign this consent and I further certify that I understand that by signing this consent I am subject to the penalties of perjury as set forth in section 609.48 as if I had signed this consent under oath.

Signed: _____

Position: _____ Daytime Phone: _____

INSTRUCTIONS

1. Complete one form for each name already on file.
2. Filing fee: $35.00 per form.
3. Make check payable to the Secretary of State.
4. Mail or bring the completed forms to:
   Secretary of State
   Business Services Division
   180 State Office Bldg., 100 Constitution Ave.
   St. Paul, MN 55155-1299
   (651)296-2803

All of the information on this form is public and required in order to process this filing. Failure to provide the requested information will prevent the Office from approving or further processing this filing.

The Secretary of State's Office does not discriminate on the basis of race, creed, color, sex, sexual orientation, national origin, age, marital status, disability, religion, reliance on public assistance, or political opinions or affiliations in employment or the provision of services. This document can be made available in alternative formats, such as large print, Braille or audio tape, by calling (651)296-2803/Voice. For TTY communication, contact the Minnesota Relay Sevice at 1-800-627-3529 and ask them to place a call to (651)296-2803.

08950913 11/98

MINNESOTA SECRETARY OF STATE

AFFIDAVIT FOR THE REGISTRATION OF A NAME

Please type or print in dark black ink for archival purposes.

Instructions: Complete this side if you are unable to locate the holder of a name already on file to obtain consent to register a name. You may be able to register the name by fulfilling **ALL** of the requirements listed below.

1. Name You Wish to Register: _____

2. Name Already on File: _____

Address: _____

I hereby certify that I have the right to register the desired name because I have fulfilled ALL of the requirements of Minnesota Statutes listed below:

- A. I have determined that the entity or person holding the conflicting name has not filed any document under that name with the Office of the Secretary of State of Minnesota during the preceding three years.
- B. I have sent written notice to this entity or person at the last registered office or business address as listed with the Secretary of State, and that notice was sent by certified mail and has been returned as undeliverable.
- C. After diligent inquiry, I have been unable to find any telephone listing for that entity or person in the county in which that registered office or business address is located; and
- D. I have no personal knowledge that the entity or business is currently engaged in business in this state.

I certify that I am authorized to sign this affidavit and I further certify that I understand that by signing this affidavit, I am subject to the penalties of perjury as set forth in section 609.48 as if I had signed this affidavit under oath.

Name: _____   Signed: _____

Daytime Phone Number: _____   Position: _____

INSTRUCTIONS

1. Complete one form for each name already on file.
2. Filing fee: $35.00 per form.
3. Make check payable to the Secretary of State.
4. Mail or bring the completed forms to:

   Secretary of State
   Business Services Section
   180 State Office Bldg.
   100 Constitution Ave.
   St. Paul, MN 55155-1299
   (651)296-2803

All of the information on this form is public and required in order to process this filing. Failure to provide the requested information will prevent the Office from approving or further processing this filing.

The Secretary of State's Office does not discriminate on the basis of race, creed, color, sex, sexual orientation, national origin, age, marital status, disability, religion, reliance on public assistance or political opinions or affiliations in employment or the provision of services. This document can be made available in alternative formats, such as large print, Braille or audio tape, by calling (651)296-2803/Voice. For TTY communication, contact the Minnesota Relay Sevice at 1-800-627-3529 and ask them to place a call to (651)296-2803.

08950913 10/98

form 3

MINNESOTA SECRETARY OF STATE

CERTIFICATE OF ASSUMED NAME

Minnesota Statutes Chapter 333

Read the directions on reverse side before completing.   Filing fee: $25.00

The filing of an assumed name does not provide a user with exclusive rights to that name. The filing is required for consumer protection in order to enable consumers to be able to identify the true owner of a business.

PLEASE TYPE OR PRINT LEGIBLY IN BLACK INK FOR MICROFILMING PURPOSES.

1. State the exact assumed name under which the business is or will be conducted: (**one** business name per application)

   _____

2. State the address of the principal place of business. A complete street address or rural route and rural route box number is required; *the address cannot be a P.O.Box.*

Street	City	State	Zip code

3. List the name and complete street address of all persons conducting business under the above Assumed Name or if the business is a corporation, provide the legal corporate name and registered office address of the corporation. Attach Additional sheet(s) if necessary.

Name *(please print)*	Street	City	State	Zip

4. I certify that I am authorized to sign this certificate and I further certify that I understand that by signing this certificate, I am subject to the penalties of perjury as set forth in *Minnesota Statutes section 609.48* as if I had signed this certificate under oath.

   _____
   Signature (ONLY one person listed in #3 is required to sign.)

   _____   _____
   Date   Print Name and Title

   _____
   Contact Person   Daytime Phone Number

(05920807) rev. 2/01

111

DIRECTIONS

THIS FORM MUST BE TYPEWRITTEN OR PRINTED IN BLACK INK FOR MICROFILMING PURPOSES.

State law requires that this Certificate of Assumed Name be filed and published prior to the conduct of any business. Licensing and regulatory boards as well as private vendors and banks often require proof of the filing of this Certificate before issuing licenses, permits or entering into business relationships with the business.

WHO MUST FILE:

1) Any person conducting business under a name which is not their true full name (first and last name) must file. (Example: "John Smith Painting" need not file, however, "Smith Painting" would be required to file.)

2) A corporation, limited partnership or limited liability company conducting business under a name other than the legal name, must file (Example: Legal name; "St. Paul Painting Contractors, Inc.", Assumed Name; "St. Paul Painting".)

3) A partnership must file if the name of the partnership does not include the true full name of each partner.

STEPS TO FOLLOW:

1) State the exact business name on line 1. Only one business name may be filed per form. Assumed names that duplicate corporate, limited partnership and limited liability company names or trademarks already on file cannot be accepted for filing. Call the Business Information Line of the Office of the Secretary of State at (651)296-2803 for a preliminary determination whether the assumed name can be filed. This will reduce the possibility of rejection of the Certificate and will provide for faster filing of this Certificate.

2) State a complete street address or rural route and rural route box number of the principal place of business. A Minnesota Address is prefferable whenever available, but an out of state address is acceptable. A post office box cannot be accepted as the address of the principal place of business.

3) List the name and complete street address of all persons conducting business under the assumed name. If the business owner is a corporation doing business under an assumed name, the legal corporate name and Minnesota registered office address is required.

4) Complete line 4 with the date, the signature of **one** person listed in #3, the printed name of the person signing and the title of the signer. Please print the name and phone number of the person this office should contact if there are any questions about this form.

5) **Submit the Certificate of Assumed Name form and the $25.00 filing fee to:**
   Secretary of State, Business Services Section
   180 State Office Building, 100 Constitution Ave.
   St. Paul, MN 55155-1299

6) The Certificate of Assumed Name must be published **after filing** for two consecutive issues in the legal notices section of a qualified legal newspaper in the county where the principal place of business is located. The newspaper will return an affidavit of publication and the newspaper ad which should be retained by the assumed name holder with the Certificate of Assumed Name. Failure to publish may render the Certificate of Assumed Name invalid.

7) The filed and published Certificate of Assumed Name is valid for 10 years after the date of filing. A renewal form will be sent to the principal place of business address on file with this office six months prior to the Assumed Name expiration.

8) Any changes due to a change of business name, address, ownership, or owner's address, require the filing of a *Certificate of* **Amended** *Assumed Name* form. The Certificate of **Amended** Assumed Name form must be filed within **60** days after any change has occurred and must be published as described in paragraph 6 above.

All of the information on this form is public and required in order to process this filing. Failure to provide the requested information will prevent the Office from approving or further processing this filing. This document can be made available in alternative formats, such as large print, Braille or audio tape, by calling (651)296-2803/Voice. For TTY communication, contact Minnesota Relay Service at 1-800-627-3529 and ask them to place a call to (651)296-2803. The Secretary of State's Office does not discriminate on the basis of race, creed, color, sex, sexual orientation, national origin, age, marital status, disability, religion, reliance on public assistance or political opinions or affiliations in employment or the provision of services.

Transmittal Letter

Business Services Section
Secretary of State
180 State Office Building
100 Constitution Avenue
St. Paul, MN 55155-1299

SUBJECT: _____
(Proposed corporate name - must include suffix)

Enclosed is an original and one (1) copy of the articles of incorporation and a check for:

❑ $135.00
Filing Fee

FROM: _____
Name (Printed of typed)

_____
Address

_____
City, State & Zip

_____
Daytime Telephone number

This page intentionally left blank.

form 5
003

STATE OF MINNESOTA
SECRETARY OF STATE

ARTICLES OF INCORPORATION
Business and Nonprofit Corporations

PLEASE TYPE OR PRINT LEGIBLY IN BLACK INK.

Please read the directions on the reverse side before completing this form. All information on this form is public information.

The undersigned incorporator(s) is an (are) individual(s) 18 years of age or older and adopt the following articles of incorporation to form a (mark ONLY one):

☐ FOR-PROFIT BUSINESS CORPORATION (Chapter 302A)   ☐ NONPROFIT CORPORATION (Chapter 317A)

ARTICLE I   NAME

The name of the corporation is:

_____

(Business Corporation names must include a corporate designation such as Incorporated, Corporation, Company, Limited or an abbreviation of one of those words.)

ARTICLE II   REGISTERED OFFICE ADDRESS AND AGENT

The registered office address of the corporation is:

_____
(A complete street address or rural route and rural route box number is required; the address cannot be a P.O. Box) City State Zip

The registered agent at the above address is:

_____
Name   (**Note:** You are not required to have a registered agent.)

ARTICLE III   SHARES

The corporation is authorized to issue a total of _____ shares.
(If you are a business corporation you must authorize at least one share. Nonprofit corporations are not required to have shares.)

ARTICLE IV   INCORPORATORS

I (We), the undersigned incorporator(s) certify that I am (we are) authorized to sign these articles and that the information in these articles is true and correct. I (We) also understand that if any of this information is intentionally or knowingly misstated that criminal penalties will apply as if I (we) had signed these articles under oath. (Provide the name and address of each incorporator. Each incorporator must sign below. List the incorporators on an additional sheet if you have more than two incorporators.)

Name	Street	City	State	Zip	Signature

Print name and phone number of person to be contacted if there is a question about the filing of these articles.

_____   (____)_____
Name   Phone Number

03930254 Rev. 2/01

DIRECTIONS

THIS FORM MUST BE TYPEWRITTEN OR PRINTED IN BLACK INK.

Choose which type of corporation you are filing. A for-profit business corporation's goal is to make money for its shareholders.

A nonprofit corporation's goal is generally to return something to the community, not the financial gain of the members. In addition, a nonprofit corporation cannot pay members dividends.

ARTICLE I. State the exact corporate name. Business corporations MUST choose one of the following words or abbreviation of these words as part of the name of the business: Incorporated, Corporation, Limited or Company. The word "company" cannot be immediately preceded by "and" or "&". Nonprofit corporations may use these words but are not required to do so. Name availability may be checked on a preliminary basis by calling the Business Information Line at (651)296-2803 between 8:00 a.m. and 4:30 p.m. (CT) on any working day.

ARTICLE II. State the complete street address or rural route and rural route box number for the registered office address. Post office box numbers are NOT acceptable.

ARTICLE III. State the number of shares the corporation will be authorized to issue. Business corporations must be authorized to issue at least one share. Nonprofit corporations may (but are not required to) issue shares.

ARTICLE IV. Only one incorporator is required. If you have more than one incorporator you must state the name and complete address for each incorporator. Each incorporator must sign. List the incorporators on an additional sheet if you have more than two incorporators.

NOTE: This form is intended merely as a guide in the formation of a Minnesota corporation. It is not intended to cover all situations. If this form does not meet the specific needs and requirements of the corporation, the incorporators should draft their own articles.

A nonprofit corporation that wishes to apply to the Internal Revenue Service (IRS) for tax exempt status (501(c)(3) **cannot use this form for its articles**. The IRS has additional language requirements. That language is available from the IRS by calling (800)829-1040. After combining the IRS language with the requirements on the front of this form, submit the articles to this Office for filing. Once the articles have been filed and returned to the corporation, the application for tax exempt status can be made to the IRS.

FILING FEES: Make checks payable to the Secretary of State.

        Business Corporations - $135
        Nonprofit Corporations - $70

SEND FORM AND FEE TO: Secretary of State
                                      Business Services Section
                                      180 State Office Bldg.
                                      100 Constitution Ave.
                                      St. Paul, MN 55155-1299
                                      (651)296-2803

All of the information on this form is public and required in order to process this filing. Failure to provide the requested information will prevent the Office from approving or further processing this filing.

This document can be made available in alternative formats, such as large print, Braille or audio tape, by calling (651)296-2803/Voice. For TTY communication, contact Minnesota Relay Service at 1-800-627-3529 and ask them to place a call to (651)296-2803. The Secretary of State's Office does not discriminate on the basis of race, creed, color, sex, sexual orientation, national origin, age, marital status, disability, religion, reliance on public assistance, or political opinions or affiliations in employment or the provision of services.

form 6

MINNESOTA SECRETARY OF STATE

AMENDMENT OF ARTICLES OF INCORPORATION

READ INSTRUCTIONS LISTED BELOW, BEFORE COMPLETING THIS FORM.

1. **Type or print in black ink.**
2. **There is a $35.00 fee** payable to the Secretary of State for filing this "Amendment of Articles of Incorporation".
3. Return Completed Amendment Form and Fee to the address listed on the bottom of the form.

CORPORATE NAME: (List the name of the company prior to any desired name change)

_____

This amendment is effective on the day it is filed with the Secretary of State, unless you indicate another date, no later than 30 days **after** filing with the Secretary of State.

_____

The following amendment(s) to articles regulating the above corporation were adopted: (Insert full text of newly amended article(s) indicating which article(s) is (are) being amended or added.) If the full text of the amendment will not fit in the space provided, attach additional numbered pages. (Total number of pages including this form____.)

ARTICLE _____

This amendment has been approved pursuant to *Minnesota Statutes chapter 302A or 317A*. I certify that I am authorized to execute this amendment and I further certify that I understand that by signing this amendment, I am subject to the penalties of perjury as set forth in section 609.48 as if I had signed this amendment under oath.

_____
(Signature of Authorized Person)

Name and telephone number of contact person: _____ ( ) _____
Please print legibly

All of the information on this form is public and required in order to process this filing. Failure to provide the requested information will prevent the Office from approving or further processing this filing.

If you have any questions please contact the Secretary of State's office at **(651)296-2803**.

RETURN TO: Secretary of State
180 State Office Bldg., 100 Constitution Ave.
St. Paul, MN 55155-1299, (651)296-2803

08921340   Rev. 10/98

form 7

MINNESOTA SECRETARY OF STATE
ARTICLES OF ORGANIZATION FOR A LIMITED LIABILITY COMPANY
MINNESOTA STATUTES CHAPTER 322B

PLEASE TYPE OR PRINT IN BLACK INK.

Before Completing this Form Please Read the Instructions on the Back.   FILING FEE $135.00

1. Name of Company: _____

2. Registered Office Address: **(P.O. Box is Unacceptable)**

   _____   _____   **MN**   _____
   Complete Street Address or Rural Route and Rural Route Box Number   City   State   ZIP Code

3. Name of Registered Agent (optional): _____

4. Business Mailing Address: (if different from registered office address)

   _____   _____   _____   _____
   Address   City   State   ZIP Code

5. Desired Duration of LLC: (in years) _____ (If you do not complete this item, a perpetual duration is assumed by law)

6. Does this LLC own, lease or have any interest in agricultural land or land capable of being farmed?
   (Check One)   Yes _____   No _____

7. Name and Address of Organizer(s):

Name (print)	Complete Address	Original Signature (required)

8. Name and Telephone Number of Contact Person for this LLC:

   Name _____

   Phone (___) _____

05920791 Rev. 2/01

form 8

MINNESOTA SECRETARY OF STATE

LIMITED LIABILITY PARTNERSHIP STATEMENT OF QUALIFICATION
CHAPTER 323A

PLEASE TYPE OR PRINT IN BLACK INK.

Please read the instructions on the reverse side before completing.   Fee: $135

1. List the Partnership name: _____
_____

2. Address of the partnership's chief executive office:

_____
Complete Street Address or Rural Route and Rural Route Box Number   City   State   ZIP
  (Please note: PO Box is unacceptable)

3. List office of partnership in Minnesota, if different from item 2:

_____
Complete Street Address or Rural Route and Rural Route Box Number   City   State   ZIP
  (Please note: PO Box is unacceptable)

4. If there is no office in Minnesota, list name and address of agent of partnership in Minnesota for service of process:

Agent Name: _____

_____
Complete Street Address or Rural Route and Rural Route Box Number   City   State   ZIP
  (Please note: PO Box is unacceptable)

5. This partnership elects to be a limited liability partnership.

6. The effective date of this filing if different from the date of filing, is: _____.

7. I certify that I am a partner authorized to sign this document on behalf of this partnership and I further certify that by signing this document I am subject to the penalties of perjury as set forth in *Minnesota Statutes, section 5.15* as if I had signed this document under oath. **Note that this statement must be signed/executed by at least two (2) partners.**

_____   _____
Signature of a partner   Signature of a partner

_____   _____
Print name and daytime telephone number   Print name and daytime telephone number

10980529 Rev. 04/01

INSTRUCTIONS FOR COMPLETING 323A LLP STATEMENT OF QUALIFICATION

This Registration Must Be Typed Or Legibly Printed In Black Ink Only. An Illegible Statement of Qualification Will Be Returned Without Being Filed. This Form Is Merely A Guide. See Your Lawyer For More Information About Filings Under *Minnesota Statutes Chapter 323A*.

1. List the name of the partnership on whose behalf this statement is filed. The name of the partnership must be distinguishable from all other names on file with the Office of the Secretary of State, must be in English characters, and must not imply an illegal purpose. Name availability may be checked by calling the Business Information Phone Lines at (651) 296-2803 between 8 a.m. and 4:30 p.m. (CST)

2. List the address of the principal place of business of the partnership, regardless of its location.

3. If the partnership has an office in Minnesota different from the chief executive office, list the Minnesota address (including zip codes) here.

4. If the partnership has neither its chief executive office nor any other office in Minnesota, list the name and address of the agent of the partnership for service of process in this item.

5. This statement is required by law.

6. If you wish to have a different effective date for this statement, you must list that date here.

7. The document must be signed by at least two partners who are authorized to sign the registration.

GENERAL INFORMATION

A copy of this statement must promptly be sent to every non-filing partner and to any other person named as partner in the statement. This statement is valid until otherwise amended or cancelled.

Return the completed form and the $135 fee to:

Business Services Division
Office of the Secretary of State
180 State Office Bldg.
100 Constitution Ave.
St. Paul MN 55155-1299
(651) 296-2803

This document can be made available in alternative formats, such as large print, Braille or audio tape, by calling (651) 296-2803 Voice. For TTY communication, contact the Minnesota Relay Service at 1-800-627-3529 and ask them to place a call to (651) 296-2803. The Secretary of State's Office does not discriminate on the basis of race, creed, color, sex, sexual orientation, national origin, age marital status, disability, religion, reliance on public assistance or political opinions or affiliations in employment or the provision of services.

form 9

MINNESOTA SECRETARY OF STATE

**CERTIFICATE OF LIMITED PARTNERSHIP
CHAPTER 322A**

DIRECTIONS:

- Type or print in dark black ink.
- Please complete all parts. Use additional sheets if needed.
- Filing fee: $100.00 ($50.00 filing fee plus $50.00 initial fee).
- Make check payable to the "Secretary of State".

The undersigned partner(s) desire to form a limited partnership under Minnesota Statutes, Chapter 322A (known as the Uniform Limited Partnership Act) and adopt the following:

NOTE: This form is intended merely as a guide in the formation of a Minnesota limited partnership under Minnesota Statutes Chapter 322A. It is not intended to cover all situations anticipated by that statute.

If this form does not meet the specific needs and requirements of the limited partnership being formed, the partners should draft a certificate specifically listing the modifications or denials of each provision to which they wish to be subject, or from which they wish to be exempt.

**ARTICLE I
NAME OF LIMITED PARTNERSHIP**

The name of this limited partnership is:

_____

**ARTICLE II
ADDRESS OF RECORDS: NAME AND ADDRESS OF AGENT**

The office address where records are to be maintained is:

_____

| Street address | City, State, Zip | County |

The name and address of the agent for service of process is:

_____

**ARTICLE III
GENERAL PARTNERS**

Name	Name
Address	Address
City, State, Zip	City, State, Zip

- OVER -

Name	Name
Address	Address
City, State, Zip	City, State, Zip

ARTICLE IV
DISSOLUTION

Describe the latest date upon which the limited partnership is to dissolve:

_____
_____
_____
_____
_____

I certify that I am authorized to execute this certificate and I further certify that I understand that by signing this certificate, I am subject to the penalties of perjury as set forth in section 609.48 as if I had signed this certificate under oath.

Date: _____ Signed: _____
                                           General Partner

All of the information on this form is public and required in order to process this filing. Failure to provide the requested information will prevent the Office from approving or further processing this filing.

This document can be made available in alternative formats, such as large print, Braille or audio tape, by calling (651)296-2803/ Voice. For TTY communication, contact Minnesota Relay Service at 1-800-627-3529 and ask them to place a call to (651)296-2803. The Secretary of State's Office does not discriminate on the basis of race, creed, color, sex, sexual orientation, national origin, age, marital status, disability, religion, reliance on public assistance or political opinions or affiliations in employment or the provision of services.

certlp Rev 11/99

form 10

MINNESOTA SECRETARY OF STATE

APPLICATION FOR LEGAL NEWSPAPER STATUS

MUST BE FILED BETWEEN SEPTEMBER 1 AND DECEMBER 31, EACH YEAR

Please read the instructions on the reverse side before completing this form.

1. CURRENT NAME AND KNOWN OFFICE OF ISSUE ADDRESS OF NEWSPAPER:

Name

Street

City   State   Zip Code

2. IF CHANGED, LIST THE NEW NAME AND/OR ADDRESS OF KNOWN OFFICE OF ISSUE (must be a complete street address or rural route and rural route box number):

_____
NAME OF NEWSPAPER

_____
STREET ADDRESS   CITY   STATE   ZIP CODE

3. COUNTY OF KNOWN OFFICE OF ISSUE: _____

4. NAME AND TELEPHONE NUMBER OF A CONTACT PERSON:

_____(_____)_____

I do hereby certify that the above listed publication has met the filing requirement for legal newspaper as set forth in Minnesota Statutes Section 331A.02, subd. 1(i).

5. _____
   Signature of Authorized Representative

IN ORDER TO PROCESS THIS APPLICATION FOR LEGAL NEWSPAPER REGISTRATION YOU MUST RETURN THE COMPLETED APPLICATION ALONG WITH THE $25.00 FILING FEE MADE PAYABLE TO THE SECRETARY OF STATE.

08111238   Rev. 9/01

INSTRUCTIONS

This registration must be filed between September 1 and December 31, each year if you wish to qualify for an entire calendar year. Applications received in our office after January 1, are effective from the date when they are filed and processed by this office.

1. Check the newspaper name and known office of issue address listed in item 1. If that information has changed, complete item 2.

2. List the name and address of the newspaper's known office of issue if it has changed. The known office of issue is the principle office maintained by the publisher or managing officer during the newspaper's regular business hours to gather news and sell advertisements and subscriptions, whether or not printing or any other operations of the newspaper are conducted at or from the office, and devoted primarily to business related to the newspaper.

3. List the name of the county in which the known office of issue is located.

4. List the name and telephone number of a person the Office of the Secretary of State can contact if there are any questions about this application.

5. The application must be signed by a person authorized to act on behalf of the newspaper.

Return the completed form and $25 filing fee to:

Secretary of State
Business Services Division
180 State Office Building
100 Constitution Ave.
St. Paul, MN 55155-1299

MAKE CHECKS PAYABLE TO THE SECRETARY OF STATE

If you have any further questions about filing this application for legal newspaper status, please contact the Business Services Division of the Secretary of State at (651)296-2803.

The Secretary of State's Office does not discriminate on the basis of race, creed, color, sex, sexual orientation, national origin, age, marital status, disability, religion, reliance on public assistance or political opinions or affiliations in employment or the provision of services. This document can be made available in alternative formats, such as large print, Braille or audio tape, by calling (651)296-2803/Voice, or on our Web site at www.sos.state.mn.us. For TTY communication, contact the Minnesota Relay Service at 1-800-627-3529 and ask them to place a call to (651)296-2803.

form 11

Form SS-4
Application for Employer Identification Number
(For use by employers, corporations, partnerships, trusts, estates, churches, government agencies, certain individuals, and others. See instructions.)

▶ Keep a copy for your records.

(Rev. April 2000)
Department of the Treasury
Internal Revenue Service

EIN
OMB No. 1545-0003

Please type or print clearly.

1 Name of applicant (legal name) (see instructions)

2 Trade name of business (if different from name on line 1)

3 Executor, trustee, "care of" name

4a Mailing address (street address) (room, apt., or suite no.)

5a Business address (if different from address on lines 4a and 4b)

4b City, state, and ZIP code

5b City, state, and ZIP code

6 County and state where principal business is located

7 Name of principal officer, general partner, grantor, owner, or trustor—SSN or ITIN may be required (see instructions) ▶

8a Type of entity (Check only one box.) (see instructions)
Caution: *If applicant is a limited liability company, see the instructions for line 8a.*

☐ Sole proprietor (SSN) _____
☐ Partnership
☐ REMIC
☐ State/local government
☐ Church or church-controlled organization
☐ Other nonprofit organization (specify) ▶ _____
☐ Other (specify) ▶

☐ Personal service corp.
☐ National Guard
☐ Farmers' cooperative

☐ Estate (SSN of decedent) _____
☐ Plan administrator (SSN) _____
☐ Other corporation (specify) ▶ _____
☐ Trust
☐ Federal government/military
(enter GEN if applicable) _____

8b If a corporation, name the state or foreign country (if applicable) where incorporated
State | Foreign country

9 Reason for applying (Check only one box.) (see instructions)
☐ Started new business (specify type) ▶ _____
☐ Hired employees (Check the box and see line 12.)
☐ Created a pension plan (specify type) ▶
☐ Banking purpose (specify purpose) ▶ _____
☐ Changed type of organization (specify new type) ▶ _____
☐ Purchased going business
☐ Created a trust (specify type) ▶ _____
☐ Other (specify) ▶

10 Date business started or acquired (month, day, year) (see instructions)

11 Closing month of accounting year (see instructions)

12 First date wages or annuities were paid or will be paid (month, day, year). **Note:** *If applicant is a withholding agent, enter date income will first be paid to nonresident alien. (month, day, year)* . . . . ▶

13 Highest number of employees expected in the next 12 months. **Note:** *If the applicant does not expect to have any employees during the period, enter -0-. (see instructions)* . . . . ▶
| Nonagricultural | Agricultural | Household |

14 Principal activity (see instructions) ▶

15 Is the principal business activity manufacturing? . . . . ☐ Yes ☐ No
If "Yes," principal product and raw material used ▶

16 To whom are most of the products or services sold? Please check one box.
☐ Public (retail) ☐ Other (specify) ▶
☐ Business (wholesale) ☐ N/A

17a Has the applicant ever applied for an employer identification number for this or any other business? . . . . ☐ Yes ☐ No
Note: *If "Yes," please complete lines 17b and 17c.*

17b If you checked "Yes" on line 17a, give applicant's legal name and trade name shown on prior application, if different from line 1 or 2 above.
Legal name ▶   Trade name ▶

17c Approximate date when and city and state where the application was filed. Enter previous employer identification number if known.
Approximate date when filed (mo., day, year) | City and state where filed | Previous EIN

Under penalties of perjury, I declare that I have examined this application, and to the best of my knowledge and belief, it is true, correct, and complete.

Business telephone number (include area code)
(   )

Fax telephone number (include area code)
(   )

Name and title (Please type or print clearly.) ▶

Signature ▶   Date ▶

Note: *Do not write below this line. For official use only.*

| Please leave blank ▶ | Geo. | Ind. | Class | Size | Reason for applying |

For Privacy Act and Paperwork Reduction Act Notice, see page 4.   Cat. No. 16055N   Form **SS-4** (Rev. 4-2000)

125

General Instructions

Section references are to the Internal Revenue Code unless otherwise noted.

Purpose of Form

Use Form SS-4 to apply for an employer identification number (EIN). An EIN is a nine-digit number (for example, 12-3456789) assigned to sole proprietors, corporations, partnerships, estates, trusts, and other entities for tax filing and reporting purposes. The information you provide on this form will establish your business tax account.

Caution: *An EIN is for use in connection with your business activities only. Do **not** use your EIN in place of your social security number (SSN).*

Who Must File

You must file this form if you have not been assigned an EIN before and:

- You pay wages to one or more employees including household employees.
- You are required to have an EIN to use on any return, statement, or other document, even if you are not an employer.
- You are a withholding agent required to withhold taxes on income, other than wages, paid to a nonresident alien (individual, corporation, partnership, etc.). A withholding agent may be an agent, broker, fiduciary, manager, tenant, or spouse, and is required to file **Form 1042**, Annual Withholding Tax Return for U.S. Source Income of Foreign Persons.
- You file **Schedule C**, Profit or Loss From Business, **Schedule C-EZ**, Net Profit From Business, or **Schedule F**, Profit or Loss From Farming, of **Form 1040**, U.S. Individual Income Tax Return, **and** have a Keogh plan or are required to file excise, employment, or alcohol, tobacco, or firearms returns.

The following must use EINs even if they do not have any employees:

- State and local agencies who serve as tax reporting agents for public assistance recipients, under Rev. Proc. 80-4, 1980-1 C.B. 581, should obtain a separate EIN for this reporting. See **Household employer** on page 3.
- Trusts, except the following:
    1. Certain grantor-owned trusts. (See the **Instructions for Form 1041**, U.S. Income Tax Return for Estates and Trusts.)
    2. Individual retirement arrangement (IRA) trusts, unless the trust has to file **Form 990-T**, Exempt Organization Business Income Tax Return. (See the **Instructions for Form 990-T**.)
- Estates
- Partnerships
- REMICs (real estate mortgage investment conduits) (See the **Instructions for Form 1066**, U.S. Real Estate Mortgage Investment Conduit (REMIC) Income Tax Return.)
- Corporations
- Nonprofit organizations (churches, clubs, etc.)
- Farmers' cooperatives
- Plan administrators (A plan administrator is the person or group of persons specified as the administrator by the instrument under which the plan is operated.)

When To Apply for a New EIN

New Business. If you become the new owner of an existing business, **do not** use the EIN of the former owner. **If you already have an EIN, use that number.** If you do not have an EIN, apply for one on this form. If you become the "owner" of a corporation by acquiring its stock, use the corporation's EIN.

Changes in Organization or Ownership. If you already have an EIN, you may need to get a new one if either the organization or ownership of your business changes. If you incorporate a sole proprietorship or form a partnership, you must get a new EIN. However, **do not** apply for a new EIN if:

- You change only the name of your business,
- You elected on **Form 8832**, Entity Classification Election, to change the way the entity is taxed, or
- A partnership terminates because at least 50% of the total interests in partnership capital and profits were sold or exchanged within a 12-month period. (See Regulations section 301.6109-1(d)(2)(iii).) The EIN for the terminated partnership should continue to be used.

Note: *If you are electing to be an "S corporation," be sure you file **Form 2553**, Election by a Small Business Corporation.*

File Only One Form SS-4. File only one Form SS-4, regardless of the number of businesses operated or trade names under which a business operates. However, each corporation in an affiliated group must file a separate application.

EIN Applied for, But Not Received. If you do not have an EIN by the time a return is due, write "Applied for" and the date you applied in the space shown for the number. **Do not** show your social security number (SSN) as an EIN on returns.

If you do not have an EIN by the time a tax deposit is due, send your payment to the Internal Revenue Service Center for your filing area. (See **Where To Apply** below.) Make your check or money order payable to "United States Treasury" and show your name (as shown on Form SS-4), address, type of tax, period covered, and date you applied for an EIN. Send an explanation with the deposit.

For more information about EINs, see **Pub. 583**, Starting a Business and Keeping Records, and **Pub. 1635**, Understanding Your EIN.

How To Apply

You can apply for an EIN either by mail or by telephone. You can get an EIN immediately by calling the Tele-TIN number for the service center for your state, or you can send the completed Form SS-4 directly to the service center to receive your EIN by mail.

Application by Tele-TIN. Under the Tele-TIN program, you can receive your EIN by telephone and use it immediately to file a return or make a payment. To receive an EIN by telephone, complete Form SS-4, then call the Tele-TIN number listed for your state under **Where To Apply**. The person making the call must be authorized to sign the form. (See **Signature** on page 4.)

An IRS representative will use the information from the Form SS-4 to establish your account and assign you an EIN. Write the number you are given on the upper right corner of the form and sign and date it.

Mail or fax (facsimile) the signed Form SS-4 **within 24 hours** to the Tele-TIN Unit at the service center address for your state. The IRS representative will give you the fax number. The fax numbers are also listed in Pub. 1635.

Taxpayer representatives can receive their client's EIN by telephone if they first send a fax of a completed **Form 2848**, Power of Attorney and Declaration of Representative, or **Form 8821**, Tax Information Authorization, to the Tele-TIN unit. The Form 2848 or Form 8821 will be used solely to release the EIN to the representative authorized on the form.

Application by Mail. Complete Form SS-4 at least 4 to 5 weeks before you will need an EIN. Sign and date the application and mail it to the service center address for your state. You will receive your EIN in the mail in approximately 4 weeks.

Where To Apply

The Tele-TIN numbers listed below will involve a long-distance charge to callers outside of the local calling area and can be used only to apply for an EIN. **The numbers may change without notice.** Call 1-800-829-1040 to verify a number or to ask about the status of an application by mail.

If your principal business, office or agency, or legal residence in the case of an individual, is located in:	Call the Tele-TIN number shown or file with the Internal Revenue Service Center at:
Florida, Georgia, South Carolina	Attn: Entity Control Atlanta, GA 39901 770-455-2360
New Jersey, New York (New York City and counties of Nassau, Rockland, Suffolk, and Westchester)	Attn: Entity Control Holtsville, NY 00501 631-447-4955
New York (all other counties), Connecticut, Maine, Massachusetts, New Hampshire, Rhode Island, Vermont	Attn: Entity Control Andover, MA 05501 978-474-9717
Illinois, Iowa, Minnesota, Missouri, Wisconsin	Attn: Entity Control Stop 6800 2306 E. Bannister Rd. Kansas City, MO 64999 816-823-7777
Delaware, District of Columbia, Maryland, Pennsylvania, Virginia	Attn: Entity Control Philadelphia, PA 19255 215-516-6999
Indiana, Kentucky, Michigan, Ohio, West Virginia	Attn: Entity Control Cincinnati, OH 45999 859-292-5467

Form SS-4 (Rev. 4-2000)
Page **3**

Kansas, New Mexico, Oklahoma, Texas	Attn: Entity Control Austin, TX 73301 512-460-7843
Alaska, Arizona, California (counties of Alpine, Amador, Butte, Calaveras, Colusa, Contra Costa, Del Norte, El Dorado, Glenn, Humboldt, Lake, Lassen, Marin, Mendocino, Modoc, Napa, Nevada, Placer, Plumas, Sacramento, San Joaquin, Shasta, Sierra, Siskiyou, Solano, Sonoma, Sutter, Tehama, Trinity, Yolo, and Yuba), Colorado, Idaho, Montana, Nebraska, Nevada, North Dakota, Oregon, South Dakota, Utah, Washington, Wyoming	Attn: Entity Control Mail Stop 6271 P.O. Box 9941 Ogden, UT 84201 801-620-7645
California (all other counties), Hawaii	Attn: Entity Control Fresno, CA 93888 559-452-4010
Alabama, Arkansas, Louisiana, Mississippi, North Carolina, Tennessee	Attn: Entity Control Memphis, TN 37501 901-546-3920
If you have no legal residence, principal place of business, or principal office or agency in any state	Attn: Entity Control Philadelphia, PA 19255 215-516-6999

Specific Instructions

The instructions that follow are for those items that are not self-explanatory. Enter N/A (nonapplicable) on the lines that do not apply.

Line 1. Enter the legal name of the entity applying for the EIN exactly as it appears on the social security card, charter, or other applicable legal document.

Individuals. Enter your first name, middle initial, and last name. If you are a sole proprietor, enter your individual name, not your business name. Enter your business name on line 2. Do not use abbreviations or nicknames on line 1.

Trusts. Enter the name of the trust.

Estate of a decedent. Enter the name of the estate.

Partnerships. Enter the legal name of the partnership as it appears in the partnership agreement. **Do not** list the names of the partners on line 1. See the specific instructions for line 7.

Corporations. Enter the corporate name as it appears in the corporation charter or other legal document creating it.

Plan administrators. Enter the name of the plan administrator. A plan administrator who already has an EIN should use that number.

Line 2. Enter the trade name of the business if different from the legal name. The trade name is the "doing business as" name.

Note: *Use the full legal name on line 1 on all tax returns filed for the entity. However, if you enter a trade name on line 2 and choose to use the trade name instead of the legal name, enter the trade name on all returns you file. To prevent processing delays and errors, always use either the legal name only or the trade name only on all tax returns.*

Line 3. Trusts enter the name of the trustee. Estates enter the name of the executor, administrator, or other fiduciary. If the entity applying has a designated person to receive tax information, enter that person's name as the "care of" person. Print or type the first name, middle initial, and last name.

Line 7. Enter the first name, middle initial, last name, and SSN of a principal officer if the business is a corporation; of a general partner if a partnership; of the owner of a single member entity that is disregarded as an entity separate from its owner; or of a grantor, owner, or trustor if a trust. If the person in question is an alien individual with a previously assigned individual taxpayer identification number (ITIN), enter the ITIN in the space provided, instead of an SSN. You are not required to enter an SSN or ITIN if the reason you are applying for an EIN is to make an entity classification election (see Regulations section 301.7701-1 through 301.7701-3), and you are a nonresident alien with no effectively connected income from sources within the United States.

Line 8a. Check the box that best describes the type of entity applying for the EIN. If you are an alien individual with an ITIN previously assigned to you, enter the ITIN in place of a requested SSN.

Caution: *This is not an election for a tax classification of an entity. See "Limited liability company (LLC)" below.*

If not specifically mentioned, check the "Other" box, enter the type of entity and the type of return that will be filed (for example, common trust fund, Form 1065). Do not enter N/A. If you are an alien individual applying for an EIN, see the **Line 7** instructions above.

Sole proprietor. Check this box if you file Schedule C, C-EZ, or F (Form 1040) and have a qualified plan, or are required to file excise, employment, or alcohol, tobacco, or firearms returns, or are a payer of gambling winnings. Enter your SSN (or ITIN) in the space provided. If you are a nonresident alien with are a nonresident alien with no effectively connected income from sources within the United States, you do not need to enter an SSN or ITIN.

REMIC. Check this box if the entity has elected to be treated as a real estate mortgage investment conduit (REMIC). See the Instructions for Form 1066 for more information.

Other nonprofit organization. Check this box if the nonprofit organization is other than a church or church-controlled organization and specify the type of nonprofit organization (for example, an educational organization).

If the organization also seeks tax-exempt status, you must file either **Package 1023**, Application for Recognition of Exemption, or **Package 1024**, Application for Recognition of Exemption Under Section 501(a). Get **Pub. 557**, Tax Exempt Status for Your Organization, for more information.

Group exemption number (GEN). If the organization is covered by a group exemption letter, enter the four-digit GEN. (Do not confuse the GEN with the nine-digit EIN.) If you do not know the GEN, contact the parent organization. Get Pub. 557 for more information about group exemption numbers.

Withholding agent. If you are a withholding agent required to file Form 1042, check the "Other" box and enter "Withholding agent."

Personal service corporation. Check this box if the entity is a personal service corporation. An entity is a personal service corporation for a tax year only if:

● The principal activity of the entity during the testing period (prior tax year) for the tax year is the performance of personal services substantially by employee-owners, and

● The employee-owners own at least 10% of the fair market value of the outstanding stock in the entity on the last day of the testing period.

Personal services include performance of services in such fields as health, law, accounting, or consulting. For more information about personal service corporations, see the **Instructions for Forms 1120 and 1120-A**, and **Pub. 542**, Corporations.

Limited liability company (LLC). See the definition of limited liability company in the **Instructions for Form 1065**, U.S. Partnership Return of Income. An LLC with two or more members can be a partnership or an association taxable as a corporation. An LLC with a single owner can be an association taxable as a corporation or an entity disregarded as an entity separate from its owner. See Form 8832 for more details.

Note: *A domestic LLC with at least two members that does not file Form 8832 is classified as a partnership for Federal income tax purposes.*

● If the entity is classified as a partnership for Federal income tax purposes, check the "partnership" box.

● If the entity is classified as a corporation for Federal income tax purposes, check the "Other corporation" box and write "limited liability co." in the space provided.

● If the entity is disregarded as an entity separate from its owner, check the "Other" box and write in "disregarded entity" in the space provided.

Plan administrator. If the plan administrator is an individual, enter the plan administrator's SSN in the space provided.

Other corporation. This box is for any corporation other than a personal service corporation. If you check this box, enter the type of corporation (such as insurance company) in the space provided.

Household employer. If you are an individual, check the "Other" box and enter "Household employer" and your SSN. If you are a state or local agency serving as a tax reporting agent for public assistance recipients who become household employers, check the "Other" box and enter "Household employer agent." If you are a trust that qualifies as a household employer, you do not need a separate EIN for reporting tax information relating to household employees; use the EIN of the trust.

QSub. For a qualified subchapter S subsidiary (QSub) check the "Other" box and specify "QSub."

Line 9. Check only **one** box. Do not enter N/A.

Started new business. Check this box if you are starting a new business that requires an EIN. If you check this box, enter the type of business being started. **Do not** apply if you already have an EIN and are only adding another place of business.

Hired employees. Check this box if the existing business is requesting an EIN because it has hired or is hiring employees and is therefore required to file employment tax returns. **Do not** apply if you already have an EIN and are only hiring employees. For information on the applicable employment taxes for family members, see **Circular E**, Employer's Tax Guide (Publication 15).

Created a pension plan. Check this box if you have created a pension plan and need an EIN for reporting purposes. Also, enter the type of plan.

Note: *Check this box if you are applying for a trust EIN when a new pension plan is established.*

127

Banking purpose. Check this box if you are requesting an EIN for banking purposes only, and enter the banking purpose (for example, a bowling league for depositing dues or an investment club for dividend and interest reporting).

Changed type of organization. Check this box if the business is changing its type of organization, for example, if the business was a sole proprietorship and has been incorporated or has become a partnership. If you check this box, specify in the space provided the type of change made, for example, "from sole proprietorship to partnership."

Purchased going business. Check this box if you purchased an existing business. **Do not** use the former owner's EIN. **Do not** apply for a new EIN if you already have one. Use your own EIN.

Created a trust. Check this box if you created a trust, and enter the type of trust created. For example, indicate if the trust is a nonexempt charitable trust or a split-interest trust.

Note: *Do not check this box if you are applying for a trust EIN when a new pension plan is established. Check "Created a pension plan."*

Exception. Do **not** file this form for certain grantor-type trusts. The trustee does not need an EIN for the trust if the trustee furnishes the name and TIN of the grantor/owner and the address of the trust to all payors. See the Instructions for Form 1041 for more information.

Other (specify). Check this box if you are requesting an EIN for any other reason, and enter the reason.

Line 10. If you are starting a new business, enter the starting date of the business. If the business you acquired is already operating, enter the date you acquired the business. Trusts should enter the date the trust was legally created. Estates should enter the date of death of the decedent whose name appears on line 1 or the date when the estate was legally funded.

Line 11. Enter the last month of your accounting year or tax year. An accounting or tax year is usually 12 consecutive months, either a calendar year or a fiscal year (including a period of 52 or 53 weeks). A calendar year is 12 consecutive months ending on December 31. A fiscal year is either 12 consecutive months ending on the last day of any month other than December or a 52-53 week year. For more information on accounting periods, see **Pub. 538**, Accounting Periods and Methods.

Individuals. Your tax year generally will be a calendar year.

Partnerships. Partnerships generally must adopt one of the following tax years:
- The tax year of the majority of its partners,
- The tax year common to all of its principal partners,
- The tax year that results in the least aggregate deferral of income, or
- In certain cases, some other tax year.

See the Instructions for Form 1065 for more information.

REMIC. REMICs must have a calendar year as their tax year.

Personal service corporations. A personal service corporation generally must adopt a calendar year unless:
- It can establish a business purpose for having a different tax year, or
- It elects under section 444 to have a tax year other than a calendar year.

Trusts. Generally, a trust must adopt a calendar year except for the following:
- Tax-exempt trusts,
- Charitable trusts, and
- Grantor-owned trusts.

Line 12. If the business has or will have employees, enter the date on which the business began or will begin to pay wages. If the business does not plan to have employees, enter N/A.

Withholding agent. Enter the date you began or will begin to pay income to a nonresident alien. This also applies to individuals who are required to file Form 1042 to report alimony paid to a nonresident alien.

Line 13. For a definition of agricultural labor (farmwork), see **Circular A,** Agricultural Employer's Tax Guide (Publication 51).

Line 14. Generally, enter the exact type of business being operated (for example, advertising agency, farm, food or beverage establishment, labor union, real estate agency, steam laundry, rental of coin-operated vending machine, or investment club). Also state if the business will involve the sale or distribution of alcoholic beverages.

Governmental. Enter the type of organization (state, county, school district, municipality, etc.).

Nonprofit organization (other than governmental). Enter whether organized for religious, educational, or humane purposes, and the principal activity (for example, religious organization—hospital, charitable).

Mining and quarrying. Specify the process and the principal product (for example, mining bituminous coal, contract drilling for oil, or quarrying dimension stone).

Contract construction. Specify whether general contracting or special trade contracting. Also, show the type of work normally performed (for example, general contractor for residential buildings or electrical subcontractor).

Food or beverage establishments. Specify the type of establishment and state whether you employ workers who receive tips (for example, lounge—yes).

Trade. Specify the type of sales and the principal line of goods sold (for example, wholesale dairy products, manufacturer's representative for mining machinery, or retail hardware).

Manufacturing. Specify the type of establishment operated (for example, sawmill or vegetable cannery).

Signature. The application must be signed by (a) the individual, if the applicant is an individual, (b) the president, vice president, or other principal officer, if the applicant is a corporation, (c) a responsible and duly authorized member or officer having knowledge of its affairs, if the applicant is a partnership or other unincorporated organization, or (d) the fiduciary, if the applicant is a trust or an estate.

How To Get Forms and Publications

Phone. You can order forms, instructions, and publications by phone 24 hours a day, 7 days a week. Just call 1-800-TAX-FORM (1-800-829-3676). You should receive your order or notification of its status within 10 workdays.

Personal computer. With your personal computer and modem, you can get the forms and information you need using IRS's Internet Web Site at **www.irs.gov** or File Transfer Protocol at **ftp.irs.gov**.

CD-ROM. For small businesses, return preparers, or others who may frequently need tax forms or publications, a CD-ROM containing over 2,000 tax products (including many prior year forms) can be purchased from the National Technical Information Service (NTIS).

To order **Pub. 1796**, Federal Tax Products on CD-ROM, call **1-877-CDFORMS** (1-877-233-6767) toll free or connect to **www.irs.gov/cdorders**

Privacy Act and Paperwork Reduction Act Notice. We ask for the information on this form to carry out the Internal Revenue laws of the United States. We need it to comply with section 6109 and the regulations thereunder which generally require the inclusion of an employer identification number (EIN) on certain returns, statements, or other documents filed with the Internal Revenue Service. Information on this form may be used to determine which Federal tax returns you are required to file and to provide you with related forms and publications. We disclose this form to the Social Security Administration for their use in determining compliance with applicable laws. We will be unable to issue an EIN to you unless you provide all of the requested information which applies to your entity.

You are not required to provide the information requested on a form that is subject to the Paperwork Reduction Act unless the form displays a valid OMB control number. Books or records relating to a form or its instructions must be retained as long as their contents may become material in the administration of any Internal Revenue law. Generally, tax returns/return information are confidential, as required by section 6103.

The time needed to complete and file this form will vary depending on individual circumstances. The estimated average time is:

Recordkeeping	7 min.
Learning about the law or the form	22 min.
Preparing the form	46 min.
Copying, assembling, and sending the form to the IRS . .	20 min.

If you have comments concerning the accuracy of these time estimates or suggestions for making this form simpler, we would be happy to hear from you. You can write to the Tax Forms Committee, Western Area Distribution Center, Rancho Cordova, CA 95743-0001. **Do not** send the form to this address. Instead, see **Where To Apply** on page 2.

form 12

WAIVER OF NOTICE

OF THE ORGANIZATIONAL MEETING

OF

_____

We, the undersigned incorporators named in the certificate of incorporation of the above-named corporation hereby agree and consent that the organization meeting of the corporation be held on the date and time and place stated below and hereby waive all notice of such meeting and of any adjournment thereof.

Place of meeting: _____

Date of Meeting: _____

Time of meeting: _____

Dated: _____

_____
Incorporator

_____
Incorporator

_____
Incorporator

form 13

MINUTES OF THE ORGANIZATIONAL MEETING OF

INCORPORATORS AND DIRECTORS OF

_____

The organization meeting of the above corporation was held on _____, _____ at _____ _____ at ____ o'clock __m.

The following persons were present:
_____   _____
_____   _____
_____   _____

The Waiver of notice of this meeting was signed by all directors and incorporators named in the Articles of Incorporation and filed in the minute book.

The meeting was called to order by _____ an Incorporator named in the Articles of Incorporation. _____ was nominated and elected Chairperson and acted as such until relieved by the president. _____ was nominated and elected temporary secretary, and acted as such until relieved by the permanent secretary.

A copy of the Articles of Incorporation which was filed with the Secretary of State of the State of _____ on _____, _____ was examined by the Directors and Incorporators and filed in the minute book.

The election of officers for the coming year was then held and the following were duly nominated and elected by the Board of Directors to be the officers of the corporation, to serve until such time as their successors are elected and qualified:

President: _____
Vice President: _____
Secretary: _____
Treasurer: _____

The proposed Bylaws for the corporation were then presented to the meeting and discussed. Upon motion duly made, seconded and carried, the Bylaws were adopted and added to the minute book.

A corporate seal for the corporation was then presented to the meeting and upon motion duly made, seconded and carried, it was adopted as the seal of the corporation. An impression thereof was then made in the margin of these minutes (seal)

The necessity of opening a bank account was then discussed and upon motion duly made, seconded and carried, the following resolution was adopted:

RESOLVED that the corporation open bank accounts with _____ _____ and that the officers of the corporation are authorized to take such action as is necessary to open such accounts; that the bank's printed form of resolution is hereby adopted and incorporated into these minutes by reference and shall be placed in the minute book; that any ____ of the following persons shall have signature authority over the account:

_____   _____
_____   _____
_____   _____

Proposed stock certificates and stock transfer ledger were then presented to the meeting and examined. Upon motion duly made, seconded and carried the stock certificates and ledger were adopted as the certificates and transfer book to be used by the corporation. A sample stock certificate marked "VOID" and the stock transfer ledger were then added to the minute book. Upon motion duly made, seconded and carried, it was then resolved that the stock certificates, when issued, would be signed by the President and the Secretary of the corporation.

The tax status of the corporation was then discussed and it was moved, seconded and carried that the stock of the corporation be issued under §1244 of the Internal Revenue Code and that the officers of the corporation take the necessary action to:

1. Obtain an employer tax number by filing form SS-4,

2. ❑ Become an S-Corporation for tax purposes,
   ❑ Remain a C-Corporation for tax purposes,

The expenses of organizing the corporation were then discussed and it was moved, seconded and carried that the corporation pay in full from the corporate funds the expenses and reimburse any advances made by the incorporators upon proof of payment.

The Directors named in the Articles of Incorporation then tendered their resignations, effective upon the adjournment of this meeting. Upon motion duly made, seconded and carried, the following named persons were elected as Directors of the corporation, each to hold office until the first annual meeting of shareholders, and until a successor of each shall have been elected and qualified.

_____

_____

_____

There were presented to the corporation, the following offer(s) to purchase shares of capital stock:

FROM	NO. OF SHARES	CONSIDERATION
_____	_____	_____
_____	_____	_____
_____	_____	_____

The offers were discussed and after motion duly made, seconded and carried were approved. It was further resolved that the Board of Directors has determined that the consideration was valued at least equal to the value of the shares to be issued and that upon tender of the consideration, fully paid non-assessable shares of the corporation be issued.

There being no further business before the meeting, on motion duly made, seconded and carried, the meeting adjourned.

DATED: _____

_____
President

_____
Secretary

BYLAWS OF

_____

A MINNESOTA CORPORATION

ARTICLE I - OFFICES

The principal office of the Corporation shall be located in the City of _____ and the State of _____. The Corporation may also maintain offices at such other places as the Board of Directors may, from time to time, determine.

ARTICLE II - SHAREHOLDERS

Section 1 - Annual Meetings: The annual meeting of the shareholders of the Corporation shall be held each year on _____ at _____m. at the principal office of the Corporation or at such other places, within or without the State of Minnesota, as the Board may authorize, for the purpose of electing directors, and transacting such other business as may properly come before the meeting.

Section 2 - Special Meetings: Special meetings of the shareholders may be called at any time by the Board, the President, or by the holders of twenty-five percent (25%) of the shares then outstanding and entitled to vote.

Section 3 - Place of Meetings: All meetings of shareholders shall be held at the principal office of the Corporation, or at such other places as the board shall designate in the notice of such meetings.

Section 4 - Notice of Meetings: Written or printed notice stating the place, day, and hour of the meeting and, in the case of a special meeting, the purpose of the meeting, shall be delivered personally or by mail not less than ten days, nor more than sixty days, before the date of the meeting. Notice shall be given to each Member of record entitled to vote at the meeting. If mailed, such notice shall be deemed to have been delivered when deposited in the United States Mail with postage paid and addressed to the Member at his address as it appears on the records of the Corporation.

Section 5 - Waiver of Notice: A written waiver of notice signed by a Member, whether before or after a meeting, shall be equivalent to the giving of such notice. Attendance of a Member at a meeting shall constitute a waiver of notice of such meeting, except when the Member attends for the express purpose of objecting, at the beginning of the meeting, to the transaction of any business because the meeting is not lawfully called or convened.

Section 6 - Quorum: Except as otherwise provided by Statute, or the Articles of Incorporation, at all meetings of shareholders of the Corporation, the presence at the commencement of such meetings in person or by proxy of shareholders of record holding a majority of the total number of shares of the Corporation then issued and outstanding and entitled to vote, but in no event less than one-third of the shares entitled to vote at the meeting, shall constitute a quorum for the transaction of any business. If any shareholder leaves after the commencement of a meeting, this shall have no effect on the existence of a quorum, after a quorum has been established at such meeting.

Despite the absence of a quorum at any annual or special meeting of shareholders, the shareholders, by a majority of the votes cast by the holders of shares entitled to vote thereon, may adjourn the meeting. At any such adjourned meeting at which a quorum is present, any business may be transacted at the meeting as originally called as if a quorum had been present.

Section 7 - Voting: Except as otherwise provided by Statute or by the Articles of Incorporation, any corporate action, other than the election of directors, to be taken by vote of the shareholders, shall be authorized by a majority of votes cast at a meeting of shareholders by the holders of shares entitled to vote thereon.

Except as otherwise provided by Statute or by the Articles of Incorporation, at each meeting of shareholders, each holder of record of stock of the Corporation entitled to vote thereat, shall be entitled to one vote for each share of stock registered in his name on the stock transfer books of the corporation.

Each shareholder entitled to vote may do so by proxy; provided, however, that the instrument authorizing such proxy to act shall have been executed in writing by the shareholder himself. No proxy shall be valid after the expiration of eleven months from the date of its execution, unless the person executing it shall have specified therein, the length of time it is to continue in force. Such instrument shall be exhibited to the Secretary at the meeting and shall be filed with the records of the corporation.

Any resolution in writing, signed by all of the shareholders entitled to vote thereon, shall be and constitute action by such shareholders to the effect therein expressed, with the same force and effect as if the same had been duly passed by unanimous vote at a duly called meeting of shareholders and such resolution so signed shall be inserted in the Minute Book of the Corporation under its proper date.

ARTICLE III - BOARD OF DIRECTORS

Section 1 - Number, Election and Term of Office: The number of the directors of the Corporation shall be (____) This number may be increased or decreased by the amendment of these bylaws by the Board but shall in no case be less than ____ director(s). The members of the Board, who need not be shareholders, shall be elected by a majority of the votes cast at a meeting of shareholders entitled to vote in the election. Each director shall hold office until the annual meeting of the shareholders next succeeding his election, and until his successor is elected and qualified, or until his prior death, resignation or removal.

Section 2 - Vacancies: Any vacancy in the Board shall be filled for the unexpired portion of the term by a majority vote of the remaining directors, though less than a quorum, at any regular meeting or special meeting of the Board called for that purpose. Any such director so elected may be replaced by the shareholders at a regular or special meeting of shareholders.

Section 3 - Duties and Powers: The Board shall be responsible for the control and management of the affairs, property and interests of the Corporation, and may exercise all powers of the Corporation, except as limited by statute.

Section 4 - Annual Meetings: An annual meeting of the Board shall be held immediately following the annual meeting of the shareholders, at the place of such annual meeting of shareholders. The Board from time to time, may provide by resolution for the holding of other meetings of the Board, and may fix the time and place thereof.

Section 5 - Special Meetings: Special meetings of the Board shall be held whenever called by the President or by one of the directors, at such time and place as may be specified in the respective notice or waivers of notice thereof.

Section 6 - Notice and Waiver: Notice of any special meeting shall be given at least five days prior thereto by written notice delivered personally, by mail or by telegram to each Director at his address. If mailed, such notice shall be deemed to be delivered when deposited in the United States Mail with postage prepaid. If notice is given by telegram, such notice shall be deemed to be delivered when the telegram is delivered to the telegraph company.

Any Director may waive notice of any meeting, either before, at, or after such meeting, by signing a waiver of notice. The attendance of a Director at a meeting shall constitute a waiver of notice of such meeting and a waiver of any and all objections to the place of such meeting, or the manner in which it has been called or convened, except when a Director states at the beginning of the meeting any objection to the transaction of business because the meeting is not lawfully called or convened.

Section 7 - Chairman: The Board may, at its discretion, elect a Chairman. At all meetings of the Board, the Chairman of the Board, if any and if present, shall preside. If there is no Chairman, or he is absent, then the President shall preside, and in his absence, a Chairman chosen by the directors shall preside.

Section 8 - Quorum and Adjournments: At all meetings of the Board, the presence of a majority of the entire Board shall be necessary and sufficient to constitute a quorum for the transaction of business, except as otherwise provided by law, by the Articles of Incorporation, or by these bylaws. A majority of the directors present at the time and place of any regular or special meeting, although less than a quorum, may adjourn the same from time to time without notice, until a quorum shall be present.

Section 9 - Board Action: At all meetings of the Board, each director present shall have one vote, irrespective of the number of shares of stock, if any, which he may hold. Except as otherwise provided by Statute, the action of a majority of the directors present at any meeting at which a quorum is present shall be the act of the Board. Any action authorized, in writing, by all of the Directors entitled to vote thereon and filed with the minutes of the Corporation shall be the act of the Board with the same force and effect as if the same had been passed by unanimous vote at a duly called meeting of the Board. Any action taken by the Board may be taken without a meeting if agreed to in writing by all members before or after the action is taken and if a record of such action is filed in the minute book.

Section 10 - Telephone Meetings: Directors may participate in meetings of the Board through use of a telephone if such can be arranged so that all Board members can hear all other members. The use of a telephone or videoconferencing for participation shall constitute presence in person.

Section 11 - Resignation and Removal: Any director may resign at any time by giving written notice to another Board member, the President or the Secretary of the Corporation. Unless otherwise specified in such written notice, such resignation shall take effect upon receipt thereof by the Board or by such officer, and the acceptance of such resignation shall not be necessary to make it effective. Any director may be removed with or without cause at any time by the affirmative vote of shareholders holding of record in the aggregate at least a majority of the outstanding shares of the Corporation at a special meeting of the shareholders called for that purpose, and may be removed for cause by action of the Board.

Section 12 - Compensation: No stated salary shall be paid to directors, as such for their services, but by resolution of the Board a fixed sum and/or expenses of attendance, if any, may be allowed for attendance at each regular or special meeting of the Board. Nothing herein contained shall be construed to preclude any director from serving the Corporation in any other capacity and receiving compensation therefor.

ARTICLE IV - OFFICERS

Section 1 - Number, Qualification, Election and Term: The officers of the Corporation shall consist of a President, a Secretary, a Treasurer, and such other officers, as the Board may from time to time deem advisable. Any officer may be, but is not required to be, a director of the Corporation. The officers of the Corporation shall be elected by the Board at the regular annual meeting of the Board. Each officer shall hold office until the annual meeting of the Board next succeeding his election, and until his successor shall have been elected and qualified, or until his death, resignation or removal.

Section 2 - Resignation and Removal: Any officer may resign at any time by giving written notice of such resignation to the President or the Secretary of the Corporation or to a member of the Board. Unless otherwise specified in such written notice, such resignation shall take effect upon receipt thereof by the Board member or by such officer, and the acceptance of such resignation shall not be necessary to make it effective. Any officer may be removed, either with or without cause, and a successor elected by a majority vote of the Board at any time.

Section 3 - Vacancies: A vacancy in any office may at any time be filled for the unexpired portion of the term by a majority vote of the Board.

Section 4 - Duties of Officers: Officers of the Corporation shall, unless otherwise provided by the Board, each have such powers and duties as generally pertain to their respective offices as well as such powers and duties as may from time to time be specifically decided by the Board. The President shall be the chief executive officer of the Corporation.

Section 5 - Compensation: The officers of the Corporation shall be entitled to such compensation as the Board shall from time to time determine.

Section 6 - Delegation of Duties: In the absence or disability of any Officer of the Corporation or for any other reason deemed sufficient by the Board of Directors, the Board may delegate his powers or duties to any other Officer or to any other Director.

Section 7 - Shares of Other Corporations: Whenever the Corporation is the holder of shares of any other Corporation, any right or power of the Corporation as such shareholder (including the attendance, acting and voting at shareholders' meetings and execution of waivers, consents, proxies or other instruments) may be exercised on behalf of the Corporation by the President, any Vice President, or such other person as the Board may authorize.

ARTICLE V - COMMITTEES

The Board of Directors may, by resolution, designate an Executive Committee and one or more other committees. Such committees shall have such functions and may exercise such power of the Board of Directors as can be lawfully delegated, and to the extent provided in the resolution or resolutions creating such committee or committees. Meetings of committees may be held without notice at such time and at such place as shall from time to time be determined by the committees. The committees of the corporation shall keep regular minutes of their proceedings, and report these minutes to the Board of Directors when required.

ARTICLE VI - BOOKS, RECORDS AND REPORTS

Section 1 - Annual Report: The Corporation shall send an annual report to the Members of the Corporation not later than _____ months after the close of each fiscal year of the Corporation. Such report shall include a balance sheet as of the close of the fiscal year of the Corporation and a revenue and disbursement statement for the year ending on such closing date. Such financial statements shall be prepared from and in accordance with the books of the Corporation, and in conformity with generally accepted accounting principles applied on a consistent basis.

Section 2 - Permanent Records: The corporation shall keep current and correct records of the accounts, minutes of the meetings and proceedings and membership records of the corporation. Such records shall be kept at the registered office or the principal place of business of the corporation. Any such records shall be in written form or in a form capable of being converted into written form.

Section 3 - Inspection of Corporate Records: Any person who is a Voting Member of the Corporation shall have the right at any reasonable time, and on written demand stating the purpose thereof, to examine and make copies from the relevant books and records of accounts, minutes, and records of the Corporation. Upon the written request of any Voting Member, the Corporation shall mail to such Member a copy of the most recent balance sheet and revenue and disbursement statement.

ARTICLE VII- SHARES OF STOCK

Section 1 - Certificates: Each shareholder of the corporation shall be entitled to have a certificate representing all shares which he or she owns. The form of such certificate shall be adopted by a majority vote of the Board of Directors and shall be signed by the President and Secretary of the Corporation and sealed with the seal of the corporation, if the Board of Directors shall designate a seal. No certificate representing shares shall be issued until the full amount of consideration therefore has been paid.

Section 2 - Stock Ledger: The corporation shall maintain a ledger of the stock records of the Corporation. Transfers of shares of the Corporation shall be made on the stock ledger of the Corporation only at the direction of the holder of record upon surrender of the outstanding certificate(s). The Corporation shall be entitled to treat the holder of record of any share or shares as the absolute owner thereof for all purposes and, accordingly, shall not be bound to recognize any legal, equitable or other claim to, or interest in, such share or shares on the part of any other person, whether or not it shall have express or other notice thereof, except as otherwise expressly provided by law.

ARTICLE VIII - DIVIDENDS

Upon approval by the Board of Directors the corporation may pay dividends on its shares in the form of cash, property or additional shares at any time that the corporation is solvent and if such dividends would not render the corporation insolvent.

ARTICLE IX - FISCAL YEAR

The fiscal year of the Corporation shall be the period selected by the Board of Directors as the tax year of the Corporation for federal income tax purposes.

ARTICLE X - CORPORATE SEAL

The Board of Directors may adopt, use and modify a corporate seal. Failure to affix the seal to corporate documents shall not affect the validity of such document.

ARTICLE XI - AMENDMENTS

The Articles of Incorporation may be amended by the Shareholders as provided by _____ statutes. These Bylaws may be altered, amended, or replaced by the Board of Directors; provided, however, that any Bylaws or amendments thereto as adopted by the Board of Directors may be altered, amended, or repealed by vote of the Shareholders. Bylaws adopted by the Members may not be amended or repealed by the Board.

ARTICLE XII - INDEMNIFICATION

Any officer, director or employee of the Corporation shall be indemnified to the full extent allowed by the laws of the State of Minnesota.

Certified to be the Bylaws of the corporation adopted by the Board of Directors on _____, _____.

_____
Secretary

This page intentionally left blank.

form 15

BYLAWS OF
_____

A MINNESOTA PROFESSIONAL FIRM
(whether an LLC, LLP, or other form)

ARTICLE I - OFFICES

The principal office of the Corporation shall be located at _____ in the City of _____ and the State of Minnesota. The Corporation may also maintain offices at such other places as the Board of Directors may, from time to time, determine.

ARTICLE II - PURPOSES

The business purpose of the Corporation shall be to engage in all aspects of the practice of _____ and its fields of specialization. The Corporation shall render professional services only through its legally authorized officers, agents and employees.

ARTICLE III - SHAREHOLDERS

Section 1 - Qualifications: Only persons who are duly licensed and in good standing in the profession by the State of Minnesota may be shareholders of the Corporation. Neither the Corporation nor the shareholders may transfer any shares to persons who are not duly licensed. All share certificates of the corporation shall contain a notice that the transfer is restricted by the bylaws of the Corporation. If any shareholder shall become disqualified to practice the profession, he or she shall immediately make arrangements to transfer his or her shares to a qualified person or to the Corporation and shall no longer participate in the profits of the Corporation related to the profession.

Section 2 - Annual Meetings: The annual meeting of the shareholders of the Corporation shall be held each year on_____ at _____m. at the principal office of the Corporation or at such other places, within or without the State of Minnesota, as the Board may authorize, for the purpose of electing directors, and transacting such other business as may properly come before the meeting.

Section 3 - Special Meetings: Special meetings of the shareholders may be called at any time by the Board, the President, or by the holders of twenty-five percent (25%) of the shares then outstanding and entitled to vote.

Section 4 - Place of Meetings: All meetings of shareholders shall be held at the principal office of the Corporation, or at such other places as the Board shall designate in the notice of such meetings.

Section 5 - Notice of Meetings: Written or printed notice stating the place, day, and hour of the meeting and, in the case of a special meeting, the purpose of the meeting, shall be delivered personally or by mail not less than ten days, nor more than sixty days, before the date of the meeting. Notice shall be given to each Member of record entitled to vote at the meeting. If mailed, such notice shall be deemed to have been delivered when deposited in the United States Mail with postage paid and addressed to the Member at his address as it appears on the records of the Corporation.

Section 6 - Waiver of Notice: A written waiver of notice signed by a Member, whether before or after a meeting, shall be equivalent to the giving of such notice. Attendance of a Member at a meeting shall constitute a waiver of notice of such meeting, except when the Member attends for the express purpose of objecting, at the beginning of the meeting, to the transaction of any business because the meeting is not lawfully called or convened.

Section 7 - Quorum: Except as otherwise provided by Statute, or the by Articles of Incorporation, at all meetings of shareholders of the Corporation, the presence at the commencement of such meetings of shareholders of record holding a majority of the total number of shares of the Corporation then issued and outstanding and entitled to vote, but in no event less than one-third of the shares entitled to vote at the meeting, shall constitute a quorum for the transaction of any business. If any shareholder leaves after the commencement of a meeting, this shall have no effect on the existence of a quorum, after a quorum has been established at such meeting.

Despite the absence of a quorum at any annual or special meeting of shareholders, the shareholders, by a majority of the votes cast by the holders of shares entitled to vote thereon, may adjourn the meeting. At any such adjourned meeting at which a quorum is present, any business may be transacted at the meeting as originally called as if a quorum had been present.

Section 8 - Voting: Except as otherwise provided by Statute or by the Articles of Incorporation, any corporate action, other than the election of directors, to be taken by vote of the shareholders, shall be authorized by a majority of votes cast at a meeting of shareholders by the holders of shares entitled to vote thereon.

Except as otherwise provided by Statute or by the Articles of Incorporation, at each meeting of shareholders, each holder of record of stock of the Corporation entitled to vote thereat, shall be entitled to one vote for each share of stock registered in his name on the stock transfer books of the corporation.

Any resolution in writing, signed by all of the shareholders entitled to vote thereon, shall be and constitute action by such shareholders to the effect therein expressed, with the same force and effect as if the same had been duly passed by unanimous vote at a duly called meeting of shareholders and such resolution so signed shall be inserted in the Minute Book of the Corporation under its proper date.

Section 9 - Proxies: Shareholders may not at any time vote by proxy or enter into any voting trust or other agreement vesting another person with the voting power of his stock.

ARTICLE IV - BOARD OF DIRECTORS

Section 1 Qualifications: Only persons who are duly licensed and in good standing in the profession by the State of Minnesota may be directors of the Corporation. If any director shall become disqualified from practicing the profession, he or she shall immediately resign his or her directorship and any other employment with the Corporation.

Section 2 - Number, Election and Term of Office: The number of the directors of the Corporation shall be (____) This number may be increased or decreased by the amendment of these bylaws by the Board but shall in no case be less than one director. The members of the Board, who need not be shareholders, shall be elected by a majority of the votes cast at a meeting of shareholders entitled to vote in the election. Each director shall hold office until the annual meeting of the shareholders next succeeding his election, and until his successor is elected and qualified, or until his prior death, resignation or removal.

Section 3 - Vacancies: Any vacancy in the Board shall be filled for the unexpired portion of the term by a majority vote of the remaining directors, though less than a quorum, at any regular meeting or special meeting of the Board called for that purpose. Any such director so elected may be replaced by the shareholders at a regular or special meeting of shareholders.

Section 4 - Duties and Powers: The Board shall be responsible for the control and management of the affairs, property and interests of the Corporation, and may exercise all powers of the Corporation, except as limited by statute.

Section 5 - Annual Meetings: An annual meeting of the Board shall be held immediately following the annual meeting of the shareholders, at the place of such annual meeting of shareholders. The Board, from time to time, may provide by resolution for the holding of other meetings of the Board, and may fix the time and place thereof, within Minnesota or elsewhere.

Section 6 - Special Meetings: Special meetings of the Board shall be held whenever called by the President or by one of the directors, at such time and place as may be specified in the respective notice or waivers of notice thereof.

Section 7 - Notice and Waiver: Notice of any special meeting shall be given at least five days prior thereto by written notice delivered personally, by mail or by telegram to each director at his address. If mailed, such notice shall be deemed to be delivered when deposited in the United States Mail with postage prepaid. If notice is given by telegram, such notice shall be deemed to be delivered when the telegram is delivered to the telegraph company.

Any director may waive notice of any meeting, either before, at, or after such meeting, by signing a waiver of notice. The attendance of a director at a meeting shall constitute a waiver of notice of such meeting and a waiver of any and all objections to the place of such meeting, or the manner in which it has been called or convened, except when a director states at the beginning of the meeting any objection to the transaction of business because the meeting is not lawfully called or convened.

Section 8 - Chairman: The Board may, at its discretion, elect a Chairman. At all meetings of the Board, the Chairman of the Board, if any and if present, shall preside. If there is no Chairman, or he is absent, then the President shall preside, and in his absence, a Chairman chosen by the directors shall preside.

Section 9 - Quorum and Adjournments: At all meetings of the Board, the presence of a majority of the entire Board shall be necessary and sufficient to constitute a quorum for the transaction of business, except as otherwise provided by law, by the Articles of Incorporation, or by these bylaws. A majority of the directors present at the time and place of any regular or special meeting, although less than a quorum, may adjourn the same from time to time without notice, until a quorum shall be present.

Section 10 - Board Action: At all meetings of the Board, each director present shall have one vote, irrespective of the number of shares of stock, if any, which he may hold. Except as otherwise provided by Statute, the action of a majority of the directors present at any meeting at which a quorum is present shall be the act of the Board. Any action authorized, in writing, by all of the Directors entitled to vote thereon and filed with the minutes of the Corporation shall be the act of the Board with the same force and effect as if the same had been passed by unanimous vote at a duly called meeting of the Board. Any action taken by the Board may be taken without a meeting if agreed to in writing by all members before or after the action is taken and if a record of such action is filed in the Minute Book.

Section 11 - Telephone Meetings: Directors may participate in meetings of the Board through use of a telephone or videoconference if such can be arranged so that all Board members can hear all other members. The use of a telephone or videoconference for participation shall constitute presence in person.

Section 12 - Resignation and Removal: Any director may resign at any time by giving written notice to another Board member, the President or the Secretary of the Corporation. Unless otherwise specified in such written notice, such resignation shall take effect upon receipt thereof by the Board or by such officer, and the acceptance of such resignation shall not be necessary to make it effective. Any director may be removed with or without cause at any time by the affirmative vote of shareholders holding of record in the aggregate at least a majority of the outstanding shares of the Corporation at a special meeting of the shareholders called for that purpose, and may be removed for cause by action of the Board.

Section 13 - Compensation: No stated salary shall be paid to directors, as such for their services, but by resolution of the Board a fixed sum and/or expenses of attendance, if any, may be allowed for attendance at each regular or special meeting of the Board. Nothing herein contained shall be construed to preclude any director from serving the Corporation in any other capacity and receiving compensation therefor.

ARTICLE V - OFFICERS

Section 1 Qualifications: Only persons who are duly licensed and in good standing in the profession by the State of Minnesota may be officers of the Corporation. If any director shall become disqualified from practicing the profession, he or she shall immediately resign his or her directorship and any other employment with the corporation.

Section 2 - Number, Election and Term: The officers of the Corporation shall consist of a President, a Secretary, a Treasurer, and such other officers, as the Board may from time to time deem advisable. Any officer may be, but is not required to be, a director of the Corporation. Any two or more offices may be held by the same person. The officers of the Corporation shall be elected by the Board at the regular annual meeting of the Board. Each officer shall hold office until the annual meeting of the Board next succeeding his election, and until his successor shall have been elected and qualified, or until his death, resignation or removal.

Section 3 - Resignation and Removal: Any officer may resign at any time by giving written notice of such resignation to the President or the Secretary of the Corporation or to a member of the Board. Unless otherwise specified in such written notice, such resignation shall take effect upon receipt thereof by the Board member or by such officer, and the acceptance of such resignation shall not be necessary to make it effective. Any officer may be removed, either with or without cause, and a successor elected by a majority vote of the Board at any time.

Section 4 - Vacancies: A vacancy in any office may at any time be filled for the unexpired portion of the term by a majority vote of the Board.

Section 5 - Duties of Officers: The officers of the Corporation shall, unless otherwise provided by the Board, each have such powers and duties as generally pertain to their respective offices as well as such powers and duties as may from time to time be specifically decided by the Board. The President shall be the chief executive officer of the Corporation.

Section 6 - Compensation: The officers of the Corporation shall be entitled to such compensation as the Board shall from time to time determine.

Section 7 - Delegation of Duties: In the absence or disability of any Officer of the Corporation or for any other reason deemed sufficient by the Board of Directors, the Board may delegate his powers or duties to any other Officer or to any other director.

Section 8 - Shares of Other Corporations: Whenever the Corporation is the holder of shares of any other Corporation, any right or power of the Corporation as such shareholder (including the attendance, acting and voting at shareholders' meetings and execution of waivers, consents, proxies or other instruments) may be exercised on behalf of the Corporation by the President, any Vice President, or such other person as the Board may authorize.

ARTICLE VI - COMMITTEES

The Board of Directors may, by resolution, designate an Executive Committee and one or more other committees. Such committees shall have such functions and may exercise such power of the Board of Directors as can be lawfully delegated, and to the extent provided in the resolution or resolutions creating such committee or committees. Meetings of committees may be held without notice at such time and at such place as shall from time to time be determined by the committees. The committees of the corporation shall keep regular minutes of their proceedings, and report these minutes to the Board of Directors when required.

ARTICLE VII - BOOKS, RECORDS AND REPORTS

Section 1 - Annual Report: The Corporation shall send an annual report to the Members of the Corporation not later than four months after the close of each fiscal year of the Corporation. Such report shall include a balance sheet as of the close of the fiscal year of the Corporation and a revenue and disbursement statement for the year ending on such closing date. Such financial statements shall be prepared from and in accordance with the books of the Corporation, and in conformity with generally accepted accounting principles applied on a consistent basis.

Section 2 - Permanent Records: The Corporation shall keep current and correct records of the accounts, minutes of the meetings and proceedings and membership records of the Corporation. Such records shall be kept at the registered office or the principal place of business of the Corporation. Any such records shall be in written form or in a form capable of being converted into written form.

Section 3 - Inspection of Corporate Records: Any person who is a Voting Member of the Corporation shall have the right at any reasonable time, and on written demand stating the purpose thereof, to examine and make copies from the relevant books and records of accounts, minutes, and records of the Corporation. Upon the written request of any Voting Member, the Corporation shall mail to such Member a copy of the most recent balance sheet and revenue and disbursement statement.

ARTICLE VIII- SHARES OF STOCK

Section 1 - Authorized shares: The Corporation shall be authorized to issue _____ shares of stock in one class only, each with a par value of $_____.

Section 2 - Certificates: Each shareholder of the Corporation shall be entitled to have a certificate representing all shares which he or she owns. The form of such certificate shall be adopted by a majority vote of the Board of Directors and shall be signed by the President and Secretary of the Corporation and sealed with the seal of the Corporation. No certificate representing shares shall be issued until the full amount of consideration therefore has been paid.

Section 3 - Stock Ledger: The Corporation shall maintain a ledger of the stock records of the Corporation. Transfers of shares of the Corporation shall be made on the stock ledger of the Corporation only at the direction of the holder of record upon surrender of the outstanding certificate(s). The Corporation shall be entitled to treat the holder of record of any share or shares as the absolute owner thereof for all purposes and, accordingly, shall not be bound to recognize any legal, equitable or other claim to, or interest in, such share or shares on the part of any other person, whether or not it shall have express or other notice thereof, except as otherwise expressly provided by law.

ARTICLE IX - DIVIDENDS

Upon approval by the Board of Directors the corporation may pay dividends on its shares in the form of cash, property or additional shares at any time that the Corporation is solvent and if such dividends would not render the Corporation insolvent.

ARTICLE X - FISCAL YEAR

The fiscal year of the Corporation shall be the period selected by the Board of Directors as the tax year of the Corporation for federal income tax purposes.

ARTICLE XI - CORPORATE SEAL

The Board of Directors may adopt, use and modify a corporate seal. Failure to affix the seal to corporate documents shall not affect the validity of such document.

ARTICLE XII - AMENDMENTS

The Articles of Incorporation may be amended by the shareholders as provided by Minnesota statutes. These bylaws may be altered, amended, or replaced by the Board of Directors; provided, however, that any bylaws or amendments thereto as adopted by the Board of Directors may be altered, amended, or repealed by vote of the shareholders. Bylaws adopted by the Members may not be amended or repealed by the Board.

ARTICLE XIII - INDEMNIFICATION

Any officer, director or employee of the Corporation shall be indemnified to the full extent allowed by the laws of the State of Minnesota.

Certified to be the bylaws of the corporation adopted by the Board of Directors on _____, _____.

_____
Secretary

form 16

*Banking Resolution of

_____

    The undersigned, being the corporate secretary of the above corporation, hereby certifies that on the _____ day of _____, _____ the Board of Directors of the corporation adopted the following resolution:

    RESOLVED that the corporation open bank accounts with _____ _____ and that the officers of the corporation are authorized to take such action as is necessary to open such accounts; that the bank's printed form of resolution is hereby adopted and incorporated into these minutes by reference and shall be placed in the minute book; that any ____ of the following persons shall have signature authority over the account:

_____   _____

_____   _____

and that said resolution has not been modified or rescinded.

Date: _____

_____
Corporate Secretary

(Seal)
if the corporation has one

*use only if bank does not have a blank one for you to use.

145

This page intentionally left blank.

form 17

Offer to Purchase Stock

Part A: Offer to Purchase Stock

Date: _____

To the Board of Directors of

_____

    The undersigned, hereby offers to purchase _____ shares of the _____ stock of your corporation at a total purchase price of _____.

Very truly yours,

_____

Part B: Offer to Sell Stock
Pursuant to Sec. 1244 I.R.C.

Date: _____

To: _____

Dear

    The corporation hereby offers to sell to you _____ shares of its common stock at a price of $_____ per share. These shares are issued pursuant to Section 1244 of the Internal Revenue Code.

    Your signature below shall constitute an acceptance of our offer as of the date it is received by the corporation.

Very truly yours,

_____

By:_____

Accepted:

_____

This page intentionally left blank.

form 18

Resolution
of
_____
a Minnesota Corporation

RESOLVED that the corporation shall reimburse the following parties for the organizational expenses of the organizers of this corporation and that the corporation shall amortize or deduct these expenses as allowed by IRS regulations.

Name	Expense	Amount
_____	_____	$_____
_____	_____	$_____
_____	_____	$_____
_____	_____	$_____
_____	_____	$_____

Date:_____

_____

_____

_____

_____

This page intentionally left blank.

Bill of Sale

The undersigned, in consideration of the issuance of _____ shares of common stock of _____, a Florida corporation, hereby grants, bargains, sells, transfers and delivers unto said corporation the following goods and chattels:

To have and to hold the same forever.

And the undersigned, their heirs, successors and administrators, covenant and warrant that they are the lawful owners of the said goods and chattels and that they are free from all encumbrances. That the undersigned have the right to sell this property and that they will warrant and defend the sale of said property against the lawful claims and demands of all persons. IN WITNESS whereof the undersigned have executed this Bill of Sale this ____ day of _____, _____.

This page intentionally left blank.

form 20

Form 2553
(Rev. January 2001)
Department of the Treasury
Internal Revenue Service

Election by a Small Business Corporation
(Under section 1362 of the Internal Revenue Code)
▶ See Parts II and III on back and the separate instructions.
▶ The corporation may either send or fax this form to the IRS. See page 1 of the instructions.

OMB No. 1545-0146

Notes:
1. This election to be an S corporation can be accepted only if all the tests are met under **Who May Elect** on page 1 of the instructions; all signatures in Parts I and III are originals (no photocopies); and the exact name and address of the corporation and other required form information are provided.
2. Do not file **Form 1120S**, U.S. Income Tax Return for an S Corporation, for any tax year before the year the election takes effect.
3. If the corporation was in existence before the effective date of this election, see **Taxes an S Corporation May Owe** on page 1 of the instructions.

Part I   Election Information

Please Type or Print

Name of corporation (see instructions)	**A** Employer identification number
Number, street, and room or suite no. (If a P.O. box, see instructions.)	**B** Date incorporated
City or town, state, and ZIP code	**C** State of incorporation

D Election is to be effective for tax year beginning (month, day, year) ▶ / /

E Name and title of officer or legal representative who the IRS may call for more information

F Telephone number of officer or legal representative ( )

G If the corporation changed its name or address after applying for the EIN shown in **A** above, check this box ▶ ☐

H If this election takes effect for the first tax year the corporation exists, enter month, day, and year of the **earliest** of the following: (1) date the corporation first had shareholders, (2) date the corporation first had assets, or (3) date the corporation began doing business ▶ / /

I Selected tax year: Annual return will be filed for tax year ending (month and day) ▶ ....
If the tax year ends on any date other than December 31, except for an automatic 52-53-week tax year ending with reference to the month of December, you **must** complete Part II on the back. If the date you enter is the ending date of an automatic 52-53-week tax year, write "52-53-week year" to the right of the date. See Temporary Regulations section 1.441-2T(e)(3).

J Name and address of each shareholder; shareholder's spouse having a community property interest in the corporation's stock; and each tenant in common, joint tenant, and tenant by the entirety. (A husband and wife (and their estates) are counted as one shareholder in determining the number of shareholders without regard to the manner in which the stock is owned.)	K Shareholders' Consent Statement. Under penalties of perjury, we declare that we consent to the election of the above-named corporation to be an S corporation under section 1362(a) and that we have examined this consent statement, including accompanying schedules and statements, and to the best of our knowledge and belief, it is true, correct, and complete. We understand our consent is binding and may not be withdrawn after the corporation has made a valid election. (Shareholders sign and date below.)		L Stock owned		M Social security number or employer identification number (see instructions)	N Shareholder's tax year ends (month and day)
	Signature	Date	Number of shares	Dates acquired		

Under penalties of perjury, I declare that I have examined this election, including accompanying schedules and statements, and to the best of my knowledge and belief, it is true, correct, and complete.

Signature of officer ▶   Title ▶   Date ▶

For Paperwork Reduction Act Notice, see page 4 of the instructions.   Cat. No. 18629R   Form **2553** (Rev. 1-2001)

153

Form 2553 (Rev. 1-2001) Page **2**

Part II Selection of Fiscal Tax Year (All corporations using this part must complete item O and item P, Q, or R.)

O Check the applicable box to indicate whether the corporation is:
  1. ☐ A new corporation adopting the tax year entered in item I, Part I.
  2. ☐ An existing corporation retaining the tax year entered in item I, Part I.
  3. ☐ An existing corporation changing to the tax year entered in item I, Part I.

P Complete item P if the corporation is using the expeditious approval provisions of Rev. Proc. 87-32, 1987-2 C.B. 396, to request **(1)** a natural business year (as defined in section 4.01(1) of Rev. Proc. 87-32) or **(2)** a year that satisfies the ownership tax year test in section 4.01(2) of Rev. Proc. 87-32. Check the applicable box below to indicate the representation statement the corporation is making as required under section 4 of Rev. Proc. 87-32.

  1. Natural Business Year ▶ ☐ I represent that the corporation is retaining or changing to a tax year that coincides with its natural business year as defined in section 4.01(1) of Rev. Proc. 87-32 and as verified by its satisfaction of the requirements of section 4.02(1) of Rev. Proc. 87-32. In addition, if the corporation is changing to a natural business year as defined in section 4.01(1), I further represent that such tax year results in less deferral of income to the owners than the corporation's present tax year. I also represent that the corporation is not described in section 3.01(2) of Rev. Proc. 87-32. (See instructions for additional information that must be attached.)

  2. Ownership Tax Year ▶ ☐ I represent that shareholders holding more than half of the shares of the stock (as of the first day of the tax year to which the request relates) of the corporation have the same tax year or are concurrently changing to the tax year that the corporation adopts, retains, or changes to per item I, Part I. I also represent that the corporation is not described in section 3.01(2) of Rev. Proc. 87-32.

Note: *If you do not use item P and the corporation wants a fiscal tax year, complete either item Q or R below. Item Q is used to request a fiscal tax year based on a business purpose and to make a back-up section 444 election. Item R is used to make a regular section 444 election.*

Q Business Purpose—To request a fiscal tax year based on a business purpose, you must check box Q1 and pay a user fee. See instructions for details. You may also check box Q2 and/or box Q3.

  1. Check here ▶ ☐ if the fiscal year entered in item I, Part I, is requested under the provisions of section 6.03 of Rev. Proc. 87-32. Attach to Form 2553 a statement showing the business purpose for the requested fiscal year. See instructions for additional information that must be attached.

  2. Check here ▶ ☐ to show that the corporation intends to make a back-up section 444 election in the event the corporation's business purpose request is not approved by the IRS. (See instructions for more information.)

  3. Check here ▶ ☐ to show that the corporation agrees to adopt or change to a tax year ending December 31 if necessary for the IRS to accept this election for S corporation status in the event (1) the corporation's business purpose request is not approved and the corporation makes a back-up section 444 election, but is ultimately not qualified to make a section 444 election, or (2) the corporation's business purpose request is not approved and the corporation did not make a back-up section 444 election.

R Section 444 Election—To make a section 444 election, you must check box R1 and you may also check box R2.

  1. Check here ▶ ☐ to show the corporation will make, if qualified, a section 444 election to have the fiscal tax year shown in item I, Part I. To make the election, you must complete **Form 8716,** Election To Have a Tax Year Other Than a Required Tax Year, and either attach it to Form 2553 or file it separately.

  2. Check here ▶ ☐ to show that the corporation agrees to adopt or change to a tax year ending December 31 if necessary for the IRS to accept this election for S corporation status in the event the corporation is ultimately not qualified to make a section 444 election.

Part III Qualified Subchapter S Trust (QSST) Election Under Section 1361(d)(2)*

Income beneficiary's name and address	Social security number
Trust's name and address	Employer identification number

Date on which stock of the corporation was transferred to the trust (month, day, year) . . . . ▶ / /

In order for the trust named above to be a QSST and thus a qualifying shareholder of the S corporation for which this Form 2553 is filed, I hereby make the election under section 1361(d)(2). Under penalties of perjury, I certify that the trust meets the definitional requirements of section 1361(d)(3) and that all other information provided in Part III is true, correct, and complete.

Signature of income beneficiary or signature and title of legal representative or other qualified person making the election   Date

*Use Part III to make the QSST election only if stock of the corporation has been transferred to the trust on or before the date on which the corporation makes its election to be an S corporation. The QSST election must be made and filed separately if stock of the corporation is transferred to the trust after the date on which the corporation makes the S election.

Form **2553** (Rev. 1-2001)

Instructions for Form 2553
(Revised January 2001)

Department of the Treasury
Internal Revenue Service

Election by a Small Business Corporation

Section references are to the Internal Revenue Code unless otherwise noted.

A Change To Note

Corporations may be mailing forms and elections to different service centers in 2001 and again in 2002 because the IRS has changed the filing location for several areas.

General Instructions

Purpose

To elect to be an S corporation, a corporation must file Form 2553. The election permits the income of the S corporation to be taxed to the shareholders of the corporation rather than to the corporation itself, except as noted below under **Taxes an S Corporation May Owe.**

Who May Elect

A corporation may elect to be an S corporation only if it meets all of the following tests:

1. It is a domestic corporation.

2. It has no more than 75 shareholders. A husband and wife (and their estates) are treated as one shareholder for this requirement. All other persons are treated as separate shareholders.

3. Its only shareholders are individuals, estates, exempt organizations described in section 401(a) or 501(c)(3), or certain trusts described in section 1361(c)(2)(A). See the instructions for Part III regarding qualified subchapter S trusts (QSSTs).

A trustee of a trust wanting to make an election under section 1361(e)(3) to be an electing small business trust (ESBT) should see Notice 97-12, 1997-1 C.B. 385. Also see Rev. Proc. 98-23, 1998-1 C.B. 662, for guidance on how to convert a QSST to an ESBT. If there was an inadvertent failure to timely file an ESBT election, see the relief provisions under Rev. Proc. 98-55, 1998-2 C.B. 643.

4. It has no nonresident alien shareholders.

5. It has only one class of stock (disregarding differences in voting rights). Generally, a corporation is treated as having only one class of stock if all outstanding shares of the corporation's stock confer identical rights to distribution and liquidation proceeds. See Regulations section 1.1361-1(l) for details.

6. It is not one of the following ineligible corporations:

   a. A bank or thrift institution that uses the reserve method of accounting for bad debts under section 585,

   b. An insurance company subject to tax under the rules of subchapter L of the Code,

   c. A corporation that has elected to be treated as a possessions corporation under section 936, or

   d. A domestic international sales corporation (DISC) or former DISC.

7. It has a permitted tax year as required by section 1378 or makes a section 444 election to have a tax year other than a permitted tax year. Section 1378 defines a permitted tax year as a tax year ending December 31, or any other tax year for which the corporation establishes a business purpose to the satisfaction of the IRS. See Part II for details on requesting a fiscal tax year based on a business purpose or on making a section 444 election.

8. Each shareholder consents as explained in the instructions for column K.

See sections 1361, 1362, and 1378 for additional information on the above tests.

A parent S corporation can elect to treat an eligible wholly-owned subsidiary as a qualified subchapter S subsidiary (QSub). If the election is made, the assets, liabilities, and items of income, deduction, and credit of the QSub are treated as those of the parent. To make the election, get **Form 8869,** Qualified Subchapter S Subsidiary Election. If the QSub election was not timely filed, the corporation may be entitled to relief under Rev. Proc. 98-55.

Taxes an S Corporation May Owe

An S corporation may owe income tax in the following instances:

1. If, at the end of any tax year, the corporation had accumulated earnings and profits, and its passive investment income under section 1362(d)(3) is more than 25% of its gross receipts, the corporation may owe tax on its excess net passive income.

2. A corporation with net recognized built-in gain (as defined in section 1374(d)(2)) may owe tax on its built-in gains.

3. A corporation that claimed investment credit before its first year as an S corporation will be liable for any investment credit recapture tax.

4. A corporation that used the LIFO inventory method for the year immediately preceding its first year as an S corporation may owe an additional tax due to LIFO recapture. The tax is paid in four equal installments, the first of which must be paid by the due date (not including extensions) of the corporation's income tax return for its last tax year as a C corporation.

For more details on these taxes, see the Instructions for Form 1120S.

Where To File

Send or fax this election to the Internal Revenue Service Center listed on page 2. If the corporation files this election by fax, keep the original Form 2553 with the corporation's permanent records.

Cat. No. 49978N

⚠️ *Use the list below if filing the election before January 1, 2002. Use the list in the second column if filing the election after December 31, 2001.*

If the corporation's principal business, office, or agency is located in	Use the following Internal Revenue Service Center address or fax number
New York (New York City and counties of Nassau, Rockland, Suffolk, and Westchester)	Holtsville, NY 00501 (631) 654-6567
New York (all other counties), Connecticut, Maine, Massachusetts, New Hampshire, Rhode Island, Vermont	Andover, MA 05501 (978) 474-5633
Florida, Georgia	Atlanta, GA 39901 (770) 454-1607
Delaware, District of Columbia, Indiana, Kentucky, Maryland, Michigan, New Jersey, North Carolina, Ohio, Pennsylvania, South Carolina, West Virginia, Wisconsin	Cincinnati, OH 45999 (859) 292-5289
Kansas, New Mexico, Oklahoma	Austin, TX 73301 (512) 460-4046
Alaska, Arizona, Arkansas, California (counties of Alpine, Amador, Butte, Calaveras, Colusa, Contra Costa, Del Norte, El Dorado, Glenn, Humboldt, Lake, Lassen, Marin, Mendocino, Modoc, Napa, Nevada, Placer, Plumas, Sacramento, San Joaquin, Shasta, Sierra, Siskiyou, Solano, Sonoma, Sutter, Tehama, Trinity, Yolo, and Yuba), Colorado, Hawaii, Idaho, Iowa, Louisiana, Minnesota, Mississippi, Missouri, Montana, Nebraska, Nevada, North Dakota, Oregon, South Dakota, Texas, Utah, Washington, Wyoming	Ogden, UT 84201 (801) 620-7116
California (all other counties)	Fresno, CA 93888 (559) 443-5030
Illinois	Kansas City, MO 64999 (816) 823-7861
Alabama, Tennessee	Memphis, TN 37501 (901) 546-3900
Virginia	Philadelphia, PA 19255 (215) 516-3048

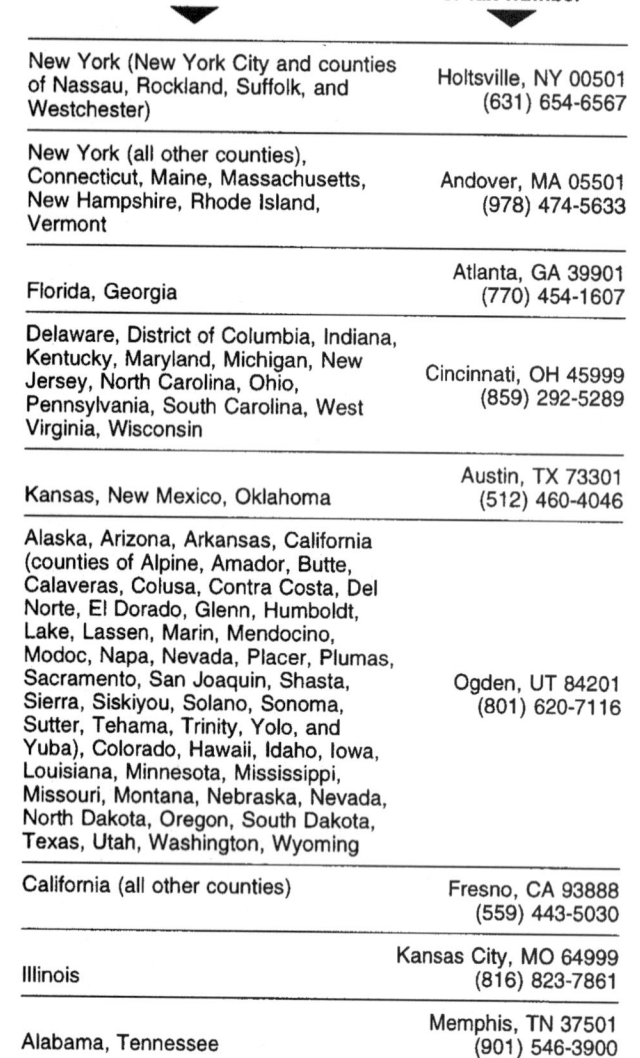

⚠️ *Use the list below **only** for elections filed after December 31, 2001.*

If the corporation's principal business, office, or agency is located in	Use the following Internal Revenue Service Center address or fax number
Connecticut, Delaware, District of Columbia, Illinois, Indiana, Kentucky, Maine, Maryland, Massachusetts, Michigan, New Hampshire, New Jersey, New York, North Carolina, Ohio, Pennsylvania, Rhode Island, South Carolina, Vermont, Virginia, West Virginia, Wisconsin	Cincinnati, OH 45999 (859) 292-5289
Alabama, Alaska, Arizona, Arkansas, California, Colorado, Florida, Georgia, Hawaii, Idaho, Iowa, Kansas, Louisiana, Minnesota, Mississippi, Missouri, Montana, Nebraska, Nevada, New Mexico, North Dakota, Oklahoma, Oregon, South Dakota, Tennessee, Texas, Utah, Washington, Wyoming	Ogden, UT 84201 (801) 620-7116

When To Make the Election

Complete and file Form 2553 **(a)** at any time before the 16th day of the 3rd month of the tax year, if filed during the tax year the election is to take effect, or **(b)** at any time during the preceding tax year. An election made no later than 2 months and 15 days after the beginning of a tax year that is less than 2½ months long is treated as timely made for that tax year. An election made after the 15th day of the 3rd month but before the end of the tax year is effective for the next year. For example, if a calendar tax year corporation makes the election in April 2001, it is effective for the corporation's 2002 calendar tax year.

However, an election made after the due date will be accepted as timely filed if the corporation can show that the failure to file on time was due to reasonable cause. To request relief for a late election, the corporation generally must request a private letter ruling and pay a user fee in accordance with Rev. Proc. 2000-1, 2000-1 I.R.B. 4 (or its successor). But if the election is filed within 12 months of its due date and the original due date for filing the corporation's initial Form 1120S has not passed, the ruling and user fee requirements do not apply. To request relief in this case, write "FILED PURSUANT TO REV. PROC. 98-55" at the top of page 1 of Form 2553, attach a statement explaining the reason for failing to file the election on time, and file Form 2553 as otherwise instructed. See Rev. Proc. 98-55 for more details.

See Regulations section 1.1362-6(b)(3)(iii) for how to obtain relief for an inadvertent invalid election if the corporation filed a timely election, but one or more shareholders did not file a timely consent.

Acceptance or Nonacceptance of Election

The service center will notify the corporation if its election is accepted and when it will take effect. The corporation will also be notified if its election is not accepted. The corporation should generally receive a determination on its election within 60 days after it has filed Form 2553. If box Q1 in Part II is checked on page 2, the corporation will receive a ruling letter from the IRS in Washington, DC, that either approves or denies the selected tax year. When box Q1 is checked, it will generally take an additional 90 days for the Form 2553 to be accepted.

Do not file Form 1120S for any tax year before the year the election takes effect. If the corporation is now required to file **Form 1120,** U.S. Corporation Income Tax Return, or any other applicable tax return, continue filing it until the election takes effect.

Care should be exercised to ensure that the IRS receives the election. If the corporation is not notified of acceptance or nonacceptance of its election within 3 months of the date of filing (date mailed), or within 6 months if box Q1 is checked, take follow-up action by corresponding with the service center where the corporation filed the election.

If the IRS questions whether Form 2553 was filed, an acceptable proof of filing is **(a)** certified or registered mail receipt (timely postmarked) from the U.S. Postal Service, or its equivalent from a designated private delivery service (see Notice 99-41, 1999–35 I.R.B. 325); **(b)** Form 2553 with accepted stamp; **(c)** Form 2553 with stamped IRS received date; or **(d)** IRS letter stating that Form 2553 has been accepted.

End of Election

Once the election is made, it stays in effect until it is terminated. If the election is terminated in a tax year beginning after 1996, IRS consent is generally required for another election by the corporation (or a successor corporation) on Form 2553 for any tax year before the 5th tax year after the first tax year in which the termination took effect. See Regulations section 1.1362-5 for details.

Specific Instructions

Part I (*All corporations must complete.*)

Name and Address of Corporation

Enter the true corporate name as stated in the corporate charter or other legal document creating it. If the corporation's mailing address is the same as someone else's, such as a shareholder's, enter "c/o" and this person's name following the name of the corporation. Include the suite, room, or other unit number after the street address. If the Post Office does not deliver to the street address and the corporation has a P.O. box, show the box number instead of the street address. If the corporation changed its name or address after applying for its employer identification number, be sure to check the box in item G of Part I.

Item A. Employer Identification Number (EIN)

If the corporation has applied for an EIN but has not received it, enter "applied for." If the corporation does not have an EIN, it should apply for one on **Form SS-4,** Application for Employer Identification Number. You can order Form SS-4 by calling 1-800-TAX-FORM (1-800-829-3676).

Item D. Effective Date of Election

Enter the beginning effective date (month, day, year) of the tax year requested for the S corporation. Generally, this will be the beginning date of the tax year for which the ending effective date is required to be shown in item I, Part I. For a new corporation (first year the corporation exists) it will generally be the date required to be shown in item H, Part I. The tax year of a new corporation starts on the date that it has shareholders, acquires assets, or begins doing business, whichever happens first. If the effective date for item D for a newly formed corporation is later than the date in item H, the corporation should file Form 1120 or Form 1120-A for the tax period between these dates.

Column K. Shareholders' Consent Statement

Each shareholder who owns (or is deemed to own) stock at the time the election is made must consent to the election. If the election is made during the corporation's tax year for which it first takes effect, any person who held stock at any time during the part of that year that occurs before the election is made, must consent to the election, even though the person may have sold or transferred his or her stock before the election is made.

An election made during the first 2½ months of the tax year is effective for the following tax year if any person who held stock in the corporation during the part of the tax year before the election was made, and who did not hold stock at the time the election was made, did not consent to the election.

Each shareholder consents by signing and dating in column K or signing and dating a separate consent statement described below. The following special rules apply in determining who must sign the consent statement.

- If a husband and wife have a community interest in the stock or in the income from it, both must consent.
- Each tenant in common, joint tenant, and tenant by the entirety must consent.
- A minor's consent is made by the minor, legal representative of the minor, or a natural or adoptive parent of the minor if no legal representative has been appointed.
- The consent of an estate is made by the executor or administrator.
- The consent of an electing small business trust is made by the trustee.
- If the stock is owned by a trust (other than an electing small business trust), the deemed owner of the trust must consent. See section 1361(c)(2) for details regarding trusts that are permitted to be shareholders and rules for determining who is the deemed owner.

Continuation sheet or separate consent statement. If you need a continuation sheet or use a separate consent statement, attach it to Form 2553. The separate consent statement must contain the name, address, and EIN of the corporation and the shareholder information requested in columns J through N of Part I. If you want, you may combine all the shareholders' consents in one statement.

Column L

Enter the number of shares of stock each shareholder owns and the dates the stock was acquired. If the election is made during the corporation's tax year for which it first takes effect, do not list the shares of stock for those shareholders who sold or transferred all of their stock before the election was made. However, these shareholders must still consent to the election for it to be effective for the tax year.

Column M

Enter the social security number of each shareholder who is an individual. Enter the EIN of each shareholder that is an estate, a qualified trust, or an exempt organization.

Column N

Enter the month and day that each shareholder's tax year ends. If a shareholder is changing his or her tax year, enter the tax year the shareholder is changing to, and attach an explanation indicating the present tax year and the basis for the change (e.g., automatic revenue procedure or letter ruling request).

Signature

Form 2553 must be signed by the president, treasurer, assistant treasurer, chief accounting officer, or other corporate officer (such as tax officer) authorized to sign.

Part II

Complete Part II if you selected a tax year ending on any date other than December 31 (other than a 52-53-week tax year ending with reference to the month of December).

Box P1

Attach a statement showing separately for each month the amount of gross receipts for the most recent 47 months as required by section 4.03(3) of Rev. Proc. 87-32, 1987-2 C. B. 396. A corporation that does not have a 47-month period of gross receipts cannot establish a natural business year under section 4.01(1).

Box Q1

For examples of an acceptable business purpose for requesting a fiscal tax year, see Rev. Rul. 87-57, 1987-2 C.B. 117.

In addition to a statement showing the business purpose for the requested fiscal year, you must attach the other information necessary to meet the ruling request requirements of Rev. Proc. 2000-1 (or its successor). Also attach a statement that shows separately the amount of gross receipts from sales or services (and inventory costs, if applicable) for each of the 36 months preceding the effective date of the election to be an S corporation. If the corporation has been in existence for fewer than 36 months, submit figures for the period of existence.

If you check box Q1, you will be charged a user fee of up to $600 (subject to change—see Rev. Proc. 2000-1 or its successor). Do not pay the fee when filing Form 2553. The service center will send Form 2553 to the IRS in Washington, DC, who, in turn, will notify the corporation that the fee is due.

Box Q2

If the corporation makes a back-up section 444 election for which it is qualified, then the election will take effect in the event the business purpose request is not approved.

In some cases, the tax year requested under the back-up section 444 election may be different than the tax year requested under business purpose. See **Form 8716,** Election To Have a Tax Year Other Than a Required Tax Year, for details on making a back-up section 444 election.

Boxes Q2 and R2

If the corporation is not qualified to make the section 444 election after making the item Q2 back-up section 444 election or indicating its intention to make the election in item R1, and therefore it later files a calendar year return, it should write "Section 444 Election Not Made" in the top left corner of the first calendar year Form 1120S it files.

Part III

Certain qualified subchapter S trusts (QSSTs) may make the QSST election required by section 1361(d)(2) in Part III. Part III may be used to make the QSST election only if corporate stock has been transferred to the trust on or before the date on which the corporation makes its election to be an S corporation. However, a statement can be used instead of Part III to make the election. If there was an inadvertent failure to timely file a QSST election, see the relief provisions under Rev. Proc. 98-55.

Note: *Use Part III only if you make the election in Part I (i.e., Form 2553 cannot be filed with only Part III completed).*

The deemed owner of the QSST must also consent to the S corporation election in column K, page 1, of Form 2553. See section 1361(c)(2).

Paperwork Reduction Act Notice. We ask for the information on this form to carry out the Internal Revenue laws of the United States. You are required to give us the information. We need it to ensure that you are complying with these laws and to allow us to figure and collect the right amount of tax.

You are not required to provide the information requested on a form that is subject to the Paperwork Reduction Act unless the form displays a valid OMB control number. Books or records relating to a form or its instructions must be retained as long as their contents may become material in the administration of any Internal Revenue law. Generally, tax returns and return information are confidential, as required by section 6103.

The time needed to complete and file this form will depend on individual circumstances. The estimated average time is:

Recordkeeping..	8 hr., 37 min.
Learning about the law or the form	3 hr., 11 min.
Preparing, copying, assembling, and sending the form to the IRS	3 hr., 28 min.

If you have comments concerning the accuracy of these time estimates or suggestions for making this form simpler, we would be happy to hear from you. You can write to the Tax Forms Committee, Western Area Distribution Center, Rancho Cordova, CA 95743-0001. **Do not** send the form to this address. Instead, see **Where To File** on page 1.

Resolution
of
_____
a Minnesota Corporation

RESOLVED that the corporation elects "S-Corporation" status for tax purposes under the Internal Revenue Code and that the officers of the corporation are directed to file IRS Form 2553 and to take any further action necessary for the corporation to qualify for S-corporation status.

Shareholders' Consent

The undersigned shareholders being all of the shareholders of the above corporation, a _____ corporation hereby consent to the election of the corporation to obtain S-corporation status

Name and Address of Shareholder	Shares Owned	Date Acquired
_____	_____	_____
_____	_____	_____
_____	_____	_____

Date:_____

_____

_____

_____

_____

form 22

WAIVER OF NOTICE OF THE ANNUAL MEETING OF
THE BOARD OF DIRECTORS OF

_____

    The undersigned, being all the Directors of the Corporation, hereby agree and consent that an annual meeting of the Board of Directors of the Corporation be held on the ____ day of _____, _____ at ___ o'clock __m at _____ _____ and do hereby waive all notice whatsoever of such meeting and of any adjournment or adjournments thereof.

    We do further agree and consent that any and all lawful business may be transacted at such meeting or at any adjournment or adjournments thereof as may be deemed advisable by the Directors present. Any business transacted at such meeting or at any adjournment or adjournments thereof shall be as valid and legal as if such meeting or adjourned meeting were held after notice.

Date: _____

_____
Director

_____
Director

_____
Director

_____
Director

form 23

MINUTES OF THE ANNUAL MEETING OF
THE BOARD OF DIRECTORS OF

_____

The annual meeting of the Board of Directors of the Corporation was held on the date and at the time and place set forth in the written waiver of notice signed by the directors, and attached to the minutes of this meeting.

The following were present, being all the directors of the Corporation:

_____   _____
_____   _____

The meeting was called to order and it was moved, seconded and unanimously carried that _____ act as Chairman and that _____ act as Secretary.

The minutes of the last meeting of the Board of Directors which was held on _____, _____ were read and approved by the Board.

Upon motion duly made, seconded and carried, the following were elected officers for the following year and until their successors are elected and qualify:

President:
Vice President:
Secretary
Treasurer:

There being no further business to come before the meeting, upon motion duly made, seconded and unanimously carried, it was adjourned.

_____
Secretary

Directors:

_____

_____

_____

form 24

WAIVER OF NOTICE OF THE ANNUAL MEETING OF THE SHAREHOLDERS OF

_____

    The undersigned, being all the shareholders of the Corporation, hereby agree and consent that an annual meeting of the shareholders of the Corporation be held on the ____ day of _____, _____ at ___ o'clock __m at _____ _____ and do hereby waive all notice whatsoever of such meeting and of any adjournment or adjournments thereof.

    We do further agree and consent that any and all lawful business may be transacted at such meeting or at any adjournment or adjournments thereof. Any business transacted at such meeting or at any adjournment or adjournments thereof shall be as valid and legal as if such meeting or adjourned meeting were held after notice.

Date: _____

_____
Shareholder

_____
Shareholder

_____
Shareholder

_____
Shareholder

form 25

MINUTES OF THE ANNUAL MEETING OF
SHAREHOLDERS OF

_____

The annual meeting of Shareholders of the Corporation was held on the date and at the time and place set forth in the written waiver of notice signed by the shareholders, and attached to the minutes of this meeting.

There were present the following shareholders:

Shareholder	No. of Shares
_____	_____
_____	_____
_____	_____
_____	_____

The meeting was called to order and it was moved, seconded and unanimously carried that _____ act as Chairman and that _____ act as Secretary.

A roll call was taken and the Chairman noted that all of the outstanding shares of the Corporation were represented in person or by proxy. Any proxies were attached to these minutes.

The minutes of the last meeting of the shareholders which was held on _____, _____ were read and approved by the shareholders.

Upon motion duly made, seconded and carried, the following were elected directors for the following year:

_____   _____
_____   _____

There being no further business to come before the meeting, upon motion duly made, seconded and unanimously carried, it was adjourned.

_____
Secretary

Shareholders:

_____

_____

_____

_____

form 26

WAIVER OF NOTICE OF SPECIAL MEETING OF
THE BOARD OF DIRECTORS OF

_____

    The undersigned, being all the Directors of the Corporation, hereby agree and consent that a special meeting of the Board of Directors of the Corporation be held on the ____ day of _____, _____ at ____ o'clock ___m at _____ _____ and do hereby waive all notice whatsoever of such meeting and of any adjournment or adjournments thereof.

    The purpose of the meeting is:

    We do further agree and consent that any and all lawful business may be transacted at such meeting or at any adjournment or adjournments thereof as may be deemed advisable by the Directors present. Any business transacted at such meeting or at any adjournment or adjournments thereof shall be as valid and legal as if such meeting or adjourned meeting were held after notice.

Date: _____

_____
Director

_____
Director

_____
Director

_____
Director

form 27

MINUTES OF SPECIAL MEETING OF
THE BOARD OF DIRECTORS OF

_____

    A special meeting of the Board of Directors of the Corporation was held on the date and at the time and place set forth in the written waiver of notice signed by the directors, and attached to the minutes of this meeting.

    The following were present, being all the directors of the Corporation:

_____   _____
_____   _____

    The meeting was called to order and it was moved, seconded and unanimously carried that _____ act as Chairman and that _____ act as Secretary.

    The minutes of the last meeting of the Board of Directors which was held on _____, _____ were read and approved by the Board.

    Upon motion duly made, seconded and carried, the following resolution was adopted:

    There being no further business to come before the meeting, upon motion duly made, seconded and unanimously carried, it was adjourned.

                                                             _____
                                                             Secretary

Directors:

_____

_____

_____

form 28

WAIVER OF NOTICE OF SPECIAL MEETING OF
THE SHAREHOLDERS OF

_____

    The undersigned, being all the shareholders of the Corporation, hereby agree and consent that a special meeting of the shareholders of the Corporation be held on the ____ day of _____, _____ at ___ o'clock __m at _____ _____ and do hereby waive all notice whatsoever of such meeting and of any adjournment or adjournments thereof.

    The purpose of the meeting is

    We do further agree and consent that any and all lawful business may be transacted at such meeting or at any adjournment or adjournments thereof. Any business transacted at such meeting or at any adjournment or adjournments thereof shall be as valid and legal as if such meeting or adjourned meeting were held after notice.

Date: _____

                                                      _____
                                                      Shareholder

                                                      _____
                                                      Shareholder

                                                      _____
                                                      Shareholder

                                                      _____
                                                      Shareholder

form 29

MINUTES OF SPECIAL MEETING OF SHAREHOLDERS OF

_____

A special meeting of Shareholders of the Corporation was held on the date and at the time and place set forth in the written waiver of notice signed by the shareholders, and attached to the minutes of this meeting.

There were present the following shareholders:

Shareholder	No. of Shares
_____	_____
_____	_____
_____	_____
_____	_____

The meeting was called to order and it was moved, seconded and unanimously carried that _____ act as Chairman and that _____ act as Secretary.

A roll call was taken and the Chairman noted that all of the outstanding shares of the Corporation were represented in person or by proxy. Any proxies were attached to these minutes.

The minutes of the last meeting of the shareholders which was held on _____, _____ were read and approved by the shareholders.

Upon motion duly made, seconded and carried, the following resolution was adopted:

There being no further business to come before the meeting, upon motion duly made, seconded and unanimously carried, it was adjourned.

_____
Secretary

Shareholders:

_____

_____

_____

This page intentionally left blank.

form 30

MINNESOTA SECRETARY OF STATE
ARTICLES OF DISSOLUTION
MSA 302A.711

Articles of Dissolution under MSA 302A.711 can only be used to dissolve a corporation that has not issued shares.

_____
Name of Corporation

_____
Date of Incorporation

No shares have been issued.

All consideration recieved from subscribers for shares to be issued, less expenses incurred in the organization of the corporation, have been returned to the subscribers.

No debts remain unpaid.

I certify that the foregoing is true and accurte and that I have the authority to sign this document, and I further certify that I understand that by signing this document, I am subject to the penalties of perjury as set forth in section 609.49 as if I had signed this reservation under oath.

_____
Signed (the Articles of Dissolution must be signed by a majority of the incorporators or directors of the corporation.)

_____
Position

_____( )_____
Name and telephone number of contact person

Please print legibly

All of the information on this form is public and required in order to process this filing. Failure to provide the requested information will prevent the Office from approving or further processing this filing

INSTRUCTIONS
Type or print with dark black ink.
Filing fee: $35.00
Make check payable to: Secretary of State
Mail or bring completed forms to:
Secretary of State
Business Services Division
180 State Office Bldg., 100 Constitution Ave.
St. Paul, MN 55155-1299, (612) 296-2803

This page intentionally left blank.

MINNESOTA SECRETARY OF STATE

form 31

NOTICE OF CHANGE OF REGISTERED OFFICE/ REGISTERED AGENT

Please read the instructions on the back before completing this form.

1. Entity Name:

   _____

2. Registered Office Address (No. & Street): List a complete street address or rural route and rural route box number. **A post office box is not acceptable**.

		MN	
Street	City	State	Zip Code

3. Registered Agent (Registered agents are required for foreign entities but optional for **Minnesota** entities):

   _____

   If you do not wish to designate an agent, you must list "NONE" in this box. **DO NOT LIST THE ENTITY NAME**.

In compliance with *Minnesota Statutes, Section 302A.123, 303.10, 308A.025, 317A.123* or *322B.135* I certify that the above listed company has resolved to change the entity's registered office and/or agent as listed above.

I certify that I am authorized to execute this notice and I further certify that I understand that by signing this notice I am subject to the penalties of perjury as set forth in *Minnesota Statutes Section 609.48* as if I had signed this notice under oath.

_____
Signature of Authorized Person

Name and Telephone Number of a Contact Person: _____(_____)_____
please print legibly

Filing Fee: Minnesota Corporations, Cooperatives and Limited Liability Companies: $35.00.

Non-Minnesota Corporations: $50.00.

Make checks payable to **Secretary of State**

Return to: Minnesota Secretary of State
180 State Office Bldg.
100 Constitution Ave.
St. Paul, MN 55155-1299
(651)296-2803

03930275 Rev. 11/98

INSTRUCTIONS FOR COMPLETING THE "NOTICE OF CHANGE OF REGISTERED OFFICE/REGISTERED AGENT" FORM

This form is used for changing the registered office address and/or registered agent listed with the Office of the Secretary of State.

Please read ALL of the directions before filling out this form.

Line 1

Fill in the name of the entity exactly as it appears in the original organizing document or subsequent amendments.

Line 2

The registered office address is the legal location for service of process or notice(s) sent to the entity. If you are using this form to change the registered office address, list the new address on this line. The registered office address must be a complete street address, or rural route AND rural route box number. A post office box number is not acceptable. This MUST be a Minnesota address.

Line 3

Registered Agents are required for foreign entities but optional for Minnesota entities. The registered agent accepts service of process or notice(s) sent to the entity. The registered agent must be a person residing in Minnesota, a Minnesota entity, or a foreign entity authorized to do business in this state. Do not list your entity name on this line because an entity may not act as its own agent.

Sign the form

Minnesota Statutes require that an officer or representative sign the form.

Contact person

Print the name and telephone number of the person who may be contacted if there are any questions about this filing.

Return the completed form and $35.00 (for Minnesota entities) or $50.00 (for non-Minnesota entities) filing fee to:

> Office of the Secretary of State
> 180 State Office Building
> 100 Constitution Ave.
> St. Paul, MN 55155-1299
> (651)296-2803

All of the information on this form is public and required in order to process this filing. Failure to provide the requested information will prevent the Office from approving or further processing this filing.

This document can be made available in alternative formats, such as large print, Braille or audio tape, by calling (651)296-2803/ Voice. For TTY communication, contact the Minnesota Relay Service at 1-800-627-3529 and ask them to place a call to (651)296-2803. The Secretary of State's Office does not discriminate on the basis of race, creed, color, sex, sexual orientation, national origin, age, marital status, disability, religion, reliance on public assistance or political opinions or affiliations in employment or the provision of services.

form 32

Stock Ledger

Certificates Issued

Cert. No.	No. of Shares	Date of Acquisition	Shareholder Name and Address	From Whom Transferred	Amount Paid

Transfer of Shares

Date of Transfer	To Whom Transferred	Cert. No. Surrendered	No. of Shares Transferred	Cert. No.

173

This page intentionally left blank.

form 33

Certificate No. _____
No. of shares _____
Dated _____
Issued to: _____
_____
_____

☐ Original issue ☐ Transferred from:
_____
_____
Date: _____
Original   Original   No. of Shares
Cert. No. No. Shares Transferred
_____ _____   _____

Received Cert. No. _____
No. of shares _____
New certificates issued:
Cert. No.   No. of Shares
_____   _____
_____   _____

Certificate No. _____
No. of shares _____
Dated _____
Issued to: _____
_____
_____

☐ Original issue ☐ Transferred from:
_____
_____
Date: _____
Original   Original   No. of Shares
Cert. No. No. Shares Transferred
_____ _____   _____

Received Cert. No. _____
No. of shares _____
New certificates issued:
Cert. No.   No. of Shares
_____   _____
_____   _____

Certificate No. _____
No. of shares _____
Dated _____
Issued to: _____
_____
_____

☐ Original issue ☐ Transferred from:
_____
_____
Date: _____
Original   Original   No. of Shares
Cert. No. No. Shares Transferred
_____ _____   _____

Received Cert. No. _____
No. of shares _____
New certificates issued:
Cert. No.   No. of Shares
_____   _____
_____   _____

Certificate No. _____
No. of shares _____
Dated _____
Issued to: _____
_____
_____

☐ Original issue

☐ Transferred from:
_____
Date: _____
Original Original No. of Shares
Cert. No. No. Shares Transferred
_____ _____ _____

Received Cert. No. _____
No. of shares _____
New certificates issued:
Cert. No.   No. of Shares
_____   _____
_____   _____

Certificate No. _____
No. of shares _____
Dated _____
Issued to: _____
_____
_____

☐ Original issue

☐ Transferred from:
_____
Date: _____
Original Original No. of Shares
Cert. No. No. Shares Transferred
_____ _____ _____

Received Cert. No. _____
No. of shares _____
New certificates issued:
Cert. No.   No. of Shares
_____   _____
_____   _____

Certificate No. _____
No. of shares _____
Dated _____
Issued to: _____
_____
_____

☐ Original issue

☐ Transferred from:
_____
Date: _____
Original Original No. of Shares
Cert. No. No. Shares Transferred
_____ _____ _____

Received Cert. No. _____
No. of shares _____
New certificates issued:
Cert. No.   No. of Shares
_____   _____
_____   _____

form 34

Certificate No.			Shares	

The shares represented by this certificate have not been registered under state or federal securities laws. Therefore, they may not be transferred until the corporation determines that such transfer will not adversely affect the exemptions relied upon.

Organized under the laws of Minnesota

This certifies that _____ *is the holder of record of* _____ *shares of* _____ *stock of* _____ *transferable only on the books of the corporation by the holder hereof in person or by Attorney upon surrender of this certificate properly endorsed.*

In witness whereof, the said corporation has caused this certificate to be signed by its duly authorized officers and its corporate seal to be hereto affixed this _____ *day of* _____ .

_____

_____

177

For value received, _____ *hereby sell, assign and transfer unto* _____, _____ *shares represented by this certificate and do hereby irrevocably constitute and appoint* _____ *attorney to transfer the said shares on the books of the corporation with full power of substitution in the premises.*

Dated _____

_____

Witness:

_____

The shares represented by this certificate have not been registered under state or federal securities laws. Therefore, they may not be transferred until the corporation determines that such transfer will not adversely affect the exemptions relied upon.

Certificate No. _____

Shares _____

Organized under the laws of Minnesota

This certifies that _____ *is the holder of record of* _____ *shares of* _____ *stock of* _____ *transferable only on the books of the corporation by the holder hereof in person or by Attorney upon surrender of this certificate properly endorsed.*

In witness whereof, the said corporation has caused this certificate to be signed by its duly authorized officers and its corporate seal to be hereto affixed this _____ *day of* _____.

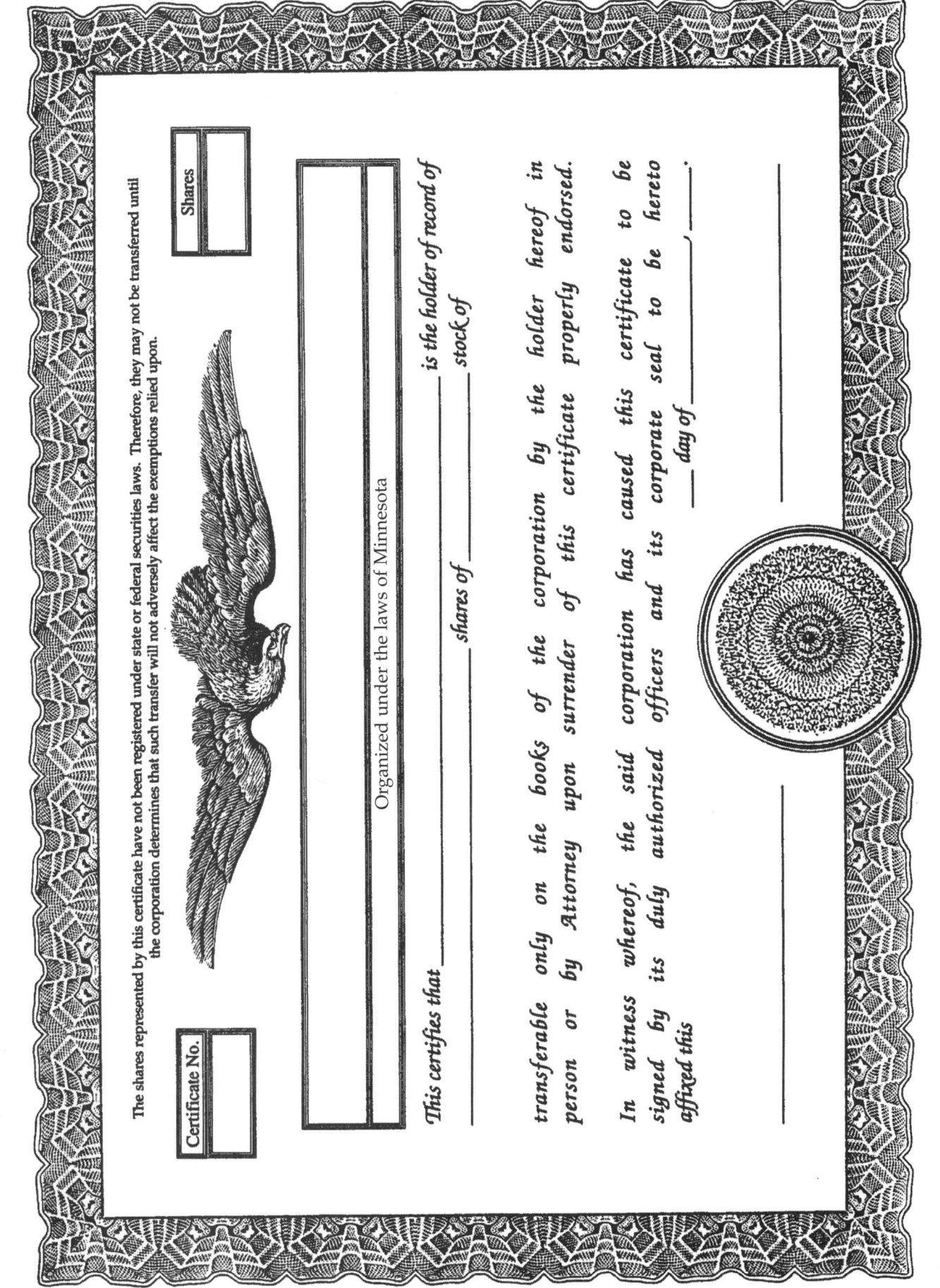

For value received, ____ hereby sell, assign and transfer unto _____, _____ shares represented by this certificate and do hereby irrevocably constitute and appoint _____ attorney to transfer the said shares on the books of the corporation with full power of substitution in the premises.

Dated _____

_____

Witness:

_____

The shares represented by this certificate have not been registered under state or federal securities laws. Therefore, they may not be transferred until the corporation determines that such transfer will not adversely affect the exemptions relied upon.

Certificate No. ____

Shares ____

Organized under the laws of Minnesota

This certifies that _____ *is the holder of record of* _____ *shares of* _____ *stock of*

transferable only on the books of the corporation by the holder hereof in person or by Attorney upon surrender of this certificate properly endorsed.

In witness whereof, the said corporation has caused this certificate to be signed by its duly authorized officers and its corporate seal to be hereto affixed this _____ *day of* _____, _____.

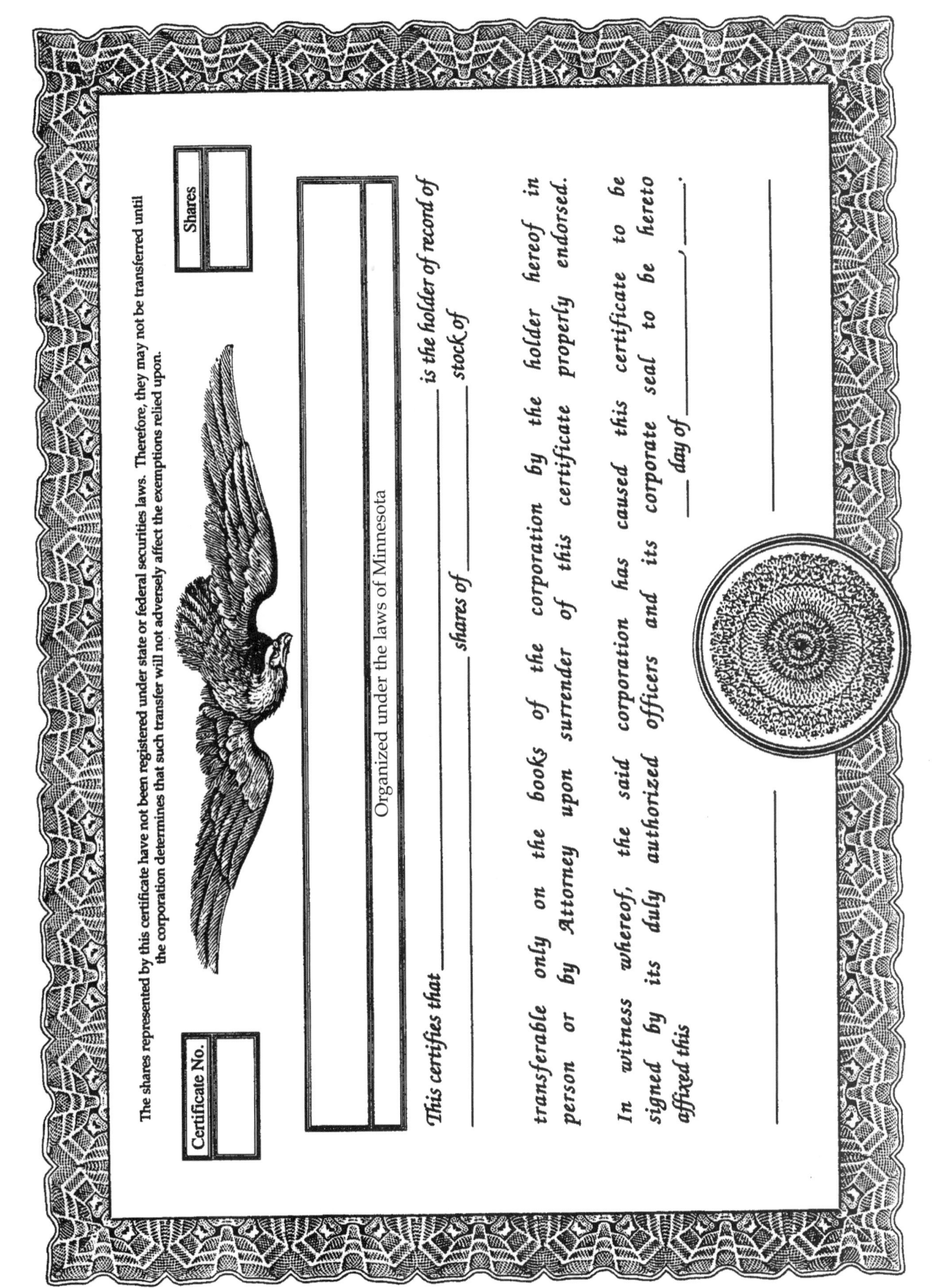

For value received, ____ *hereby sell, assign and transfer unto* _____, _____ *shares represented by this certificate and do hereby irrevocably constitute and appoint* _____ *attorney to transfer the said shares on the books of the corporation with full power of substitution in the premises.*

Dated _____

_____

Witness:

_____

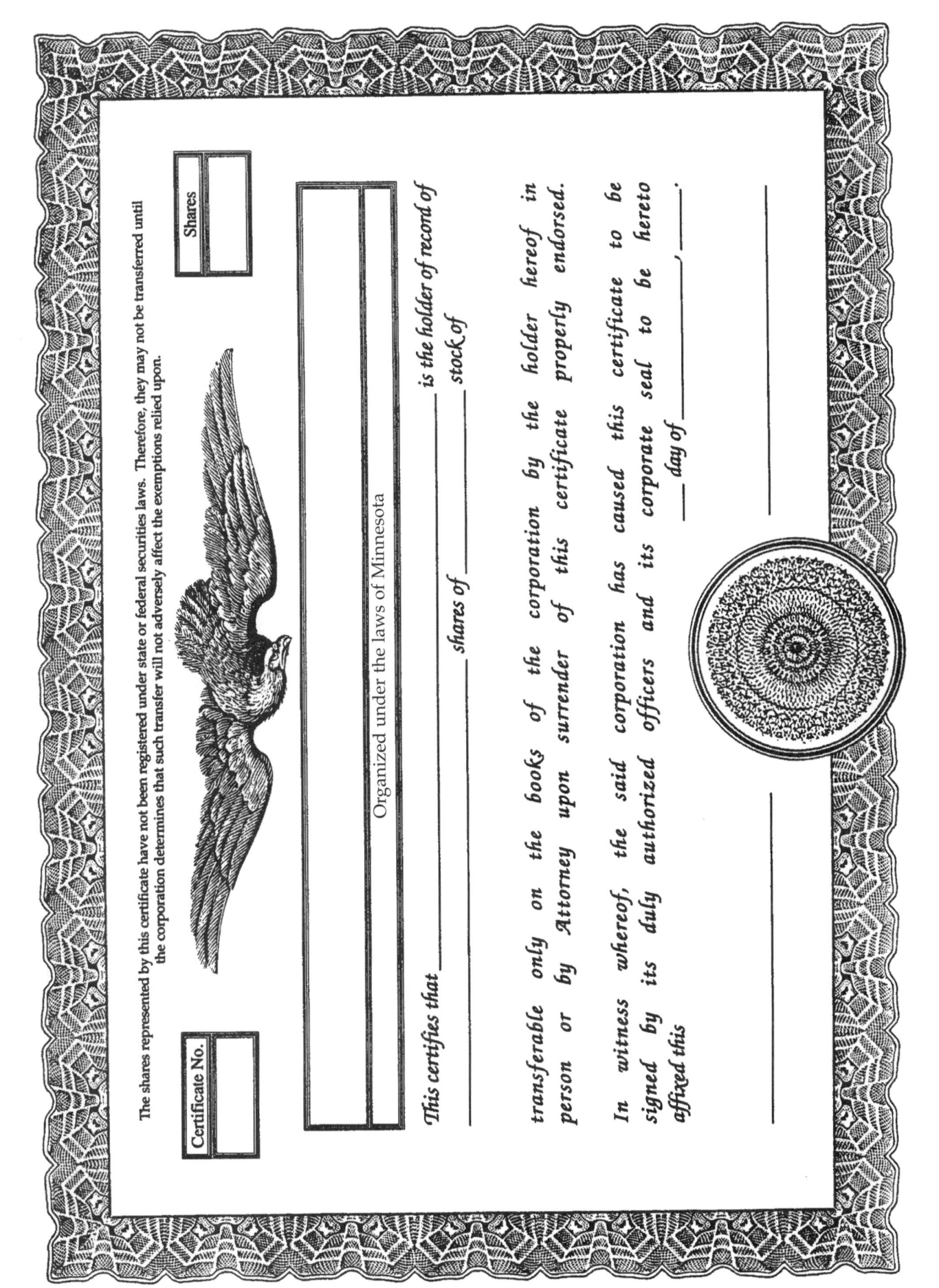

Certificate No.		Shares	

The shares represented by this certificate have not been registered under state or federal securities laws. Therefore, they may not be transferred until the corporation determines that such transfer will not adversely affect the exemptions relied upon.

Organized under the laws of Minnesota

This certifies that _____ *is the holder of record of* _____ *shares of* _____ *stock of* _____ *transferable only on the books of the corporation by the holder hereof in person or by Attorney upon surrender of this certificate properly endorsed.*

In witness whereof, the said corporation has caused this certificate to be signed by its duly authorized officers and its corporate seal to be hereto affixed this _____ *day of* _____.

For value received, ____ *hereby sell, assign and transfer unto* _____
_____,
_____ *shares represented by this certificate and do hereby irrevocably constitute and appoint* _____ *attorney to transfer the said shares on the books of the corporation with full power of substitution in the premises.*

Dated _____

_____

Witness:

_____

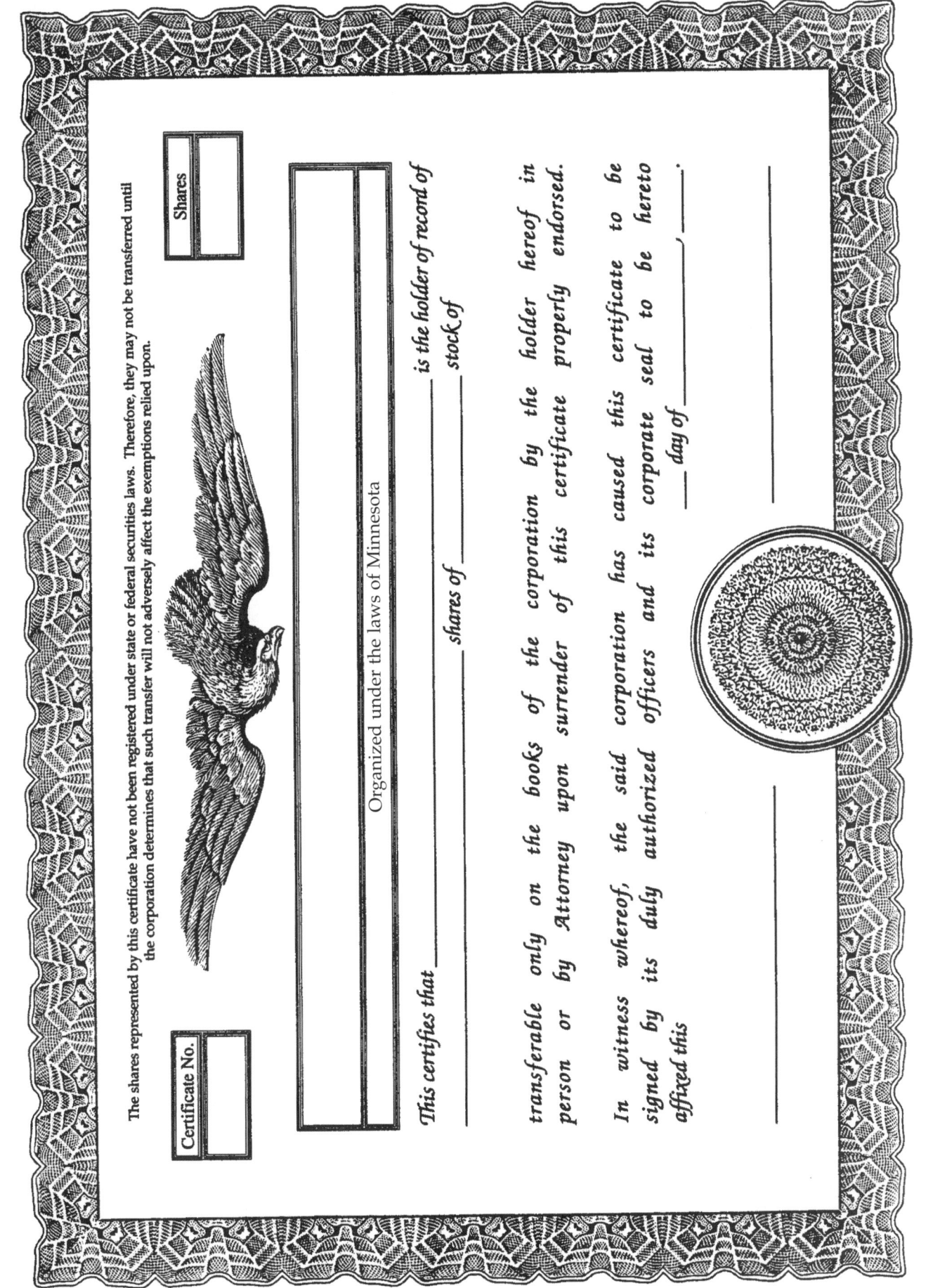

Certificate No.			Shares	

The shares represented by this certificate have not been registered under state or federal securities laws. Therefore, they may not be transferred until the corporation determines that such transfer will not adversely affect the exemptions relied upon.

Organized under the laws of Minnesota

This certifies that _____ *is the holder of record of* _____ *shares of* _____ *stock of* _____

transferable only on the books of the corporation by the holder hereof in person or by Attorney upon surrender of this certificate properly endorsed.

In witness whereof, the said corporation has caused this certificate to be signed by its duly authorized officers and its corporate seal to be hereto affixed this _____ *day of* _____ .

For value received, ____ hereby sell, assign and transfer unto _____, _____ shares represented by this certificate and do hereby irrevocably constitute and appoint _____ attorney to transfer the said shares on the books of the corporation with full power of substitution in the premises.

Dated _____

_____

Witness:

_____

MINNESOTA SECRETARY OF STATE

form 35

DOMESTIC CORPORATION ANNUAL REGISTRATION
Minnesota Statutes Chapter 302A/319B
Must be filed by December 31

READ INSTRUCTIONS ON BACK BEFORE COMPLETING THIS FORM

TO:

CURRENT INFORMATION ON FILE:

1. Charter#:   2. State of Incorporation: **MINNESOTA**

3. Corporate Name:

4. Registered Agent/ Registered Office Address:

5. Principal Executive Office Address: (PO Box Not Acceptable)	**INFORMATION YOU WISH TO CHANGE:** Principal Executive Office Address: (PO Box Not Acceptable)
6. Name and Business Address of C.E.O.:	Name and Business Address of C.E.O.:

7. Does this corporation own, lease, or have any financial interest in agricultural land or land capable of being farmed?
     ____ Yes   ____ No

8. Name and **daytime** telephone number and/or e-mail address of contact person:

Name: _____ (____)_____ Ext. _____

E-Mail Address: _____

NOTICE: Failure to file this form by December 31 of this year will result in this corporation losing its good standing without further notice from the Secretary of State. To regain good standing, the corporation must file this form and pay a $25 fee.

Failure to file the annual registration for 3 consecutive years will result in the dissolution of the corporation unless a registration with a $25 fee is submitted, pursuant to *Minnesota Statute* 302A.821. A postcard notice will be sent prior to dissolution.

A CORPORATION THAT HAS BEEN DISSOLVED PURSUANT TO MINNESOTA STATUTES 302A.821, MUST REINCORPORATE TO BE REGISTERED AS A BUSINESS IN THIS STATE.

302a319b.p65 Rev. 11/00

INSTRUCTIONS FOR COMPLETING THIS FORM

All business corporations governed under chapter 302A/319B are required to file an annual registration once every calendar year.

If pre-printed, items 1 through 6 list current information on file with the Office of the Secretary of State. If there are any changes to lines 3 or 4, you must amend your articles of incorporation separately. If amending, an amendment form and $35 fee must be included with your annual registration.

You may obtain the necessary forms by calling the Office of the Secretary of State at (651) 296-2803, or from our WEB site at www.sos.state.mn.us.

1. **Charter Number:** If the form is pre-printed, the charter number issued by the Minnesota Secretary of State appears here. Otherwise, provide the charter number and all other information required on this form.

2. **State of Incorporation:** This form is to be filed only if the state of incorporation is Minnesota.

3. **Corporate Name:** If changes to the corporate name are necessary an amendment form and $35 fee must be included with the annual registration.

4. **Registered Agent, if any and Registered Office Address:** If changes to the registered agent name or address are necessary an amendment form and $35 fee must be included with the annual registration.

5. **Principal Executive Office Address:** (Must Complete) Fill in the address of the principal executive office. Minnesota law requires a full street address or rural route and rural route box number. A post office box alone is not acceptable. Changes in this information may be made on this form at no charge.

6. **Name and Business Address of Chief Executive Officer:** (Must Complete) Fill in the name and complete business address of the Chief Executive Officer or other person who carries out the functions as C.E.O. of the corporation. Changes in this information may be made on this form at no charge.

7. **Does the corporation own, lease, or have any financial interest in agricultural land or land capable of being farmed?** This question is optional. Check Yes or No.

8. **Name and daytime telephone number or e-mail address of contact person for the corporation:** Please list a name and daytime telephone number and/or an e-mail address of a person who can be contacted about this form.

If you have any questions, please contact the Secretary of State's Office at (651)296-2803.

RETURN TO:

If NO FEE(S) are due:
Secretary of State
Public Information Division
555 Park Street #402
St. Paul, MN 55103-2141

IF FEE(S) are due:
Secretary of State
180 State Office Building
100 Constitution Avenue
St Paul, MN 55155-1299

MAKE CHECKS PAYABLE TO THE "SECRETARY OF STATE"

All of the information on this form is public and required in order to process this filing. Failure to provide the requested information will prevent the Office from approving or further processing this filing. This document can be made available in alternative formats, such as large print, Braille or audio tape, by calling (651)296-2803/Voice. For TTY communication, contact the Minnesota Relay Service at 1-800-627-3529 and ask them to place a call to (651)296-2803. The Secretary of State's Office does not discriminate on the basis of race, creed, color, sex, sexual orientation, national origin, age, marital status, disability, religion, reliance on public assistance or political opinions or affiliations in employment or the provision of services.

form 36

MINNESOTA SECRETARY OF STATE
APPLICATION FOR
TRADEMARK, SERVICE MARK
CERTIFICATION MARK OR
COLLECTIVE MARK

PLEASE TYPE OR PRINT LEGIBLY IN BLACK INK
Please read the Instructions on the back before completing this form. To expedite the return of your documents please submit a stamped self-addressed envelope. All information on this form is public information.

1. State the words or phrase to be registered: _____
_____

2. Provide a <u>written</u> description of the logo design (if none, leave blank). Stylized letters are not a logo design:
_____
_____

3. Trade/Service Mark Classification Number (see instruction 3 on the back of this form before completing this item): _____
   NOTE: A separate application and fee is required for each classification desired.

4. State the SPECIFIC goods or services within the above classification for which the mark is used:
_____

5. How and where is the mark displayed on the goods or services listed in Item 4?
_____

6. State the date on which this mark was first used in commerce by the applicant or their predecessor(s) in Minnesota:
   (must have been used prior to registration)

   _____
   Month   Day   Year

7. Name of individual, firm, partnership, corporation, association, union or other organization applying for this mark:

_____
Name   State of Incorporation

_____
Street Address   City   State   ZIP

I certify that I am the applicant or that I am authorized to sign this application on behalf of the applicant, that the applicant understands the above application and its contents, that the facts set out in the application are true, that the applicant believes that he, she or it is the owner of the mark and that no other person, firm, partnership, association, union, corporation or other organization has the right to use the mark in Minnesota, either in an identical form or in such a manner that might deceive or be mistaken for this mark. The specimen or facsimile filed with this application is a true and correct example of the mark as used. I further certify that I understand that by signing this application, I am subject to the penalties of perjury as set forth in section 609.48 as if I had signed this application under oath.

_____
Signature

_____
Print Name and Phone Number of Contact Person for this Mark.

09921549   Rev. 10/98

INSTRUCTIONS

1) State the words or phrase to be registered, if any. The words or phrase must be listed exactly as it appears on the specimens submitted with this application. A separate application is needed for each phrase to be registered.

2) Provide a <u>written</u> description of the <u>logo design</u> to be registered, if any. This description must depict the design as it appears on the accompanying specimen. Only one logo design is permitted per application. If none, leave blank.

3) Indicate the classification number under which this mark falls. A list of the International system of trade and service mark classifications is available from the Office of the Secretary of State. Leave blank if unknown and this office will fill it in. <u>A separate application and fee is required for each classification in which you wish to register a mark.</u>

4) State the SPECIFIC goods or services represented by the mark. DO NOT use indefinite terms, such as "accessories", "products," or the like. Use language that would be readily understandable to the general public. For example, "t-shirts" or "dry cleaning services".

If the applicant identifies the goods or services too broadly as, for example, "advertising and business," or just "products," or "services," the application will be returned.

The identification of goods or services must NOT describe the mode of use of the mark, such as on labels, stationery, business cards, menus, signs or in advertising.

5) State the way the mark appears on the goods, i.e., "on containers," "on tags or labels affixed to the goods", " by stamping it on the goods".

6) In order to register a mark in Minnesota, it must have been used commercially prior to registration. State the date the mark was first used in Minnesota. If it has not yet been used in Minnesota you cannot register the mark with the Secretary of State.

7) State the name and complete address of the applicant. If the applicant is a corporation, list the state of incorporation and the principal place of business in that state.

FURTHER REQUIREMENTS

* You must submit one specimen or facsimile of the mark as you have actually used it in commerce.
* Copies are acceptable.
* A typewritten statement of the mark would not be acceptable, since it would not have been in use with the public. Acceptable examples would be a business card, letterhead, clipping from an advertisement, label, picture or copies of such materials.

Submit the application, one specimen and $50.00 filing fee to:

Secretary of State
Business Services Division
180 State Office Building
100 Constitution Ave.
St. Paul, MN 55155-1299

Once accepted, this registration is valid for 10 years. A renewal notice will be sent by this office prior to the expiration date, to the name holder at the address on file with this office. If there is any change in address, please notify this office of the new address of the mark holder.

If you have any questions regarding trademarks or this application, contact the Office of the Secretary of State at (651)296-2803. Information regarding Federal trademarks can be obtained by calling (703)308-4357 or visiting the US patent & Trademark Office website at www.uspto.gov.

All of the information on this form is public and required in order to process this filing. Failure to provide the requested information will prevent the Office from approving or further processing this filing. This document can be made available in alternative formats, such as large print, Braille or audio tape, by calling (651)296-2803/Voice. For TTY communication, contact Minnesota Relay Service at 1-800-627-3529 and ask them to place a call to (651)296-2803. The Secretary of State's Office does not discriminate on the basis of race, creed, color, sex, sexual orientation, national origin, age, marital status, disability, religion, reliance on public assistance or political opinions or affiliations in employment or the provision of services.

SHAREHOLDER AGREEMENT

WHEREAS the undersigned shareholders are forming a Corporation and wish to protect their interests and those of the Corporation, in consideration of the mutual promises and conditions set out below, the parties agree as follows:

1. ***Best Efforts.*** Each shareholder agrees to devote his or her best efforts to the development of the Corporation. No shareholder shall participate in any enterprise which competes in any way with the activities of the Corporation.

2. ***Right to Serve as Director or Officer.*** Each shareholder shall, so long as he owns shares in the Corporation, have the right to serve as a director of the Corporation or to designate some responsible person to serve as his nominee.

The officers of the Corporation shall be the following shareholders, each of whom shall continue to serve as long as he owns shares:

President _____

Vice President _____

Treasurer _____

Secretary _____

Any officer or director who ceases to be a shareholder shall no longer be an officer or director upon the transfer of shares.

3. ***Salary.*** The Corporation shall employ the shareholders and pay salaries to them as follows:

Name of Shareholder and initial salary

_____ $_____

_____ $_____

_____ $_____

The salary received by any shareholder as an officer or employee or in any other function or for any other service shall serve as compensation for all services or functions the shareholder performs for the Corporation. The directors may increase or decrease the salaries from time to time, upon unanimous vote.

4. ***Additional Shares.*** The Corporation shall not, without consent of all of the shareholders, do any of the following: (a) issue additional shares of any class or any securities convertible

into shares of any class; (b) merge or participate in a share exchange with any other Corporation; or (c) transfer all or substantially all of the assets of the Corporation for any consideration other than cash.

In the event the shareholders agree to issue additional shares or securities convertible into shares, then each of the shareholders shall have the right to purchase any such securities so offered at a future date in proportion to his then respective interest in the Corporation at the time of such offer.

5. *Transfer of Shares.* No shares shall be transferred in any manner or by any means except upon unanimous consent of the shareholders. If a proposed sale is not agreed to by unanimous consent, a shareholder may resign from his positions with the corporation and be bought out by the corporation as provided below.

6. *Buyout.* Upon the death, resignation, adjudication of incompetency, or bankruptcy by any shareholder, or the transfer, agreement to transfer, or attachment of any shares, the Corporation shall purchase all of the shares of the shareholder so affected at the value of shares described below. Payment by the corporation for such buyout shall be within thirty days of the determination of value and the transferring shareholder shall execute all documents necessary to transfer his or her shares.

7. *Value of Shares*. The parties agree that upon execution of this agreement the value of each share of stock is $_____. This value shall be reviewed and updated once each year and at any time that a sale of shares is contemplated. New value shall be set by a unanimous vote of the shareholders. If the shareholders cannot agree, then the corporation's accountant shall be asked to set a value. If any shareholder disagrees with the corporation's accountant's value, he or she may get the value of another accountant. If the two accountants cannot agree to an acceptable value, they shall choose a third accountant to set the final value.

8. *S Corporation Status.* If the Corporation is an S corporation and if it reasonably determines that any proposed transferee is not eligible as a shareholder of a Subchapter S Corporation or that such transfer would cause the Corporation to lose its qualification as a Subchapter S Corporation, then the Corporation may so notify the shareholder of that determination and thereby forbid the consummation of the transfer.

9. *Endorsement.* The certificates for shares of the Corporation shall be endorsed as follows: "The shares represented by this certificate are subject to and are transferable only on compliance with a Shareholders Agreement a copy of which is on file in the office of the Secretary of the Corporation."

10. *Formalities*. Whenever under this Agreement notice is required to be given, it shall be given in writing served in person or by certified or registered mail, return receipt requested, to the address of the shareholder listed in the stock ledger of the corporation, and it shall be deemed to have been given upon personal delivery or on the date notice is posted.

11. *Termination*. This Agreement shall terminate and all rights and obligations hereunder shall cease upon the happening of any one of the following events:

(a) The adjudication of the Corporation as bankrupt, the execution by it of any assignment for the benefit of creditors, or the appointment of a receiver for the Corporation;

(b) The voluntary or involuntary dissolution of the Corporation;

(c) By a written Agreement signed by all the shareholders to terminate this Agreement.

12. *Entire Agreement*. This Agreement embodies the entire representations, Agreements and conditions in relation to the subject matter hereof and no representations, understandings or Agreements, oral or otherwise, in relation thereto exist between the parties except as herein expressly set forth. The Agreement may not be amended or terminated orally but only as expressly provided herein or by an instrument in writing duly executed by the parties hereto.

13. *Heirs and Assigns*. This Agreement and the various rights and obligations arising under it shall inure to the benefit of and be binding upon the parties hereto and their respective heirs, successors and assigns.

14. *Severability*. The invalidity or unenforceability of any term or provision of this Agreement or the non-application of such term or provision to any person or circumstance shall not impair or affect the remainder of this Agreement, and its application to other persons and circumstances and the remaining terms and provisions hereof shall not be invalidated but shall remain in full force and effect.

15. *Gender*. Whenever in this Agreement any pronoun is used in reference to any shareholder, purchaser or other person or entity, natural or otherwise, the singular shall include the plural, and the masculine shall include the feminine or the neuter, as required by context.

16. *Dispute Resolution.* All disputes between shareholders or between the corporation and one or more shareholders shall first be settled through good faith negotiations. If negotiations fail, the dispute shall be settled in mediation with the assistance of a mediator chosen by agreement of the parties to the dispute. If some or all of the dispute is not resolved in mediation, then the parties will submit the dispute to binding arbitration under the rules of the American Arbitration Association. The parties waive any rights to bring action in any court

except to enforce an arbitration decision.

17. **Choice of Law.** This Agreement shall be governed by and construed in accordance with the laws of the State of Minnesota.

IN WITNESS WHEREOF, the parties hereto have executed this Agreement the date and place first above mentioned.

_____ (Name of Corporation)

By: _____,
President

                                                       _____ Shareholder

                                                       _____ Shareholder

                                                       _____ Shareholder

                                                       _____ Shareholder

Index

A

amendment of articles of incorporation, 59
application for business registration, 35
application for employer identification number (IRS Form SS-4), 34-35, 40, 125
application for legal newspaper status, 123
application for trademark, servicemark, certification mark or collective mark, 189
arbitration, 31
articles of dissolution, 62, 169
articles of incorporation, 3, 21, 23-27, 40, 42, 54, 56, 57, 59-60, 115
    amendments, 23, 54, 59-60, 117
articles of organization for a limited liability company, 118
assets, 5, 6, 7, 30
attorneys, 3, 9, 15, 24, 25, 28, 31, 46, 50, 54, 62

B

bank accounts, 8, 10, 41-43
    checks, 10
banking resolution, 34, 39, 43, 145
bankruptcy, 9, 28, 61, 62
banks, 34, 41
bill of sale, 39, 151
board of directors. *See* directors
bonds, 16
buy-out, 29
bylaws, 3, 15, 23, 24, 31, 33, 37, 38, 39, 40, 54, 56, 57, 60, 133, 139
    amendments, 54

C

C Corporation, 12-15
capital, 8, 25, 38, 46
certificate of assumed name, 19, 111
certificate of limited partnership, 121
change of registered office/registered agent, 60, 171
closely held corporation. *See* corporation
committee, 58
consent to the use of a name, 109
corporate kits, 36
corporate seal, 33, 36-37
corporation, 1-3, 5-10, 11-17, 27, 31, 36, 37, 41, 53-58, 59-60, 61-62
    closely held, 15
    Delaware, 11
    family, 28
    for profit, 16, 17
    foreign, 11-12
    Nevada, 11-12
    nonprofit, 16, 17
court, 6, 12, 30, 44, 55
credit, 9
    rating, 9
creditors, 5, 34, 62

D

debts, 1, 5, 45, 62
department of revenue, 35
depreciation, 12
directors, 2, 14, 25, 32, 33, 34, 37, 38, 53, 54, 55, 56, 57, 59, 62
dissolution, 6, 61-62
    automatic, 61

formal, 62
dividends, 14
domestic corporation annual registration, 9, 58, 187

E

election by a small business corporation (IRS form 2553), 13, 35, 153
employees, 14
employer identification number, 34, 35
endorsement, 30
estate planning, 8
expenses, 8, 9-10, 12, 14, 31, 39

F

foreign. See corporation

G

goods, 21, 22, 35

H

home business, 43-44

I

income, 12, 13, 14, 38
incorporator, 25, 26, 32, 38, 59, 62
insurance, 8, 13, 14, 15
    accident, 14
    health, 13, 14
    life, 13, 14, 15
    medical, 8
    unemployment, 9
interest, 13, 41
Internal Revenue Service (IRS), 13, 35, 38
Internet, 20, 50
investments, 1, 16, 28, 45, 50
investors, 1, 13, 45, 48, 49

L

lawsuits, 30
lawyers. See attorneys
legal forms
    form 1, 107
    form 2, 109
    form 3, 111
    form 4, 26, 113
    form 5, 23, 26, 115
    form 6, 59, 117
    form 7, 118
    form 8, 119
    form 9, 121
    form 10, 123
    form 11, 34, 125
    form 12, 32, 39, 129
    form 13, 33, 130
    form 14, 31, 39, 133
    form 15, 31, 32, 39, 139
    form 16, 34, 39, 43, 145
    form 17, 38, 39, 147
    form 18, 149
    form 19, 39, 151
    form 20, 13, 35, 153
    form 21, 34, 35, 159
    form 22, 32, 160
    form 23, 57, 161
    form 24, 32, 162
    form 25, 55, 163
    form 26, 32, 164
    form 27, 57, 165
    form 28, 32, 166
    form 29, 167
    form 30, 62, 169
    form 31, 60, 171
    form 32, 40, 173
    form 33, 40, 175
    form 34, 37, 39, 177
    form 35, 187
    form 36, 189
    form 37, 27, 28, 191
liability, 1, 5-6, 17, 25, 53
    limited, 5-6, 17
    personal, 6, 53
    unlimited, 1
licenses, 7, 15, 22, 43-44
    occupational, 43
limited liability companies, 16, 27
limited liability partnership statement of qualification, 119
loans, 46

M

mediation, 30
mediator, 30
meetings, 32, 33, 34, 36, 38-40, 54, 55-58
    annual, 32, 55, 56
    directors, 56-58
    formal, 34, 56, 57

index

notice, 56, 57
organizational, 32, 34, 38-40
shareholders, 55-56
special, 32, 55, 56, 57
merger, 17, 30
Minnesota Department of Revenue, 14
Minnesota Employer's Unemployment Handbook, 10
Minnesota Unemployment Insurance Trust Fund., 9
minutes, 9, 31, 33-34, 35, 36, 39, 40-41, 53, 54, 55, 56
minutes of annual meeting of board of directors, 161
minutes of annual meeting of shareholders, 163
minutes of organizational meeting of incorporators and directors, 40, 130
minutes of special meeting of the board of directors, 57
minutes of the annual meetings of the board of directors, 57
minutes of the organizational meeting of incorporators and directors, 33
minutes of special meeting of board of directors, 165
minutes of special meeting of shareholders, 167
mortgage, 16

N

names, 16, 19-23, 24, 27, 36, 37, 40, 54
assumed, 16, 19-20, 27
business, 20
corporate, 24
fictitious, 36, 40
forbidden, 22
registering, 19
reservation, 21
similar, 21
trade, 20
nonprofit corporation. *See* corporation

O

offer to purchase stock, 37-38, 39, 40, 147
officers, 2, 14, 33, 37, 38, 39, 41, 54, 55, 57, 62

P

partners, 6
partnership, 5, 9, 12, 13, 16, 27
Patent and Trademark Depository Libraries, 20
pension. *See* retirement
permits, 7

piercing the corporate veil, 6, 56, 57
professional firms, 15-17, 26, 27, 37
profits, 1, 7, 8, 13, 14, 15, 17, 45
property, 13, 14, 39, 43, 50, 51
real, 16

Q

quorum, 56, 57, 60

R

real estate. *See* property
records, 8, 9, 36, 53-55
registered agent, 2-3, 12, 24, 25, 60
registered office, 25, 60
regulation D, 48
request for reservation of a name, 107
resolution, 15, 34, 39, 54
resolution (adopting S corporation status), 34, 35, 159
resolution (to reimburse expenses), 149
retirement, 8
royalties, 13

S

S Corporation, 12-15, 35, 38
salary, 9, 14, 15, 17, 28, 29
secretary of state, 26
securities, 13, 15, 38, 45-47, 47-49, 50
exemptions, 46, 47-48
Securities and Exchange Commission (SEC), 46, 47, 48
services, 22, 35
shareholder agreement, 27-31, 191
shareholders, 2, 13, 14, 15, 16, 17, 25, 27-31, 32, 33, 34, 37, 39, 54, 55, 56, 58, 59, 60
shares. *See* stocks
sole proprietorship, 5, 7, 9
stock certificate stubs, 40, 41, 175
stock certificates, 15, 33, 36, 37-38, 39, 40, 177
stock transfer ledger, 40, 41, 173
stockholders. *See* shareholders
stocks, 2, 7, 12, 15, 16, 24, 25, 36, 37-38, 45-51, 54
classes, 13, 24, 37
common, 24, 45
par value, 25, 50
preferred, 24, 37, 45
pro-rata, 30
voting, 7

197

T

taxes, 1, 8, 9, 10, 12, 13, 14, 15, 17, 34-35, 39, 40-41, 51
- advantages, 17
- corporate, 12, 14
- deductions, 14
- double, 12, 14
- federal, 10, 17, 42
- income, 12, 14
- license, 43
- return, 9
- sales, 35
- shareholders, 12
- unemployment, 10, 17

taxpayer identification number. *See* employer identification number
trademark, 20-21, 22-23, 27, 40
transmittal letter, 26, 113

U

unemployment compensation, 9
United States Patent and Trademark Office (USPTO), 20, 23

V

voting, 56, 57-58

W

wages. *See* salary
waiver of notice of annual meeting of board of directors, 160
waiver of notice of annual meeting of shareholders, 162
waiver of notice of organizational meeting, 39, 40, 129
waiver of notice of special meeting of board of directors, 164
waiver of notice of special meeting of shareholders, 166

Z

zoning, 44

Your #1 Source for Real World Legal Information...

SPHINX® PUBLISHING
An Imprint of Sourcebooks, Inc.®

- Written by lawyers
- Simple English explanation of the law
- Forms and instructions included

HOW TO FILE FOR DIVORCE IN MINNESOTA

Whether you plan to use a lawyer or not, protect yourself by getting all the information you need about divorce laws and your legal rights in Minnesota. Includes forms with step-by-step instructions to simplify filing for divorce, obtaining support, and settling parenting arrangements.

296 pages; $21.95;
ISBN 1-57248-142-0

HOW TO MAKE A MINNESOTA WILL, 2 ED.

This book gives a basic understanding of the laws regarding wills, joint property, and other types of ownership that affect estate planning. Includes sample filled-in forms and blank tear-out forms for easy use.

128 pages; $16.95;
ISBN 1-57248-178-1

See the following order form for books written specifically for California, Florida, Georgia, Illinois, Massachusetts, Michigan, Minnesota, New York, North Carolina, Ohio, Pennsylvania, and Texas!

What our customers say about our books:

"It couldn't be more clear for the lay person." —R.D.

"I want you to know I really appreciate your book. It has saved me a lot of time and money." —L.T.

"Your real estate contracts book has saved me nearly $12,000.00 in closing costs over the past year." —A.B.

"...many of the legal questions that I have had over the years were answered clearly and concisely through your plain English interpretation of the law." —C.E.H.

"If there weren't people out there like you I'd be lost. You have the best books of this type out there." —S.B.

"...your forms and directions are easy to follow." —C.V.M.

*Sphinx Publishing's Legal Survival Guides
are directly available from Sourcebooks, Inc., or from your local bookstores.
For credit card orders call 1–800–432–7444, write P.O. Box 4410, Naperville, IL 60567-4410,
or fax 630-961-2168*

SPHINX® PUBLISHING'S NATIONAL TITLES
Valid in All 50 States

Legal Survival in Business

The Complete Book of Corporate Forms	$24.95
How to Form a Delaware Corporation from Any State	$24.95
How to Form a Limited Liability Company	$22.95
Incorporate in Nevada from Any State	$24.95
How to Form a Nonprofit Corporation	$24.95
How to Form Your Own Corporation (3E)	$24.95
How to Form Your Own Partnership	$22.95
How to Register Your Own Copyright (3E)	$21.95
How to Register Your Own Trademark (3E)	$21.95
Most Valuable Business Legal Forms You'll Ever Need (3E)	$21.95

Legal Survival in Court

Crime Victim's Guide to Justice (2E)	$21.95
Grandparents' Rights (3E)	$24.95
Help Your Lawyer Win Your Case (2E)	$14.95
Jurors' Rights (2E)	$12.95
Legal Research Made Easy (2E)	$16.95
Winning Your Personal Injury Claim (2E)	$24.95
Your Rights When You Owe Too Much	$16.95

Legal Survival in Real Estate

Essential Guide to Real Estate Contracts	$18.95
Essential Guide to Real Estate Leases	$18.95
How to Buy a Condominium or Townhome	$19.95

Legal Survival in Personal Affairs

Cómo Hacer su Propio Testamento	$16.95
Guía de Inmigración a Estados Unidos (3E)	$24.95
Cómo Solicitar su Propio Divorcio	$24.95
How to File Your Own Bankruptcy (4E)	$21.95
How to File Your Own Divorce (4E)	$24.95
How to Make Your Own Will (2E)	$16.95
How to Write Your Own Living Will (2E)	$16.95
How to Write Your Own Premarital Agreement (2E)	$21.95
How to Win Your Unemployment Compensation Claim	$21.95
Living Trusts and Simple Ways to Avoid Probate (2E)	$22.95
Most Valuable Personal Legal Forms You'll Ever Need	$24.95
Neighbor v. Neighbor (2E)	$16.95
The Nanny and Domestic Help Legal Kit	$22.95
The Power of Attorney Handbook (3E)	$19.95
Repair Your Own Credit and Deal with Debt	$18.95
The Social Security Benefits Handbook (3E)	$18.95
Unmarried Parents' Rights	$19.95
U.S.A. Immigration Guide (3E)	$19.95
Your Right to Child Custody, Visitation and Support (2E)	$24.95

Legal Survival Guides are directly available from Sourcebooks, Inc., or from your local bookstores. Prices are subject to change without notice.

For credit card orders call 1–800–432–7444, write P.O. Box 4410, Naperville, IL 60567-4410 or fax 630-961-2168

SPHINX® PUBLISHING ORDER FORM

BILL TO:		SHIP TO:	
Phone #	Terms	F.O.B. Chicago, IL	Ship Date

Charge my: ☐ VISA ☐ MasterCard ☐ American Express

☐ Money Order or Personal Check

Credit Card Number

Expiration Date

Qty	ISBN	Title	Retail	Ext.
		SPHINX PUBLISHING NATIONAL TITLES		
	1-57248-148-X	Cómo Hacer su Propio Testamento	$16.95	
	1-57248-147-1	Cómo Solicitar su Propio Divorcio	$24.95	
	1-57248-166-8	The Complete Book of Corporate Forms	$24.95	
	1-57248-163-3	Crime Victim's Guide to Justice (2E)	$21.95	
	1-57248-159-5	Essential Guide to Real Estate Contracts	$18.95	
	1-57248-160-9	Essential Guide to Real Estate Leases	$18.95	
	1-57248-139-0	Grandparents' Rights (3E)	$24.95	
	1-57248-188-9	Guía de Inmigración a Estados Unidos (3E)	$24.95	
	1-57248-103-X	Help Your Lawyer Win Your Case (2E)	$14.95	
	1-57071-164-X	How to Buy a Condominium or Townhome	$19.95	
	1-57071-223-9	How to File Your Own Bankruptcy (4E)	$21.95	
	1-57248-132-3	How to File Your Own Divorce (4E)	$24.95	
	1-57248-100-5	How to Form a DE Corporation from Any State	$24.95	
	1-57248-083-1	How to Form a Limited Liability Company	$22.95	
	1-57248-099-8	How to Form a Nonprofit Corporation	$24.95	
	1-57248-133-1	How to Form Your Own Corporation (3E)	$24.95	
	1-57071-343-X	How to Form Your Own Partnership	$22.95	
	1-57248-119-6	How to Make Your Own Will (2E)	$16.95	
	1-57248-124-2	How to Register Your Own Copyright (3E)	$21.95	
	1-57248-104-8	How to Register Your Own Trademark (3E)	$21.95	
	1-57071-349-9	How to Win Your Unemployment Compensation Claim	$21.95	
	1-57248-118-8	How to Write Your Own Living Will (2E)	$16.95	
	1-57071-344-8	How to Write Your Own Premarital Agreement (2E)	$21.95	
	1-57248-158-7	Incorporate in Nevada from Any State	$24.95	
	1-57071-333-2	Jurors' Rights (2E)	$12.95	
	1-57071-400-2	Legal Research Made Easy (2E)	$16.95	
	1-57071-336-7	Living Trusts and Simple Ways to Avoid Probate (2E)	$22.95	

Qty	ISBN	Title	Retail	Ext.
	1-57248-167-6	Most Valuable Bus. Legal Forms You'll Ever Need (3E)	$21.95	
	1-57248-130-7	Most Valuable Personal Legal Forms You'll Ever Need	$24.95	
	1-57248-098-X	The Nanny and Domestic Help Legal Kit	$22.95	
	1-57248-089-0	Neighbor v. Neighbor (2E)	$16.95	
	1-57071-348-0	The Power of Attorney Handbook (3E)	$19.95	
	1-57248-149-8	Repair Your Own Credit and Deal with Debt	$18.95	
	1-57248-168-4	The Social Security Benefits Handbook (3E)	$18.95	
	1-57071-399-5	Unmarried Parents' Rights	$19.95	
	1-57071-354-5	U.S.A. Immigration Guide (3E)	$19.95	
	1-57248-138-2	Winning Your Personal Injury Claim (2E)	$24.95	
	1-57248-162-5	Your Right to Child Custody, Visitation and Support (2E)	$24.95	
	1-57248-157-9	Your Rights When You Owe Too Much	$16.95	
		CALIFORNIA TITLES		
	1-57248-150-1	CA Power of Attorney Handbook (2E)	$18.95	
	1-57248-151-X	How to File for Divorce in CA (3E)	$26.95	
	1-57071-356-1	How to Make a CA Will	$16.95	
	1-57248-145-5	How to Probate and Settle an Estate in California	$26.95	
	1-57248-146-3	How to Start a Business in CA	$18.95	
	1-57071-358-8	How to Win in Small Claims Court in CA	$16.95	
	1-57071-359-6	Landlords' Rights and Duties in CA	$21.95	
		FLORIDA TITLES		
	1-57071-363-4	Florida Power of Attorney Handbook (2E)	$16.95	
	1-57248-176-5	How to File for Divorce in FL (7E)	$26.95	
	1-57248-177-3	How to Form a Corporation in FL (5E)	$24.95	
	1-57248-086-6	How to Form a Limited Liability Co. in FL	$22.95	
	1-57071-401-0	How to Form a Partnership in FL	$22.95	
	1-57248-113-7	How to Make a FL Will (6E)	$16.95	

Form Continued on Following Page   **SUBTOTAL**

To order, call Sourcebooks at 1-800-432-7444 or FAX (630) 961-2168 (Bookstores, libraries, wholesalers—please call for discount)

Prices are subject to change without notice.

SPHINX® PUBLISHING ORDER FORM

Qty	ISBN	Title	Retail	Ext.
	1-57248-088-2	How to Modify Your FL Divorce Judgment (4E)	$24.95	
	1-57248-144-7	How to Probate and Settle an Estate in FL (4E)	$26.95	
	1-57248-081-5	How to Start a Business in FL (5E)	$16.95	
	1-57071-362-6	How to Win in Small Claims Court in FL (6E)	$16.95	
	1-57248-123-4	Landlords' Rights and Duties in FL (8E)	$21.95	
GEORGIA TITLES				
	1-57248-137-4	How to File for Divorce in GA (4E)	$21.95	
	1-57248-075-0	How to Make a GA Will (3E)	$16.95	
	1-57248-140-4	How to Start a Business in Georgia (2E)	$16.95	
ILLINOIS TITLES				
	1-57071-405-3	How to File for Divorce in IL (2E)	$21.95	
	1-57071-415-0	How to Make an IL Will (2E)	$16.95	
	1-57071-416-9	How to Start a Business in IL (2E)	$18.95	
	1-57248-078-5	Landlords' Rights & Duties in IL	$21.95	
MASSACHUSETTS TITLES				
	1-57248-128-5	How to File for Divorce in MA (3E)	$24.95	
	1-57248-115-3	How to Form a Corporation in MA	$24.95	
	1-57248-108-0	How to Make a MA Will (2E)	$16.95	
	1-57248-106-4	How to Start a Business in MA (2E)	$18.95	
	1-57248-107-2	Landlords' Rights and Duties in MA (2E)	$21.95	
MICHIGAN TITLES				
	1-57071-409-6	How to File for Divorce in MI (2E)	$21.95	
	1-57248-077-7	How to Make a MI Will (2E)	$16.95	
	1-57071-407-X	How to Start a Business in MI (2E)	$16.95	
MINNESOTA TITLES				
	1-57248-142-0	How to File for Divorce in MN	$21.95	
	1-57248-179-X	How to Form a Corporation in MN	$24.95	
	1-57248-178-1	How to Make a MN Will (2E)	$16.95	
NEW YORK TITLES				
	1-57248-141-2	How to File for Divorce in NY (2E)	$26.95	
	1-57248-105-6	How to Form a Corporation in NY	$24.95	
	1-57248-095-5	How to Make a NY Will (2E)	$16.95	
	1-57071-185-2	How to Start a Business in NY	$18.95	
	1-57071-187-9	How to Win in Small Claims Court in NY	$16.95	

Qty	ISBN	Title	Retail	Ext.
	1-57071-186-0	Landlords' Rights and Duties in NY	$21.95	
	1-57071-188-7	New York Power of Attorney Handbook	$19.95	
	1-57248-122-6	Tenants' Rights in NY	$21.95	
NORTH CAROLINA TITLES				
	1-57248-185-4	How to File for Divorce in NC (3E)	$22.95	
	1-57248-129-3	How to Make a NC Will (3E)	$16.95	
	1-57248-184-6	How to Start a Business in NC (3E)	$18.95	
	1-57248-091-2	Landlords' Rights & Duties in NC	$21.95	
OHIO TITLES				
	1-57248-190-0	How to File for Divorce in OH (2E)	$24.95	
	1-57248-174-9	How to Form a Corporation in Ohio	$24.95	
PENNSYLVANIA TITLES				
	1-57248-127-7	How to File for Divorce in PA (2E)	$24.95	
	1-57248-094-7	How to Make a PA Will (2E)	$16.95	
	1-57248-112-9	How to Start a Business in PA (2E)	$18.95	
	1-57071-179-8	Landlords' Rights and Duties in PA	$19.95	
TEXAS TITLES				
	1-57248-171-4	Child Custody, Visitation, and Support in TX	$22.95	
	1-57071-330-8	How to File for Divorce in TX (2E)	$21.95	
	1-57248-114-5	How to Form a Corporation in TX (2E)	$24.95	
	1-57071-417-7	How to Make a TX Will (2E)	$16.95	
	1-57071-418-5	How to Probate an Estate in TX (2E)	$22.95	
	1-57071-365-0	How to Start a Business in TX (2E)	$18.95	
	1-57248-111-0	How to Win in Small Claims Court in TX (2E)	$16.95	
	1-57248-110-2	Landlords' Rights and Duties in TX (2E)	$21.95	

SUBTOTAL THIS PAGE _____

SUBTOTAL PREVIOUS PAGE _____

Shipping — $5.00 for 1st book, $1.00 each additional _____

Illinois residents add 6.75% sales tax _____

Connecticut residents add 6.00% sales tax _____

TOTAL _____

To order, call Sourcebooks at 1-800-432-7444 or FAX (630) 961-2168 (Bookstores, libraries, wholesalers—please call for discount)

Prices are subject to change without notice.